Kaplan Publishing are constantly findi[...] difference to your studies and our exc[...] lly do offer something different to students [...]

This book comes with free MyKaplan c[...] so that you can study anytime, anywhere. **This free online resource is not sold separately and is included in the price of the book.**

Having purchased this book, you have access to the following online study materials:

CONTENT	AAT	
	Text	Kit
Electronic version of the book	✓	✓
Progress tests with instant answers	✓	
Mock assessments online	✓	✓
Material updates	✓	✓

How to access your online resources

Kaplan Financial students will already have a MyKaplan account and these extra resources will be available to you online. You do not need to register again, as this process was completed when you enrolled. If you are having problems accessing online materials, please ask your course administrator.

If you are not studying with Kaplan and did not purchase your book via a Kaplan website, to unlock your extra online resources please go to www.mykaplan.co.uk/addabook (even if you have set up an account and registered books previously). You will then need to enter the ISBN number (on the title page and back cover) and the unique pass key number contained in the scratch panel below to gain access. You will also be required to enter additional information during this process to set up or confirm your account details.

If you purchased through the Kaplan Publishing website you will automatically receive an e-mail invitation to MyKaplan. Please register your details using this email to gain access to your content. If you do not receive the e-mail or book content, please contact Kaplan Publishing.

Your Code and Information

This code can only be used once for the registration of one book online. This registration and your online content will expire when the final sittings for the examinations covered by this book have taken place. Please allow one hour from the time you submit your book details for us to process your request.

Please scratch the film to access your unique code.

Please be aware that this code is case-sensitive and you will need to include the dashes within the passcode, but not when entering the ISBN.

KAPLAN PUBLISHING

FINANCIAL STATEMENTS OF LIMITED COMPANIES

STUDY TEXT

Qualifications and Credit Framework

AQ2016

This Study Text supports study for the following AAT qualifications:

AAT Professional Diploma in Accounting – Level 4

AAT Level 4 Diploma in Business Skills

AAT Professional Diploma in Accounting at SCQF – Level 8

Published by:

Kaplan Publishing UK
Unit 2 The Business Centre
Molly Millar's Lane
Wokingham
Berkshire
RG41 2QZ

ISBN 978-1-78740-785-5

Acknowledgements

This Product includes propriety content of the International Accounting Standards Board which is overseen by the IFRS Foundation, and is used with the express permission of the IFRS Foundation under licence. All rights reserved. No part of this publication may be reproduced, stored in a retrieval system, or transmitted in any form or by any means, electronic, mechanical, photocopying, recording, or otherwise, without prior written permission of Kaplan Publishing and the IFRS Foundation.

CONTENTS

This document references IFRS® Standards and IAS® Standards, which are authored by the International Accounting Standards Board (the Board), and published in the 2019 IFRS Standards Red Book.

FINANCIAL STATEMENTS OF LIMITED COMPANIES

STUDY TEXT

Qualifications and Credit Framework

AQ2016

This Study Text supports study for the following AAT qualifications:

AAT Professional Diploma in Accounting – Level 4

AAT Level 4 Diploma in Business Skills

AAT Professional Diploma in Accounting at SCQF – Level 8

Published by:

Kaplan Publishing UK
Unit 2 The Business Centre
Molly Millar's Lane
Wokingham
Berkshire
RG41 2QZ

ISBN 978-1-78740-785-5

Acknowledgements

This Product includes propriety content of the International Accounting Standards Board which is overseen by the IFRS Foundation, and is used with the express permission of the IFRS Foundation under licence.

INTRODUCTION

HOW TO USE THESE MATERIALS

These Kaplan Publishing learning materials have been carefully designed to make your learning experience as easy as possible and to give you the best chance of success in your AAT assessments.

They contain a number of features to help you in the study process.

The sections on the Unit Guide, the Assessment and Study Skills should be read before you commence your studies.

They are designed to familiarise you with the nature and content of the assessment and to give you tips on how best to approach your studies.

STUDY TEXT

This study text has been specially prepared for the revised AAT qualification introduced in September 2016.

It is written in a practical and interactive style:

- key terms and concepts are clearly defined
- all topics are illustrated with practical examples with clearly worked solutions based on sample tasks provided by the AAT in the new examining style
- frequent practice activities throughout the chapters ensure that what you have learnt is regularly reinforced
- 'pitfalls' and 'examination tips' help you avoid commonly made mistakes and help you focus on what is required to perform well in your examination
- 'Test your understanding' activities are included within each chapter to apply your learning and develop your understanding.

ICONS

The chapters include the following icons throughout.

They are designed to assist you in your studies by identifying key definitions and the points at which you can test yourself on the knowledge gained.

Definition

These sections explain important areas of knowledge which must be understood and reproduced in an assessment.

Example

The illustrative examples can be used to help develop an understanding of topics before attempting the test your understanding exercises.

Test your understanding

These are exercises which give the opportunity to assess your understanding of all the assessment areas.

Quality and accuracy are of the utmost importance to us so if you spot an error in any of our products, please send an email to mykaplanreporting@kaplan.com with full details.

Our Quality Co-ordinator will work with our technical team to verify the error and take action to ensure it is corrected in future editions.

Progression

There are two elements of progression that we can measure: first how quickly students move through individual topics within a subject; and second how quickly they move from one course to the next. We know that there is an optimum for both, but it can vary from subject to subject and from student to student. However, using data and our experience of student performance over many years, we can make some generalisations.

A fixed period of study set out at the start of a course with key milestones is important. This can be within a subject, for example 'I will finish this topic by 30 June', or for overall achievement, such as 'I want to be qualified by the end of next year'.

Your qualification is cumulative, as earlier papers provide a foundation for your subsequent studies, so do not allow there to be too big a gap between one subject and another.

We know that exams encourage techniques that lead to some degree of short term retention, the result being that you will simply forget much of what you have already learned unless it is refreshed (look up Ebbinghaus Forgetting Curve for more details on this). This makes it more difficult as you move from one subject to another: not only will you have to learn the new subject, you will also have to relearn all the underpinning knowledge as well. This is very inefficient and slows down your overall progression which makes it more likely you may not succeed at all.

In addition, delaying your studies slows your path to qualification which can have negative impacts on your career, postponing the opportunity to apply for higher level positions and therefore higher pay.

You can use the following diagram showing the whole structure of your qualification to help you keep track of your progress.

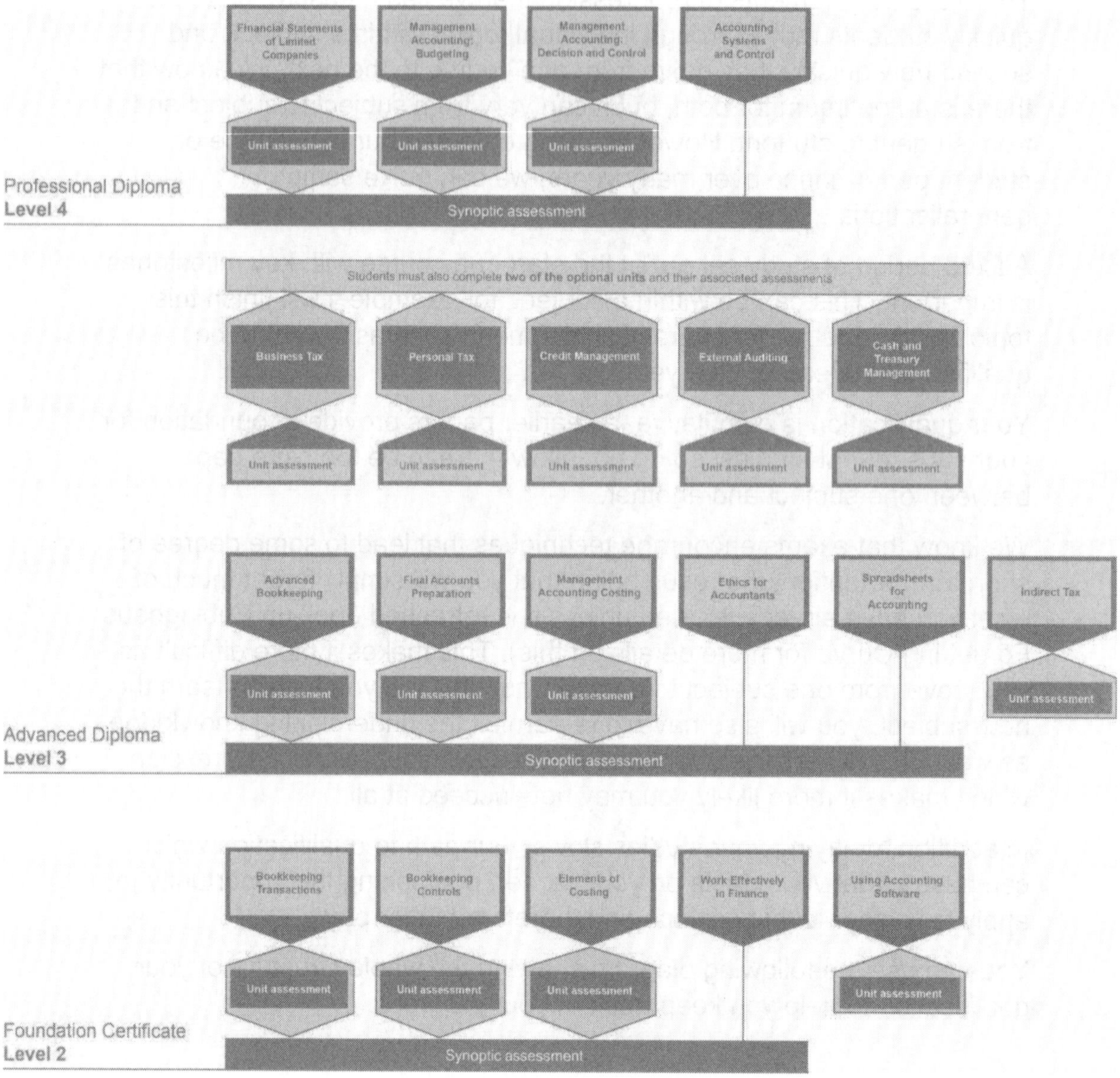
Financial Statements of Limited Companies
Management Accounting: Budgeting
Management Accounting: Decision and Control
Accounting Systems and Control
Unit assessment
Unit assessment
Unit assessment
Professional Diploma
Level 4
Synoptic assessment
Students must also complete two of the optional units and their associated assessments
Business Tax
Personal Tax
Credit Management
External Auditing
Cash and Treasury Management
Unit assessment
Unit assessment
Unit assessment
Unit assessment
Unit assessment
Advanced Bookkeeping
Final Accounts Preparation
Management Accounting Costing
Ethics for Accountants
Spreadsheets for Accounting
Indirect Tax
Unit assessment
Unit assessment
Unit assessment
Unit assessment
Advanced Diploma
Level 3
Synoptic assessment
Bookkeeping Transactions
Bookkeeping Controls
Elements of Costing
Work Effectively in Finance
Using Accounting Software
Unit assessment
Unit assessment
Unit assessment
Unit assessment
Foundation Certificate
Level 2
Synoptic assessment

UNIT GUIDE

Introduction

This unit is concerned with the drafting, analysis and interpretation of financial statements of limited companies. This builds on the Foundation and Advanced levels, where the emphasis of the financial accounting units is on identifying and recording transactions in accounts and ledgers following the principles of double-entry bookkeeping, and drafting the financial statements of unincorporated organisations from the accounts and records prepared.

On successful completion of this unit, a student could be expected to be able to draft the financial statements of single limited companies and groups of companies with little supervision. A student could also analyse and interpret financial statements of limited companies by means of ratio analysis for the purposes of assisting outside user groups in their decision making, thereby fulfilling a useful role within an accounting team.

The unit provides students with the skills and knowledge for drafting the financial statements of single limited companies and consolidated financial statements for groups of companies. It ensures that students will have a proficient level of knowledge and understanding of international accounting standards, which they will be able to apply when drafting the financial statements, and will have a sound appreciation of the regulatory and conceptual frameworks that underpin the preparation of limited company financial statements.

Finally, the unit will equip students with the tools and techniques that will enable them to analyse and interpret financial statements effectively.

Financial Statements of Limited Companies is a **mandatory** unit.

Learning outcomes

On completion of this unit the learner will be able to:

- understand the reporting frameworks and ethical principles that underpin financial reporting
- understand the key features of a published set of financial statements
- draft statutory financial statements for a limited company
- draft consolidated financial statements
- interpret financial statements using ratio analysis.

Scope of content

To perform this unit effectively you will need to know and understand the following:

		Chapter
1	**Demonstrate an understanding of the reporting frameworks and ethical principles that underpin financial reporting**	
1.1	**Explain the regulatory framework that underpins financial reporting** Students need to know: • the purpose of financial statements • the different types of business organisation (sole traders, partnerships, limited liability partnerships. Companies, not-for-profit organisations (charities, clubs and societies), public sector organisations (local authorities, central government and the National Health Service) and cooperatives • the types of limited company • how the financial statements of limited companies differ from those of sole traders and partnerships • forms of equity, reserves and loan capital • the reasons for the existence of a regulatory framework • sources of regulation: international accounting standards and company law (Companies Act 2006) • the purpose of accounting standards • the duties and responsibilities of the directors in respect of financial statements.	1, 2
1.2	**Explain the International Accounting Standards Board (IASB) Conceptual Framework that underpins financial reporting** Students need to know: • the concepts that underlie the preparation and presentation of financial statements for external users, as detailed in the guidance notes.	1, 2

		Chapter
1.3	**Discuss the ethical principles that underpin financial reporting in accordance with the AAT Code of Professional Ethics** Students need to be able to: • explain fundamental principles • identify the threats • apply the safeguards to resolve ethical conflict.	2
2	**Demonstrate an understanding of the key features of a published set of financial statements**	
2.1	**Examine the effect of international accounting standards on the preparation of financial statements** Students need to be able to: • explain the effect of international accounting standards on the presentation, valuation and disclosure of items within the financial statements • make any supporting calculations.	3 – 16
3	**Draft statutory financial statements for a limited company**	
3.1	**Draft a statement of profit or loss and other comprehensive income** Students need to be able to: • make appropriate entries in the statement in respect of information extracted from a trial balance and additional information.	3

		Chapter
3.2	**Draft a statement of financial position**	3

Students need to be able to:

- make appropriate entries in the statement in respect of information extracted from a trial balance and additional information.

3.3	**Draft a statement of changes in equity**	3

Students need to be able to:

- make appropriate entries in the statement in respect of information extracted from a trial balance and additional information or other financial statements provided.

3.4	**Draft a statement of cash flows**	14

Students need to be able to:

- make appropriate entries in the statement, using the indirect method, in respect of information extracted from a statement of profit or loss and other comprehensive income for a single year, and statements of financial position for two years, and any additional information provided.

4 Draft consolidated financial statements

4.1	**Draft a consolidated statement of profit or loss for a parent company with one partly-owned subsidiary**	16

Students need to be able to:

- consolidate each line item in the statement of profit or loss
- treat inter-company sales and other intercompany items, impairment losses on goodwill and dividends paid by a subsidiary company to its parent company
- calculate and treat unrealised profit on inventories and non-controlling interest.

		Chapter
4.2	**Draft a consolidated statement of financial position for a parent company with one partly-owned subsidiary**	15

Students need to be able to:

- consolidate each line item in the statement of financial position
- calculate and treat goodwill, non-controlling interest, pre- and post-acquisition profits, equity and unrealised profit on inventories
- treat adjustment to fair value, impairment of goodwill and intercompany balances.

5	**Interpret financial statements using ratio analysis**	
5.1	**Calculate ratios with regard to profitability, liquidity, efficient use of resources and financial position**	13

Students need to be able to:

- calculate the following ratios:

  profitability
  - return on capital employed
  - return on shareholders' funds
  - gross profit percentage
  - expense/revenue percentage
  - operating profit percentage

  liquidity
  - current ratio
  - the quick ratio or 'acid test' ratio

  use of resources
  - inventory turnover
  - inventory holding period (days)
  - trade receivables collection period
  - trade payables payment period
  - working capital cycle
  - asset turnover (net assets)
  - asset turnover (non-current assets)

  financial position
  - interest cover
  - gearing.

		Chapter
5.2	**Appraise the relationship between elements of the financial statements with regard to profitability, liquidity, efficient use of resources and financial position, by means of ratio analysis** Students need to be able to: • identify, with reasons, whether a ratio is better or worse as compared to a comparative ratio • suggest the factors that influence ratios and how they interrelate.	13
5.3	**Effectively present an analysis with recommendations** Students need to be able to: • present the key findings of their analysis to meet user requirements • suggest how ratios could be improved and the potential consequences of doing so • explain the limitations of ratio analysis.	13

Delivery guidance

The AAT have provided a comprehensive content guide for the unit in respect of the international financial reporting standards (both IFRS and IAS) which are assessable. The content that is assessable is described under each of the headings.

IFRS 3 *Business combinations*

- Definitions of acquiree, acquirer, business, business combination, control, fair value, goodwill, identifiable, non-controlling interest (Appendix A)
- identifying a business combination (3 and Appendix B5)
- the acquisition method (4 and 5), identifying the acquirer (6 and 7), determining the acquisition date (8 and 9), recognition and measurement of assets, liabilities and non-controlling interest (10 – 12)
- measurement principle (18 and 19)
- recognition and measurement of goodwill (32, 34, and 35).

IFRS 10 *Consolidated Financial Statements*

- Requirement to present consolidated financial statements (4) and definition of consolidated financial statements (Appendix A)
- Assessment of whether an entity controls an investee (5 – 7)
- Explanations of power (10), returns (15), and the link between power and returns (17)
- Need to use uniform accounting policies in consolidation (19)
- Consolidation procedures (B86)
- Presentation of non-controlling interests (22).

IFRS 15 *Revenue from Contracts with Customers*

- key definitions: Customer, income, and revenue (Appendix A)
- the core principle of IFRS 15 and the five-step model framework (IN7)
- step 1: Identifying the contract (9)
- step 2: Identifying performance obligations (22)
- step 3: Determining the transaction price (47)
- methods used to estimate the amount of variable consideration (53)
- step 4: Allocating the transaction price to performance obligations (73)
- allocation of a discount (81)
- step 5: Satisfaction of performance obligations (31)
- performance obligations satisfied over time (35, B14, B15 and B18)
- performance obligations satisfied at a point in time (38).

IFRS 16 *Leases*

- Definition of a lease (Appendix A)
- Recognition at the commencement date (22)
- Definition of a right-of-use asset (Appendix A)
- Recognition exemptions (5, 6 and 8)
- Definition of a short term lease (Appendix A)
- Leases for which the asset is of low value (B3, B4 and B8)
- Initial measurement of the right-of-use asset (23, 24 (a and b)
- Initial measurement of the lease liability (26)

- Definitions of the interest rate implicit in the lease and the lessee's incremental borrowing rate (both Appendix A)
- Subsequent measurement of the right-of-use asset (29, 30(a) and 35)
- Depreciation and impairment of the right of use asset (31, 32 and 33)
- Subsequent measurement of the lease liability (36(a and b), 37 and 38(a))

IAS 1 *Presentation of financial statements*

Purpose of financial statements (9)

Complete set of financial statements (10, 10A and 11)

- requirement for financial statements to present fairly the financial position, financial performance and cash flows of an entity (15)
- requirement to make a statement in respect of compliance with IFRS (16)
- requirement to assess going concern (25)
- requirement for accrual accounting (27)
- requirement to present each material class of similar items separately (29)
- prohibition of offsetting elements (32)
- requirement to present a complete set of financial statements at least annually (36)
- requirement for comparative information (38)
- requirement for consistency of presentation and classification (45)
- requirement to identify clearly the financial statements (49) and each component of the financial statements (51)
- requirement to display other information prominently (51)
- information to be presented on the face of the statement of financial position (54 and 55)
- requirement to separate current and non-current assets and liabilities (60)
- criteria for current assets (66) and current liabilities (69)
- sub-classifications on the face of the statement of financial position or in notes (77 and 78) and disclosure of other items on the face of the statement of financial position or the statement of changes in equity or in notes (79)

- information to be presented on the face of the statement of profit or loss and other comprehensive income (82 – 85)
- prohibition of extraordinary items (87)
- separate disclosure of material items of income and expense (97)
- requirement to analyse expenses based on nature of expenses or their function (99) and criteria of choice (99, 105) with examples of analysis in 102 – 103). [Only the form of analysis based upon functionality will be assessed]
- requirement to present a statement of changes in equity (106)
- information to be shown in the statement of changes of equity (106) and the treatment of dividends (107)
- general requirements for notes (112), cross referencing (113), disclosure of accounting policies (117) and disclosure of dividends proposed (137).

IAS 2 *Inventories*

- Definition of inventories (6)
- measurement of inventories (9) and definition of net realisable value (6)
- what is included in cost of inventories (10 and 15) and what is excluded (16)
- cost of inventories of items that are not ordinarily interchangeable (23)
- formulas that are to be used to determine the cost of inventories of items that are ordinarily interchangeable (25) and explanations of the FIFO formula and the weighted average cost formula (27)
- examples of situations that could affect the ability of an entity to recover the cost of inventories (28) and the basis by which inventories are to be written down to net realisable value (29)
- recognition as an expense when inventories sold (34).

IAS 7 *Statement of cash flows*

- Requirement for an entity to prepare a statement of cash flows in accordance with this standard (1)
- definitions of terms used in standard (6)
- requirement to report cash flows during the period classified by operating, investing and financing activities (10)

- examples of cash flows from operating activities (14)
- examples of investing activities (16)
- examples of financing activities (17)
- requirement to report cash flows from operating activities using either the direct method or the indirect method (18). Examples of both types of statement can be found in the illustrative examples which accompany the standard
- determination of the net cash flow from operating activities in accordance with the indirect method (20)
- requirement to report separately major classes of gross cash receipts and gross cash payments arising from investing and financing activities (21)
- requirement to disclose separately cash flows from interest and dividends received and paid in a consistent manner from period to period as either operating, investing or financing activities (31)
- requirement to disclose separately cash flows from taxes on income as cash flows from operating activities unless they can be specifically identified with financing and investing activities (35)
- disclosure of components of cash and cash equivalents and the reconciliation of the amounts in the statement of cash flows with the equivalent items reported in the statement of financial position (45).

IAS 10 *Events after the reporting period*

- Definitions of events after the reporting period and adjusting and non- adjusting events (3)
- requirement to adjust for adjusting events after the reporting period (8) with examples (9)
- prohibition of adjustment in respect of non-adjusting events after the reporting period (10) with examples (11)
- prohibition on recognition of dividends declared after the reporting period as a liability (12)
- prohibition on preparing financial statements on a going concern basis if there is an intention to liquidate or cease trading (14)
- requirement to disclose date when financial statements were authorised for issue (17)
- requirement to disclose material non-adjusting events (21) with examples (22).

IAS 12 *Income taxes*

- [Students need only be able to identify the amount of tax that needs to be recognised in the statement of financial position and the statement of profit or loss in respect of profit for the year, and account for any adjustments in respect of over or under-estimated tax of prior periods. Students will not be required to perform a tax computation or account for deferred tax].

IAS 16 *Property, plant and equipment*

- Definition of property, plant and equipment (6)
- recognition rule for items of property, plant and equipment (7)
- recognition rules for subsequent expenditure (12, 13 and 14)
- measurement rule at recognition (15) and of elements of cost (16, 17 and 19)
- measurement rules after recognition (29) including explanation of cost model (30) and revaluation model (31)
- rules on frequency of revaluations (34)
- rule that all assets belonging to a class must be revalued if one item in that class is revalued (36) and examples of different classes (37)
- treatment of revaluation surpluses or decreases (39 and 40)
- requirement to depreciate each part of an item of property, plant and equipment separately (43)
- depreciation charge for each period to be recognised in profit or loss (48)
- depreciable amount to be allocated on a systematic basis over the asset's useful life (50)
- requirement to review the residual value at least at the year end and any change to be accounted for as a change in accounting estimate
- rule that depreciation is required even if fair value exceeds carrying amount as long as the residual value does not exceed its carrying amount, in which case depreciation is zero, and not negated by repair and maintenance (52)
- depreciable amount determined after deducting residual value (53)
- factors determining useful life of an asset (56)
- land not depreciated (58)

- rule for determining depreciation method (60) with examples of methods (62) and need for review at least at the year end (61)
- derecognition rule (67)
- treatment of gain and loss (68) and how computed (71)
- disclosure relating to each class of property, plant and equipment (73), depreciation method and useful life or depreciation rates, depreciation and accumulated depreciation (75).

IAS 36 ***Impairment of assets***

- Definitions of carrying amount, recoverable amount, fair value, value in use and impairment loss (6)
- an asset is impaired when its carrying amount exceeds its recoverable amount (8)
- requirement to assess whether there is any indication that an asset may be impaired and requirement to estimate the recoverable amount when such an indication exists (9)
- requirement to assess intangible assets with an indefinite useful life and goodwill annually (10)
- indications of impairment (12, 13 and 14)
- explanations of how to determine fair value less costs to sell (25, 26, 27 and 28)
- recognising and measuring an impairment loss for in individual assets other than goodwill (59 and 60) and revision of depreciation charge (63)
- disclosure of impairment loss recognised in profit or loss and other comprehensive income (126a and c).

IAS 37 ***Provisions, contingent liabilities and contingent assets***

- Definitions (not onerous contracts or restructuring) (10)
- distinction between provisions and other liabilities (11), idea of being contingent in the standard (12) and distinction between provisions and contingent liabilities (13)
- requirement to recognise provisions and criteria (14)
- prohibition on recognising contingent liabilities (27) and contingent assets (31)
- measurement of provision (36 and 37)

- requirement to review provisions at the end of each reporting period to reflect current best estimate (59)
- use of provisions (61)
- disclosure of provisions (84 – 85)
- disclosure of contingent liabilities (86) and contingent assets (89).

IAS 38 *Intangible assets*

- Definition of an intangible asset, research and development (8)
- identifiability criterion in definition of an intangible asset (12)
- recognition criteria for intangible assets (21) including explanation of future economic benefits (17)
- measurement rule for intangible assets (24)
- prohibition on recognition of internally generated goodwill (48)
- rules of recognition of internally generated intangible assets including the need to classify the generation of the asset into a research phase and a development phase (52 and 53); the accounting treatment of expenditure incurred in the research phase of a project (54) and examples of research activities (56); the accounting treatment of expenditure incurred in the development phase of a project (57) and examples of development activities (59)
- prohibition of the recognition of internally generated brands and similar items (63)
- need to determine whether useful life of an intangible asset is finite or indefinite (88)
- rules for depreciation of intangible assets with finite useful lives (97), residual value (100) and review of amortisation period (104)
- prohibition of amortisation for intangible assets with indefinite useful life (107) and requirement for impairment review in accord with IAS 36 (108) and review of useful life assessment (109).

Delivering this unit

Unit name	Content links	Suggested order of delivery
Not applicable	This unit integrates with a number of other units in the qualification, all of which are concerned with financial accounting. At Foundation level, Bookkeeping Transactions and Bookkeeping Controls introduce students to basic bookkeeping skills and the books of prime entry. These units lead into the two Advanced level units, Advanced Bookkeeping and Final Accounts Preparation, which cover the theoretical foundations of financial accounting, together with practical skills for the preparation of financial statements for unincorporated traders. The knowledge and skills gained in the Foundation level and Advanced level financial accounting units are drawn on and developed at Professional level in Financial Statements of Limited Companies, which focuses on the drafting, analysis and interpretation of the financial statements of limited companies.	Students may find it useful to have studied the Foundation level and Advanced level bookkeeping units before this unit.

THE ASSESSMENT

Test specification for this unit assessment

Assessment type	Marking type	Duration of exam
Computer based unit assessment	Partially computer/ partially human marked	2 hours 30 minutes

The assessment for this unit consists of 8 compulsory tasks.

The competency level for AAT assessments is 70%.

Learning outcomes		**Weighting**
1	Understand the reporting frameworks and ethical principles that underpin financial reporting	7%
2	Understand the key features of a published set of financial statements	18%
3	Draft statutory financial statements for a limited company	27%
4	Draft consolidated financial statements	20%
5	Interpret financial statements using ratio analysis	28%
Total		**100%**

UNIT LINK TO THE SYNOPTIC ASSESSMENT

AAT AQ16 introduced a Synoptic Assessment, which students must complete if they are to achieve the appropriate qualification upon completion of a qualification. In the case of the Professional Diploma in Accounting, students must pass all of the mandatory assessments and the Synoptic Assessment to achieve the qualification.

As a Synoptic Assessment is attempted following completion of individual units, it draws upon knowledge and understanding from those units. It may be appropriate for students to retain their study materials for individual units until they have successfully completed the Synoptic Assessment for that qualification.

With specific reference to this unit, the following learning objectives are also relevant to the Professional Diploma in Accounting Synoptic Assessment:

LO1 Understand the reporting frameworks and ethical principles that underpin financial reporting

LO5 Interpret financial statements using ratio analysis

STUDY SKILLS

Preparing to study

Devise a study plan

Determine which times of the week you will study.

Split these times into sessions of at least one hour for study of new material. Any shorter periods could be used for revision or practice.

Put the times you plan to study onto a study plan for the weeks from now until the assessment and set yourself targets for each period of study – in your sessions make sure you cover the whole course, activities and the associated questions in the workbook at the back of the manual.

If you are studying more than one unit at a time, try to vary your subjects as this can help to keep you interested and see subjects as part of wider knowledge.

When working through your course, compare your progress with your plan and, if necessary, re-plan your work (perhaps including extra sessions) or, if you are ahead, do some extra revision/practice questions.

Effective studying

Active reading

You are not expected to learn the text by rote, rather, you must understand what you are reading and be able to use it to pass the assessment and develop good practice.

A good technique is to use SQ3Rs – Survey, Question, Read, Recall, Review:

1 **Survey the chapter**

Look at the headings and read the introduction, knowledge, skills and content, so as to get an overview of what the chapter deals with.

2 **Question**

Whilst undertaking the survey ask yourself the questions you hope the chapter will answer for you.

3 **Read**

Read through the chapter thoroughly working through the activities and, at the end, making sure that you can meet the learning objectives highlighted on the first page.

4 **Recall**

At the end of each section and at the end of the chapter, try to recall the main ideas of the section/chapter without referring to the text. This is best done after a short break of a couple of minutes after the reading stage.

5 **Review**

Check that your recall notes are correct.

You may also find it helpful to re-read the chapter to try and see the topic(s) it deals with as a whole.

Note taking

Taking notes is a useful way of learning, but do not simply copy out the text.

The notes must:

- be in your own words
- be concise
- cover the key points
- be well organised
- be modified as you study further chapters in this text or in related ones.

Trying to summarise a chapter without referring to the text can be a useful way of determining which areas you know and which you don't.

Three ways of taking notes

1 **Summarise the key points of a chapter**

2 **Make linear notes**

A list of headings, subdivided with sub-headings listing the key points.

If you use linear notes, you can use different colours to highlight key points and keep topic areas together.

Use plenty of space to make your notes easy to use.

3 Try a diagrammatic form

The most common of which is a mind map.

To make a mind map, put the main heading in the centre of the paper and put a circle around it.

Draw lines radiating from this to the main sub-headings which again have circles around them.

Continue the process from the sub-headings to sub-sub-headings.

Annotating the text

You may find it useful to underline or highlight key points in your study text – but do be selective.

You may also wish to make notes in the margins.

Revision phase

Kaplan has produced material specifically designed for your final examination preparation for this unit.

These include pocket revision notes and a bank of revision questions specifically in the style of the new syllabus.

Further guidance on how to approach the final stage of your studies is given in these materials.

Further reading

In addition to this text, you should also read the 'Accounting Technician' magazine every month to keep abreast of any guidance from the examiners.

Regulatory frameworks

1

Introduction

In this initial chapter we will be covering background information that is essential for your understanding of the preparation of financial statements for many types of organisation, in particular for limited companies.

ASSESSMENT CRITERIA

Explain the regulatory framework that underpins financial reporting (1.1)

Explain the International Accounting Standards Board (the Board) Conceptual Framework for Financial Reporting ('the Framework') that underpins financial reporting (1.2)

CONTENTS

1 Introduction

1.1 Background knowledge

In previous units of your accounting studies you were introduced ledger accounting, and progressed on to preparation of an extended trial balance. When preparing an extended trial balance you would have made a number of adjustments for items such as inventories, accruals, prepayments, depreciation, irrecoverable debts and allowances for receivables. Each account on the extended trial balance was then balanced and extended into either the statement of profit or loss columns or the statement of financial position columns depending upon whether the account was an item of income, expense, an asset, a liability or equity/capital.

In this unit, your knowledge of financial accounting will be developed further.

1.2 Drafting financial statements

This unit includes the drafting of the relevant financial statements for limited companies. You must be able to prepare a statement of financial position, statement of profit or loss and other comprehensive income, statement of changes in equity and statement of cash flows in accordance with all of the applicable regulations (the Companies Act 2006, accounting standards, etc.).

1.3 Interpretation of financial statements

The unit also includes interpretation of financial statements. It is concerned with being able to analyse and understand the structure and purpose of financial statements of limited companies. It requires a sound understanding of the knowledge and skills required to prepare financial statements and an ability to interpret the relationships between the various components of the financial statements by using ratio analysis.

In order to understand and interpret limited company financial statements you must be able to understand how they have been prepared. Therefore your knowledge from Bookkeeping Transactions and Advanced Bookkeeping is extremely important as the knowledge and skills from these units will assist you to understand how the financial statements of limited companies are prepared.

In this chapter and the next, however, we will consider the background to the preparation of financial statements for limited companies by considering the regulatory framework and then the Conceptual Framework for Financial Reporting ('the Framework') within which financial statements are prepared.

2 The purpose of financial statements

2.1 Introduction

The main purpose of financial statements is to provide information to a wide range of users.

The **statement of financial position** provides information on the financial position of a business (its assets and liabilities and capital/equity at a point in time).

The **statement of profit or loss and other comprehensive income** provides information on the performance of a business (the profit or loss which results from trading over a period of time) as well as gains or losses that are not recognised in profit or loss.

The **statement of changes in equity** provides information about how the equity of the company has changed over the period.

The **statement of cash flows** provides information on the financial adaptability of a business (the movement of cash into and out of the business over a period of time).

2.2 Stewardship

Financial statements also show the results of the stewardship of an organisation. Stewardship is the accountability of management for the resources entrusted to it by the owners or the Government. This applies to the financial statements of limited companies as well as to others who prepare financial statements for stakeholders, such as central and local government, National Health Service, a board of trustees for a charity or the committee of a sports and social club.

2.3 Needs of users

All users of financial statements need information on financial position, performance and financial adaptability of the organisation they are interested in. However, many different groups of people may use financial statements and each group will particular information needs.

Users of financial statements may include investors, management, employees, customers, suppliers, lenders, the government and the public. User groups are considered in more detail on the following chapter.

2.4 Legal requirements

Law in the United Kingdom (UK) and many other countries requires limited companies to prepare annual financial statements. These financial statements must be filed with the Registrar of Companies and are then available to all interested parties. Most organisations, whether incorporated or not, are required to produce financial statements for submission to HM Revenue and Customs.

In the UK, the form and content of limited company accounts is specified by the Companies Acts. The preparation of limited company accounts is also subject to regulations issued by the Financial Reporting Council if the company is applying UK accounting standards or by the International Accounting Standards Board (the Board) if the company has adopted international financial reporting standards (IFRS Standards).

3 The legal framework

3.1 Introduction

The financial statements of limited companies must be prepared within the legal framework relevant to that company. In the case of UK companies, the Companies Act 2006 contains guidance and rules on:

- formats for the financial statements
- fundamental accounting principles
- valuation of items included in the financial statements.

The Companies Act 2006 allows companies to use the format of accounts set out in IAS 1 (revised) *Presentation of Financial Statements* if they have adopted IFRS® Standards or continue to use the format in the Act if they have not.

4 Accounting standards

4.1 IFRS Standards and IAS Standards

Accounting standards give guidance in specific areas of accounting. The Financial Statements syllabus follows International standards which consist of the following:

- **International Financial Reporting Standards (IFRS® Standards)**

  IFRS Standards are issued by the International Accounting Standards Board (the Board). Many countries have used IFRS Standards for some years. In 2002, the Council of Ministers of the European Union (EU) decided that any company which is listed on a European Stock Exchange must prepare their consolidated accounts in accordance with IFRS Standards with effect from 1 January 2005.

- **International Accounting Standards (IAS® Standards)**

  IAS Standards were created by the International Accounting Standards Committee (IASC) which was the predecessor of the Board. When the Board was formed it adopted the IAS Standards then in issue. Subsequently, many IAS Standards have been withdrawn and superseded by IFRS Standards, although some remain in issue.

4.2 The structure of the regulatory bodies

The structure of the International Financial Reporting Standards Foundation and its subsidiary bodies is shown below:

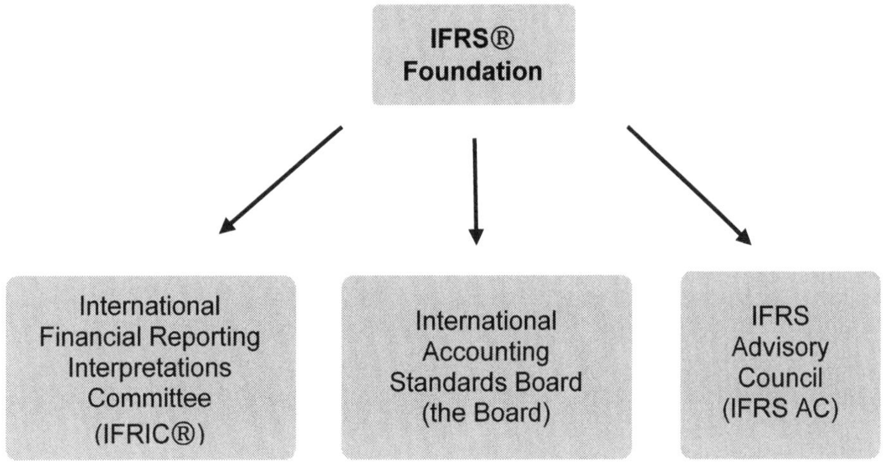

4.3 The IFRS Foundation ('the Foundation')

The IFRS Foundation is an independent not-for-profit foundation based in the USA. The Trustees of the Foundation appoint the members of the International Accounting Standards Board, the IFRS Advisory Council and the IFRS Interpretations Committee. They are also responsible for setting and approving the budgets of the various bodies, determining strategic direction and promoting IFRS Standards.

4.4 The International Accounting Standards Board ('the Board')

The Board has sole responsibility for the setting of international accounting standards. The Board's objectives are to:

(a) develop a single set of high quality, global accounting standards that require transparent and comparable information in general purpose financial statements

(b) promote the use and rigorous application of those standards, and

(c) work actively with national standard setters to bring about convergence of national accounting standards and IFRS Standards.

IFRS Standards set out the recognition, measurement, presentation and disclosure requirements of transactions and events that are important in accounting. They apply to all general purpose financial statements and any limitation in scope of a standard is stated within that standard.

The Board cooperates with other accounting standard setters with the aim of achieving harmony of accounting practice throughout the world. This has been the case in the UK as the Financial Reporting Council has adopted recently issued IFRS Standards. There will be relatively little difference in accounting practice for UK companies who have adopted IFRS Standards and those who have not.

4.5 International Financial Reporting Interpretations Committee ('IFRIC')

The aim of the IFRIC is to assist the Board in establishing and improving standards of financial accounting and reporting. It promotes the rigorous and uniform application of IFRS Standards. They provide timely guidance on:

1 newly identified financial reporting issues not specifically covered by an accounting standard, and

2 unsatisfactory interpretations that have developed or may develop.

The guidelines IFRIC publishes are called IFRIC Interpretations. If a company complies with IFRS Standards, then it is also presumed that this includes compliance with IFRIC Interpretations.

4.6 IFRS Advisory Council ('IFRS AC')

The Council provides a forum for organisations and individuals to input into the standard-setting process. Its overall objectives are to:

(a) give advice to the Board on agenda decisions and priorities

(b) inform the Board of the views of organisations and individuals, and

(c) give other advice to the Board or the Trustees.

4.7 The standard-setting process

There are a number of steps in the process to develop and issue a new accounting standard by the Board as follows:

(a) staff are asked to identify and review all issues associated with a topic and to consider the application of the Framework to the issues

(b) study of national accounting requirements and practice and an exchange of views about the issues with national standard-setters

(c) consulting the Council about the advisability of adding the topic to the Board agenda

(d) formation of an advisory group to give advice to the Board on the project

(e) publication of a discussion document for public comment

(f) publication of an 'exposure draft' for public comment which has been approved by at least eight members of the Board, including any dissenting opinions held by Board members

(g) publication within an exposure draft a basis for conclusions

(h) consideration of all comments received within the comment period on the discussion documents and exposure drafts

(i) consideration of whether to hold a public hearing and to conduct field tests and, if necessary, holding such hearings and conducting such tests

(j) approval of a standard by at least eight members of the Board and inclusion in the published standard of any dissenting opinions, and

(k) publication within a standard a basis for conclusions explaining, amongst other things, the steps in the Board due process and how the Board dealt with public comments on the exposure draft.

Test your understanding 1

1 What are the four principal financial statements that would be included in a set of financial statements?

2 What is meant by the term 'stewardship'?

3 What does IFRS stand for?

4 What is the role of the Board?

5 What is the role of IFRIC?

5 Summary

The regulatory framework for a UK company preparing financial statements in accordance with IFRS Standards consists of:

- the Companies Act which applies to all UK companies regardless of whether they follow UK or International accounting rules
- the International Accounting Standards Board ('the Board') and its associated bodies who are responsible for the development, approval and publication of IFRS Standards.

Test your understanding answers

Test your understanding 1

1 Statement of financial position, statement of profit or loss and other comprehensive income, statement of changes in equity and statement of cash flows.

2 Stewardship is the accountability of management for the resources entrusted to it by the owners of a business or the Government.

3 International Financial Reporting Standard.

4 The role of the Board is to develop, approve and publish International Financial Reporting Standards.

5 IFRIC assists the Board by producing IFRIC Interpretations which provide guidance on new accounting issues that are not covered by an IFRS Standard and provide guidance on the appropriate interpretation and application of an IFRS Standard.

The conceptual framework and ethical principles

2

Introduction

This chapter provides some essential background knowledge of the principles and concepts that underlie the preparation of financial statements for limited companies. The Board have produced a framework for the preparation and presentation of financial statements.

ASSESSMENT CRITERIA

Explain the International Accounting Standards Board (the Board) Conceptual Framework for Financial Reporting ('the Framework') that underpins financial reporting (1.2)

Discuss the ethical principles that underpin financial reporting in accordance with the AAT Code of Professional Ethics (1.3)

CONTENTS

1 User groups

1.1 The purpose of accounting

The purpose of accounting is to provide information to users of financial statements. Legally, company financial statements are drawn up for the benefit of the shareholders, so that they can assess the performance of their Board of Directors. However, in practice many other groups will use these financial statements, and these groups will all have different needs. These groups, and their needs, are described below.

1.2 Management

Management will be interested in an analysis of revenues and expenses that will provide information that is useful when plans are formulated and decisions made. Once the budget for a business is complete, the accountant can produce figures for what actually happens as the budget period unfolds, so that they can be compared with the budget.

Management will also need to know the cost consequences of a particular course of action to aid their decision making. However, this information is more likely to be found in monthly management accounts than in the published financial statements.

1.3 Shareholders and potential shareholders

This group includes the investing public at large and the stockbrokers and commentators who advise them. The shareholders should be informed of the manner in which management has used their funds that have been invested in the business. This is a matter of reporting on past events. However, both shareholders and potential shareholders are also interested in the future performance of the business and use past figures as a guide to the future if they have to vote on proposals or decide whether to sell their shares.

Financial analysts advising investors such as insurance companies, pension funds, unit trusts and investment trusts are among the most sophisticated users of accounting information, and the company contemplating a takeover bid is yet another type of potential shareholder.

1.4 Employees and their trade union representatives

These use accounting information to assess the potential performance of the business. This information is relevant to the employee, who wishes to discover whether the company can offer him safe employment and promotion through growth over a period of years, and also to the trade unionist, who uses past profits and potential profits in his calculations and claims for higher wages or better conditions. The viability of different divisions of a company is of interest to this group.

1.5 Lenders

This group includes some who have financed the business over a long period by lending money which is to be repaid at the end of a number of years, as well as short-term payables such as a bank which allows a company to overdraw its bank account for a number of months, and suppliers of raw materials, which permit a company to buy goods from them and pay in, say, four to twelve weeks' time.

Lenders are interested in the security of their loan, so they will look at an accounting statement to ensure that the company will be able to repay on the due date and meet the interest requirements before that date. The amount of cash available and the value of assets, which form a security for the debt, are of importance to this group. Credit rating agencies are interested in accounts for similar reasons.

1.6 Government agencies

These use accounting information, either when collecting statistical information to reveal trends within the economy as a whole or, in the case of HM Revenue and Customs, to assess the profit on which the company's tax liability is to be computed.

1.7 The public

From time to time other groups not included above may have an interest in the company e.g. members of a local community where the company operates, environmental pressure groups, and so on.

Conclusion

Financial statements serve a wide variety of user groups, who have different interests and also different levels of financial sophistication. This makes it particularly difficult to produce accounts that are intelligible to the layman but comprehensive for the expert.

The next section looks at how standards have been developed to try to meet these diverse needs.

2 A conceptual framework

2.1 Overview of the framework

A conceptual framework is a coherent system of inter-related objectives and fundamentals that can lead to consistent standards and that prescribes the nature, function and limits of financial accounting and financial statements. The Board's conceptual framework is known as the Conceptual Framework for Financial Reporting ('the Framework').

The basic objective of the conceptual framework is to provide a logical and sensible guide for preparing accounting standards and applying them. In effect it will be the constitution within which accountant's work, while the standards themselves will be the detailed laws enacted to apply these constitutional principles.

The Framework is not an accounting standard. Nothing in the Framework overrides a specific international financial reporting standard.

3 Conceptual Framework for Financial Reporting ('the Framework')

3.1 The matters dealt with in the Framework

The following topics are covered in the Framework:

- The objective of financial statements.
- The underlying assumption.
- Qualitative characteristics of financial statements.
- Definition of elements of financial statements.
- Recognition of the elements of financial statements.
- Measurement of the elements of financial statements.
- Concepts of capital and capital maintenance.

4 The objective of financial statements

4.1 Usefulness for particular purposes

The objective of financial statements is to provide information about the financial position, performance and changes in financial position of an entity that is useful to a wide range of users in making economic decisions. Financial statements may not provide all the information that users need to make economic decisions as they portray the effect of past events and do not always provide non-financial information.

The two most common 'economic decisions' made by users are:

- to buy or sell shares, and
- to re-elect or replace the Board of Directors.

Users need to be able to evaluate the ability of the entity to generate cash. They also need to be able to predict the timing and certainty of the cash being generated. To be able to do this users need historic information about:

- financial position
- performance
- cash flow of an entity.

(a) The financial position of an entity is affected by:

  - the economic resources it controls
  - its financial structure
  - its liquidity and solvency
  - its capacity to adapt to changes in the environment in which it operates.

  This information is normally found in the statement of financial position.

(b) Information about the performance of an entity comprises the return obtained by the entity on the resources it controls. This can be found in the statement of profit or loss and the statement of changes in equity.

(c) Information on cash flows of an entity is useful in providing the user with an additional perspective on the performance of an entity by indicating the amounts and principal sources of its cash inflows and outflows. This is provided by the statement of cash flow.

Each statement reflects different aspects of the same transactions and events. A user should study all of the statements before making any decisions.

4.2 User groups

Traditionally financial statements were prepared for the benefit of the shareholders (the owners) and the creditors. The Framework recognises that other user groups may have a reasonable right to information, and that financial statements should take their needs into account.

5 The underlying assumptions

5.1 Going concern

The going concern basis assumes that the entity will continue in operation for the foreseeable future and has neither the need nor the intention to liquidate or curtail materially the scale of its operations.

5.2 Accrual basis

Under the accrual basis the effects of transactions and other events are recognised when they occur, and not as cash is received or paid (cash basis). Events are recorded in the accounting records and reported in the financial statements of the periods to which they relate.

6 The qualitative characteristics of financial statements

6.1 Overview

The Framework identifies two fundamental qualitative characteristics of useful financial information:

- relevance, and
- faithful representation.

These are supported by four enhancing qualitative characteristics:

- comparability
- verifiability
- timeliness, and
- understandability.

Definitions

Relevance

Financial information is regarded as relevant if it is capable of influencing the decisions of users.

Faithful representation

This means that financial information must be complete, neutral and free from error.

Comparability

It should be possible to compare an entity over time and with similar information about other entities.

Verifiability

If information can be verified (e.g. through an audit) this provides assurance to the users that it is both credible and reliable.

Timeliness

Information should be provided to users within a timescale suitable for their decision making purposes.

Understandability

Information should be understandable to those that might want to review and use it. This can be facilitated through appropriate classification, characterisation and presentation of information.

6.2 True and fair view/fair presentation

Financial statements are frequently described as giving a true and fair view of, or presenting fairly, the position, performance and changes in financial position of an entity. The Framework does not define the concept of a true and fair view, but by following accounting standards as well as the qualitative characteristics above financial statements should present a true and fair view.

One of the concepts embodied in the concept of truth and fairness is that of reasonable accuracy, rather than absolute accuracy. For example, consider a large multinational corporation with revenues of hundreds of billions of dollars per year; would the users' decisions be affected by an error that overstated profits in the financial statements by one thousand dollars? Of course it would not; the financial statements would be rounded to the nearest billion dollars so the error is totally irrelevant. Would an error that understated liabilities by two billion dollars affect their decisions? The answer to this is that it might; this is a significant amount of debt missing from the statement of financial position and the debt position of a business is crucial to decision makers, particularly lenders.

This leads to the concept of materiality; to be true and fair financial statements should be free from material misstatement.

Definition

Information is material if omitting, misstating or obscuring it could reasonably be expected to influence the decisions that the primary users of general purpose financial statements make on the basis of those financial statements, which provide financial information about a specific reporting entity.

7 The elements of financial statements

7.1 Overview

The Framework identifies five elements of financial statements:

- assets
- liabilities
- equity interest
- income
- expenses.

7.2 Assets

'An asset is

- **a present economic resource controlled by the entity**
- **as a result of past events'**

(Framework, para 4.3)

'An economic resource is a right that has the potential to produce economic benefit.' (Framework, para 4.4)

7.3 Liabilities

'A liability is

- **a present obligation of the entity**
- **to transfer an economic resource as a result of past events'**

(Framework, para 4.26).

7.4 Equity interest

The Framework defines equity as:

'The residual interest in the assets of the entity after deducting all its liabilities.' (Framework, para 4.4)

In other words, equity is what is left when all liabilities have been settled. This is essentially the net assets of a business.

7.5 Income

Income consists of both revenue and gains. Revenue arises from a business's ordinary activities such as the sale of goods. Gains represent increases in economic benefits such as a gain on disposal of a non-current asset. Gains are usually shown separately from the revenue generated by the business often because they need to be disclosed separately to give a full understanding of the transaction. Note that contributions from shareholders are not income, they are part of equity.

7.6 Expenses

Expenses are losses as well as expenses that arise in the normal course of business such as cost of sales, wages and depreciation. Losses represent a decrease in economic benefits such as losses on disposal of non-current assets or disasters such as fire or flood. As with gains, losses are often shown separately in the financial statements to give a full understanding of the situation. Note that distributions (dividends) to shareholders are not expenses.

8 The accounting equation

8.1 The accounting equation

This unit requires that the elements of the financial statements should be identified and that the relationships between these elements are also identified.

Earlier in your studies you will have learned the accounting equation:

Assets – Liabilities = Capital + Profits – Drawings

When preparing company financial statements the equation is rearranged as follows:

Assets = Equity + Liabilities

Test your understanding 1

Sabrina Ltd

Statement of financial position as at 31 March 20X8

ASSETS	£
Non-current assets	
Property, plant and equipment	20,500
Current assets	17,500
Total assets	38,000
EQUITY AND LIABILITIES	
Share capital	12,000
Share premium	3,000
Retained earnings	5,000
	20,000
Non-current liabilities	5,000
Current liabilities	13,000
Total equity and liabilities	38,000

What are the monetary values of the equity, the assets and the liabilities in Sabrina Ltd as at 31 March 20X8 and how are they related in the accounting equation?

9 Recognition of the elements of financial statements

9.1 General recognition criteria

An item should be recognised in the financial statements if:

- it meets one of the definitions of an element (asset, liability, equity, income, expense).
- it is probable that any future economic benefit associated with the item will flow to or from the entity (for example, income is recognised when a sale is made, not when an order is received).
- the item has a cost or value that can be measured with reliability.

Normally the monetary amount will come straight from the sale or purchase invoice. However, reasonable, reliable and prudent estimates can be recognised, for example, a property revaluation or a warranty provision.

The recognition process

Recognition is triggered where a past event indicates that there has been a measurable change in the assets or liabilities of the entity.

The effect of uncertainty

The more evidence there is for an item, the more reliable its recognition and measurement will be.

Test your understanding 2

The conceptual framework for financial reporting states that 'the objective of financial statements is to provide information about the financial position, performance and changes in financial position of an entity.'

Additionally it states 'financial statements also show the results of the stewardship of management.'

(a) What is meant by saying that financial statements show the results of 'stewardship of management'?

(b) What is meant by 'Equity'? How is it related to other elements in the accounting equation?

10 Measurement of the elements of financial statements

10.1 Overview

The Framework identifies four possible measurement bases:

- historical cost
- current cost
- realisable value
- present value.

10.2 Historical cost

Assets are recorded at the amount of cash paid to acquire them. Sometimes the terms, cash equivalents or fair value at acquisition will be used instead.

Liabilities are recorded at the proceeds received in exchange for the obligation.

10.3 Current cost

Assets are carried at their current purchase price (i.e. their price now, not their price when originally purchased).

Liabilities are carried at the undiscounted amount currently required to settle them.

10.4 Realisable value

Assets are carried at the amount, which could currently be obtained by an orderly disposal. Liabilities are carried at their settlement values – the amount to be paid to satisfy them in the normal course of business.

10.5 Present value

Assets are carried at the present discounted value of the future net cash inflows that the item is expected to generate in the normal course of business.

Liabilities are carried at the present discounted value of the expected cash outflows necessary to settle them.

Although historical cost is the most common basis, the others are often used to modify historical cost. For example, inventories are usually carried at the lower of cost and net realisable value, investments may be carried at market value and pension liabilities are carried at their present value.

11 The potential benefits and drawbacks of an agreed conceptual framework

11.1 Potential benefits

The potential benefits of a conceptual framework are:

- A framework for setting future accounting standards.
- A basis for resolving disputes as the elements of financial statements are clearly defined.
- Fundamental principles do not have to be repeated in accounting standards.
- There should be a reduction in pressure from vested interests who wish to pursue a particular policy out of self-interest rather than satisfying the general needs of users.

11.2 Potential drawbacks

Drawbacks to a conceptual framework include:

- Due to their general nature the principles may not, in practice, reduce the options available.
- There may be further disagreement as to the contents of the framework in addition to disagreement over the contents of standards.

12 Accounting policies

12.1 Accounting policies

Accounting policies are the specific principles, bases, conventions, rules and practices applied by an entity in preparing and presenting financial statements.

Management should select and apply appropriate accounting policies so that the financial statements comply with all international standards (IFRS Standards and IAS Standards) and IFRIC Interpretations.

If there is no specific standard for a particular item then management should choose policies that are relevant and reliable. Management should refer to IFRS Standards, IAS Standards and Interpretations dealing with similar issues and to the Framework.

All material accounting policies should be disclosed and explained in the notes to the financial statements.

An entity should select and apply accounting policies consistently for similar transactions.

13 Ethical principles

13.1 Introduction

In this section we look at the ethical principles that underpin financial reporting in accordance with the Code of Ethics for Professional Accountants, the threats involved and how we can apply safeguards to resolve ethical conflict.

13.2 The Code of Ethics for Professional Accountants

The Code of Ethics for Professional Accountants, published by The International Federation of Accountants (IFAC), forms the basis for the ethical codes of many accountancy bodies, including the AAT, ICAEW, ACCA and CIMA.

The code adopts a principles-based approach. It does not attempt to cover every situation where a member may encounter professional ethical issues, prescribing the way in which he or she should respond. Instead, it adopts a value system, focusing on fundamental professional and ethical principles which are at the heart of proper professional behaviour.

The five key principles are as follows:

(a) Integrity

A person should be straightforward and honest in performing professional work and in all business relationships.

(b) Objectivity

A professional accountant should not allow bias, conflict of interest or undue influence of others to override professional or business judgments.

Test your understanding 3

Olivia, an AAT member in practice at Integrity LLP, has been offered a job by one of her audit clients.

In order to maintain her independence, what course of action should Olivia take?

- Resign immediately.
- Inform the partners at Integrity LLP and be removed from the audit of the client.
- Nothing – it is just an offer.

(c) Professional competence and due care

A professional accountant has a continuing duty to maintain professional knowledge and skill at the level required to ensure that a client or employer receives competent professional service based on current developments in practice, legislation and techniques.

(d) Confidentiality

A professional accountant should respect the confidentiality of information acquired as a result of professional and business relationships and should not disclose any such information to third parties without proper and specific authority unless there is a legal or professional right or duty to disclose.

(e) Professional behaviour

A person should not act in any way that is unprofessional or does not comply with relevant laws and regulations.

13.3 Threats

Threats to compliance with the fundamental principles can be general in nature or relate to the specific circumstances of an appointment.

General categories of threats to the principles include the following:

- **The self-interest threat** – a threat to a member's integrity or objectivity may stem from a financial or other self-interest conflict.

  This could arise, for example, from a direct or indirect interest in a client or from fear of losing an engagement or having his or her employment terminated or as a consequence of undue commercial pressure from within or outside the firm.

- **The self-review threat** – there will be a threat to objectivity if any product or judgement of the member or the firm needs to be challenged or re-evaluated by him or her subsequently.

- **The advocacy threat** – there is a threat to a member's objectivity if he or she becomes an advocate for or against the position taken by the client or employer in any adversarial proceedings or situation. The degree to which this presents a threat to objectivity will depend on the individual circumstances. The presentation of only one side of the case may be compatible with objectivity provided that it is accurate and truthful.

- **The familiarity or trust threat** – is a threat that the member may become influenced by his or her
  - knowledge of the issue
  - relationship with the client or employer
  - judgement of the qualities of the client or employer to the extent that he or she becomes too trusting.

- **The intimidation threat** – the possibility that the member may become intimidated by threat, by a dominating personality, or by other pressures, actual or feared, applied by the client or employer or by another.

Test your understanding 4

Consider each of the following threats to independence and label them according the classification given above.

- The financial statements of Hird Ltd have been prepared by Lloyd Brothers, their audit firm.
- Having audited the client firm for many years, the audit partner has become close friends with the Directors.
- Knowalot plc has intimated to the audit firm that if they do not receive an unqualified audit report for the year 20X9, they may put the audit out to tender.

13.4 Safeguards

Safeguards may eliminate or reduce such threats to an acceptable level.

They fall into two broad categories:

(i) safeguards created by the profession, legislation or regulation and

(ii) safeguards in the work environment.

Safeguards created by the profession, legislation or regulation include, but are not restricted to:

(i) educational, training and experience requirements for entry into the profession

(ii) continuing professional development requirements

(iii) corporate governance regulations

(iv) professional standards

(v) professional or regulatory monitoring and disciplinary procedures

(vi) external review of the reports, returns, communications or information produced by a member and carried out by a legally empowered third party.

Safeguards in the work environment include, but are not restricted to:

(i) the employing organisation's systems of corporate oversight or other oversight structures

(ii) the employing organisation's ethics and conduct programmes

(iii) recruitment procedures in the employing organisation emphasising the importance of employing high calibre competent staff

(iv) strong internal controls

(v) appropriate disciplinary processes

(vi) leadership that stresses the importance of ethical behaviour and the expectation that employees will act in an ethical manner

(vii) policies and procedures to implement and monitor the quality of employee performance

(viii) timely communication of the employing organisation's policies and procedures, including any changes to them, to all employees and appropriate training and education on such policies and procedures

(ix) policies and procedures to empower and encourage employees to communicate to senior levels within the employing organisation any ethical issues that concern them without fear of retribution

(x) consultation with another appropriate professional.

The nature of the safeguards to be applied will vary depending on the circumstances. In exercising professional judgement, a member should consider what a reasonable and informed third party, having knowledge of all relevant information, including the significance of the threat and the safeguards applied, would conclude to be unacceptable.

14 Other key concepts

14.1 Substance over form

Under this concept, transactions and other events are accounted for and presented in financial statements in accordance with their economic substance and financial reality and not merely with their legal form.

For example, leasehold buildings are owned by the landlord rather than the occupier, but the occupier is using them for his business in the same way as if they were freehold. Thus it may be appropriate to treat them as a fixed asset in the occupier's statement of financial position, provided that it is made clear that the premises are leasehold.

14.2 The consistency concept

Like items are treated in a similar manner within each accounting period and from one period to the next. This aids comparison of results over time.

Test your understanding 5

The accounting equation is:

Assets – Liabilities = Equity or

Assets = Equity + Liabilities

(a) Define the following elements of financial statements:

(i) Assets

(ii) Liabilities

(iii) Equity

(b) Explain why inventory is an asset of a company.

Test your understanding 6

1 Which group is seen to be the main user of financial statements?

2 What does management require from financial information?

3 What would potential shareholders' interests be in the financial statements?

4 What is a conceptual framework?

5 What is meant by the relevance of information?

6 How does the Framework define:

- assets
- liabilities?

7 What is the going concern concept?

Test your understanding 7

A major objective of published financial statements is 'to provide information about the financial position, performance and financial adaptability of an enterprise that is useful to a wide range of users for assessing the stewardship of management and for making economic decisions'.

What characteristics contribute to making financial information useful in terms of both content and presentation, and how do these characteristics fulfil their objective?

Test your understanding 8

The elements of financial statements comprise:

- Assets
- Liabilities
- Equity interest
- Income
- Expenses

Define these terms and state which of these terms comprise the 'accounting equation'.

Test your understanding 9

Data

The accounting equation of a business is as follows:

Assets £1,200 – Liabilities £800 = Equity interest £400

The business subsequently makes two transactions:

1 it purchases on credit inventories costing £120; and

2 it sells the inventories purchased in (1) for £180 cash.

Task

(a) Explain what is meant by 'assets', 'liabilities' and 'equity interest'.

(b) Explain the effect of each transaction on the elements in the statement of financial position.

(c) State the accounting equation for the business after the two transactions have taken place.

(d) Draft a simple statement of profit or loss for the two transactions.

(e) Give an example of a user who might be interested in a statement of profit or loss.

Explain how the user you have chosen might find the statement useful.

Test your understanding 10

Data

The conceptual framework for financial reporting states the following elements of the financial statements:

(a) Assets

(b) Liabilities

(c) Equity interest

(d) Income

(e) Expenses

Task

(a) (i) In which primary financial statement are 'assets', 'liabilities' and 'equity interest' shown?

(ii) What is the relationship between assets, liabilities and equity?

(b) What is meant by 'income' and 'expenses' and in which primary financial statement are they shown?

Test your understanding 11

Why are potential investors interested in company financial statements?

15 Different types of business organisation

15.1 Introduction

There are a range of organisations, of varying size, administrative structure and complexity that enter into accounting transactions. Each organisation will need to maintain some accounting records sufficient to ensure that they can report upon their financial performance and position to interested stakeholders, including owners and other providers of finance.

15.2 Sole trader

A sole trader both owns and manages the business. A sole trader takes on all of the risks and rewards associated with owning and managing the business, including unlimited liability for the debts of the business. The size and nature of the business is subject to the financial and other resources available to each individual sole trader. There is minimum formality required when setting up a business as a sole trader.

Normally, the financial accounts of sole traders and partnerships adhere to the principal requirements of financial reporting standards as a matter of good practice.

15.3 Partnership

A partnership is defined by the Partnership Act 1890 as "persons carrying on a business in common with a view of profit". The partners both own and manage the business, with each partner having unlimited personal liability for the debts of the partnership.

As with a sole trader, the size and nature of the business is subject to the financial and other resources available to the partners collectively. Normally, a partnership business is able to grow larger than a sole trader as more persons are contributing capital and other resources to the business.

Partnerships are normally subject to a partnership agreement which sets out the rights and obligations between the partners, including individual shares of profits and losses arising from running the business. It may also include individual work responsibilities and define the nature and extent of agreed business activities.

As with a sole trader, there is minimum formality required to establish a partnership and, unless agreed otherwise between the partners, the Partnership Act 1890 includes the presumption that all partners jointly own and manage the business, and will also share profits and losses equally.

15.4 Limited liability partnership (LLP)

A limited liability partnership may be formed by complying with the required procedure ('incorporation') specified in the Limited Liability Partnerships Act 2000. It is a 'half-way house' between a partnership and limited liability company. It retains much of the flexibility of a normal partnership such as:

- partners' agreeing the nature and extent of their business activities
- partners' agreeing their respective share of the annual profit or loss
- partners' agreeing their individual responsibilities e.g. having responsibility for accounting issues, marketing, staffing etc.
- each partner will be subject to income tax on their share of the partnership profit.

Note that a LLP must have one general partner who has unlimited personal liability for the debts of the partnership.

A LLP has many of the 'external characteristics' of a limited liability company, such as:

- it is formed by a formal incorporation process specified by law
- it is regarded as a separate legal entity
- it must file annual accounts at Companies House
- its annual accounts are subject to audit (unless complying with exemption criteria)
- it can own property in its own name.

15.5 Limited liability company

A limited liability company may be formed by complying with the required procedure ('incorporation') specified in the Companies Act 2006. The key features of a limited liability company are as follows:

- it is a separate legal entity, distinct from its owners and/or managers, and can own property in its own name
- there is a separation between ownership of a limited company by its members (i.e. shareholders) and its management by directors. It is possible to be both a member and a director of a company, but the law recognises distinct rights and responsibilities of each position
- it must file annual reports and accounts at Companies House
- its annual accounts are subject to audit (unless complying with exemption criteria)

- it may raise finance by the issue of a debenture, and may grant a floating charge as security for any borrowings
- it is subject to corporation tax on its profit.

There are two types of limited liability company:

(a) a private limited company, and

(b) a public limited company.

15.5.1 Private limited company

A private limited company is required to have only one member and one director, and can commence trading upon issue of the certificate of incorporation. There is no upper limit on the maximum number of members or directors.

A private company cannot offer its shares to the general public, and nor can they be publicly traded.

15.5.2 Public limited company

A public limited company is required to have a minimum of two members and two directors. Public companies are permitted to raise capital by offering shares to the general public and, therefore, are subject to additional regulation.

A public limited company must have a minimum of £50,000 issued share capital, along with a certificate of incorporation, before it can obtain a trading certificate which confirms eligibility to commence trading activities.

It cannot be exempt from annual audit and it must file its annual reports and accounts within a shorter time period than a private company.

15.6 Not-for-profit organisations

These organisations tend to have benevolent or social objectives, such as a charity or a sports or social club. They are not run to make a profit, but may undertake a range of fund-raising activities and use the proceeds generated to support their objectives.

Although many charities, clubs or societies may be local in nature, they may vary in size and complexity. For example, a charity may consist of a local support group to help disadvantaged persons, raising and spending relatively low sums of cash. It could also extend to international fund-raising and benevolent activities to provide relief in locations suffering the effects of a natural disaster or from the effects of conflict. In the UK, charities are subject to the Charities Act 2011 which defines what a charity is and the permitted purposes it may be established for.

A club or society could be a local amateur dramatic society or a local sports team.

Not-for-profit organisations will enter into transactions which need to be recorded, summarised and classified into financial reports of some kind. Normally, they will not have a statement of profit or loss, but may have a statement of income and expenditure, which summarises income received (donations, subscriptions etc.), expenditure incurred (charitable relief, maintenance of the sports facilities etc.) and whether there was a surplus or deficit for the accounting period.

15.7 Public sector organisations

These organisations tend to be for the benefit of the public as a whole and to administer central and local government activity. They can be regarded as a particular type of not-for-profit organisation as they are subject to specific laws and regulations, including accounting requirements. Invariably, they will be subject to annual external audit and may also be subject to internal audit requirements.

The accounting and reporting requirements may include reporting on 'value for money' aspects of activity, which is something not included within the annual report and accounts of commercially-focussed organisations.

Public sector organisations now apply IFRS Standards as far as practicable, subject to other specific legislative or regulatory requirements that may apply.

15.7.1 Local authorities

Local authorities receive funds from central government in addition to raising funds from locally imposed business rates, council tax on households and other sundry income such as public car park charges.

Expenditure consists of meeting obligations imposed upon local authorities by central government or by legislation, plus other locally determined commitments for the benefit of the community.

Accounting requirements focus upon reporting how financial resources have been raised and used. This may include elements of capital and fund accounting for large projects, such as projects to construct a new housing estate.

15.7.2 Central government

Central government raises funds principally from taxation imposed upon businesses and individuals. Expenditure consists of support payments to local authorities to enable them to meet their obligations and to support government departments and ministries, both at home and abroad.

Most government departments are 'spending departments' as they are responsible for accounting for the use of financial resources allocated to it by central government.

As with local authorities, accounting requirements for central government departments will focus upon reporting how financial resources have been raised and used. Including elements of capital and fund accounting for large projects, such as significant projects to maintain and support national defence.

15.7.3 National Health Service (NHS)

The NHS is funded principally from central government funds. There are many elements to the NHS, such as hospitals, support of general practice provision and other auxiliary services.

In recent years, the NHS has devolved from a centralised organisation into a number of trusts, which are legally independent and autonomous bodies with their own governance arrangements. The trusts are accountable to the local people and community they serve.

Each trust prepares annual financial reports and accounts which are subject to external audit. They are also subject to internal audit requirements, which include reporting on 'value for money' aspects of the activities of a trust.

15.7.4 Cooperatives

A cooperative is an organisation owned and run by its members. This may be on a 'not-for-profit' basis, although it could also have a commercial purpose. They may be a way to promote employee participation in the management of an organisation, or enable a group of traders to collectively improve their bargaining position with suppliers or customers.

Cooperatives must submit their annual reports and accounts in specified form to the Financial Conduct Authority. A cooperative may be required to have an annual audit, based upon either the activities it undertakes (e.g. a housing association) and/or does not meet the required financial thresholds to be exempt from audit.

16 Summary

The framework for the preparation and presentation of financial statements sets out two fundamental accounting concepts:

- going concern
- accrual basis.

The objective of financial statements is to provide information about the reporting entity's financial performance and financial position that is useful to a wide range of users for assessing the stewardship of management and for making economic decisions.

The two fundamental qualitative characteristics of financial information are:

- relevance
- faithful representation.

The four enhancing qualitative characteristics of financial information are:

- comparability
- verifiability
- timeliness
- understandability.

The elements of financial statements are:

- assets
- liabilities
- equity interest
- income
- expenses.

The importance of ethical behaviour in accounting has been reviewed within this chapter. It has focussed on the ethical principles that need to be applied when preparing financial statements and potential threats to these principles.

Test your understanding answers

Test your understanding 1

Sabrina Ltd

The monetary values are as follows:

	£
Equity	20,000
Assets	38,000
Liabilities	18,000

The figures are related in the accounting equation as follows

Assets – Liabilities = Equity

38,000 – 18,000 = 20,000 or

Assets = Equity + Liabilities

38,000 = 20,000 + 18,000

Test your understanding 2

(a) Management is accountable for the safe-keeping of the entity's resources and for their proper, efficient and profitable use.

In other words, they are the 'stewards' of the resources of the entity and are responsible to shareholders for the management of the resources to ensure that they generate adequate profit and cash flows to give them a return and to ensure that lenders to the business are repaid.

(b) Equity is 'the residual interest in the assets of the entity after deducting all its liabilities'. The equity is related to the other elements in the accounting equation as follows:

Assets – Liabilities = Equity

Test your understanding 3

Olivia should inform the partners at Integrity LLP and should be removed from the audit of the client.

Test your understanding 4

- Self-review
- Familiarity
- Intimidation

Test your understanding 5

(a) The elements of financial statements are defined by the conceptual framework for financial reporting as follows:

(i) 'Assets' are present economic resources controlled by an entity as a result of past events. An economic resource is a right that has the potential to produce economic benefit.

(ii) 'Liabilities' are present obligations of the entity to transfer an economic resource as a result of past events.

(iii) Equity is 'the residual interest in the assets of the entity after deducting all its liabilities'.

(b) Inventory fits the definition of an asset as the purchase of inventory for resale has the potential to produce economic benefits in that the entity can sell the inventory or use the inventory to manufacture products that are sold.

Test your understanding 6

1 Shareholders.

2 Management will be interested in an analysis of revenues and expenses that will provide information that is useful when plans are formulated and decisions made. Once the budget for a business is complete, the accountant can produce figures for what actually happens as the budget period unfolds, so that they can be compared with the budget. Management will also need to know the cost consequences of a particular course of action to aid their decision making.

3 The future performance of the business.

4 A conceptual framework is a coherent system of inter-related objectives and fundamentals that can lead to consistent standards and that prescribes the nature, function and limits of financial accounting and financial statements.

5 Relevant information is capable of making a different to the economic decisions made by users. Relevant information may have predictive or confirmatory value, or both.

6 An asset is a present economic resource controlled by an entity as a result of a past event. A liability is a present obligation of the entity to transfer an economic resource as a result of a past event.

7 The going concern basis assumes that the entity will continue in operation for the foreseeable future and has neither the need nor the intention to liquidate or curtail materially the scale of its operations.

Test your understanding 7

The Framework identifies two fundamental characteristics which make financial information useful:

- Relevance, and
- Faithful representation.

Relevant information is capable of influencing the economic decisions of the key users of the financial statements. Thus, if information is not relevant to a user it is unlikely to be useful. For example; the managing director's shoe size is information but it is not relevant to a shareholder's decision regarding whether to retain or sell their shares.

Faithful representation means that financial information must be complete, neutral and free from error.

It is not sufficient to only report some liabilities to users as the debt position of the business is crucial to making decisions. All liabilities must be reported to users.

Neutral information is information that is free of director/manager bias. A good example of this would be with regard to the recognition of provisions (are they probable?) and the useful life of property, plant and equipment. Managers could manipulate these figures to suit their own profit and remuneration targets so they must be (and be perceived to be) neutral when they make estimates.

Finally, information should be free from errors: users need quality information to make quality decisions. If the information is wrong then their decisions may be too.

Test your understanding 8

The Framework defines an asset as:

> *'a present economic resource controlled by the entity as a result of past events' (para 4.3).*

The Framework defines a liability as:

> *'a present obligation of the entity to transfer an economic resource as a result of past events' (para 4.26).*

The Framework defines equity as:

> *'The residual interest in the assets of the entity after deducting all its liabilities'.*

In other words, equity is what is left when all liabilities have been settled. This is essentially the net assets of a business.

Income consists of both revenue and gains. Revenue arises from a business's ordinary activities such as the sale of goods. Gains represent increases in economic benefits such as a gain on disposal of a non-current asset.

Expenses are losses as well as expenses that arise in the normal course of business such as cost of sales, wages and depreciation. Losses represent a decrease in economic benefits such as losses on disposal of non-current assets or disasters such as fire or flood.

Accounting equation

Assets less liabilities = equity interest

Test your understanding 9

(a) 'Assets' are present economic resources controlled by an entity as a result of past events.

'Liabilities' are present obligations of the entity to transfer an economic resource as a result of past events. 'Equity interest' is the residual amount found by deducting all of the entity's liabilities from all of the entity's assets.

(b) The first transaction would increase the assets (inventories) by £120 and increase the liabilities (trade payables) by £120.

The second transaction would decrease the asset (inventories), i.e. inventories at cost, by £120, but increase the asset cash by £180. This would increase net assets by £60 and equity interest, i.e. capital, by £60 (the profit on the transaction).

(c) The accounting equation would then appear as:

Assets £1,380 – Liabilities £920 = Equity Interest £460

(d) A simple statement of profit or loss would show:

	£
Revenue	180
Cost of sales	(120)
Profit	60

(e) Users identified in the Framework would include shareholders, customers, suppliers, loan payable group, employees, public, government.

For example, existing or potential shareholders would be interested in the business' profitability and it's earning potential. They may compare current performance with the previous year's performance. Using such information they may decide to invest or disinvest in the business.

Test your understanding 10

(a) The elements of assets, liabilities and equity interest are shown in the statement of financial position. The relationship between these elements is shown by the accounting equation as:

Assets – Liabilities = Equity Interest

(b) 'Income' encompasses revenue and gains. Income increases the equity interest.

Expenses' lead to a decrease in equity interest.

Both incomes and expenses are in the statement of profit or loss.

Test your understanding 11

Potential investors are interested in information that is useful to them in taking decisions about potential investment in the company.

They need information about the entity's potential return to investors and the risk inherent in those returns. Information about the entity's past financial performance helps them to assess its anticipated performance and cash-generation abilities.

Information about its financial position and structure can be useful in assessing how future cash flows will be distributed and whether the company can meets its commitments as they fall due and raise finance in the future.

Information about its financial adaptability is useful in assessing risk or benefit from unexpected changes.

3 Company financial statements

Introduction

In this chapter we will consider the presentation of financial statements for limited companies and consider the legal and regulatory requirements for the presentation of those financial statements.

ASSESSMENT CRITERIA

Explain the regulatory framework that underpins financial reporting (1.1)

Explain the International Accounting Standards Board (the Board) Conceptual Framework for Financial Reporting ('the Framework') (1.2)

Examine the effect of international accounting standards on the preparation of financial statements (2.1)

Draft a statement of profit or loss and other comprehensive income (3.1)

Draft a statement of financial position (3.2)

Draft a statement of changes in equity (3.3)

CONTENTS

1 Distinctive features of limited companies

1.1 Differences between a sole trader and a limited company

A limited company is a separate legal entity and is distinct from its owners. This is in contrast to a sole trader who in law is not a separate entity from his business, even though he is treated as such for accounting purposes.

The key advantage of this is the limited liability that an investment in shares offers the shareholder. While a sole trader has unlimited liability for the debts of his business, shareholders have limited liability for the debts of the company in which they hold shares.

1.2 Types of limited company

There are two types of limited company, public and private. A public company must include in its name the letters 'plc' standing for public limited company. Private companies must include Limited or Ltd in their name. The main difference is that a private company may not offer its shares to the public and so all companies listed on the Stock Exchange are public companies.

1.3 Advantages and disadvantages of incorporated status

There are certain advantages and disadvantages associated with trading as a company rather than as a sole trader.

The advantages are as follows:

- If a company goes into liquidation the owners of the company (the shareholders) are only liable to pay any amounts that they have not yet paid for the shares that they hold. A sole trader would be personally liable for any outstanding debts of the business.
- The shareholders can share in the profits of the business without necessarily having to work day-to-day for the business.
- Companies are in a better position when borrowing money; for example they can issue debentures.
- The company will continue in existence even if shareholders die. If a sole trader dies the business will only continue if the business is sold. This is known as 'perpetual succession'.

The disadvantages are as follows:

- A large company (i.e. one that meets certain size criteria) must normally have an audit of its accounts and therefore must pay auditors' fees. However an audit also offers benefits to the company.
- A company must prepare its accounts in a format prescribed by legislation.
- A company suffers a greater administrative burden than a sole trader. For example, it must file its accounts each year with the Registrar of Companies and must hold an Annual General Meeting of its shareholders.

1.4 Accounting distinctions between a limited company and a sole trader

There are three main differences between the final accounts of a company and those of a sole trader:

- the way in which profit and tax are dealt with in the statement of profit or loss
- the composition of capital in the statement of financial position
- the statutory requirements of the Companies Act 2006.

The accounts prepared by a company for its own internal use can be in any format that the managers choose. It is only the accounts filed publicly with the Registrar of Companies each year that have to follow the statutory formats. These formats are reproduced later in the chapter.

Test your understanding 1

What is the difference between a private and a public company?

2 Key differences between a sole trader's accounts and limited company accounts

There are a few differences between the format and content of a sole trader's accounts and the published financial statements of a limited company. The key differences are explained below.

2.1 Capital and retained earnings

The capital introduced by the shareholders is classified separately in the statement of financial position. It is split between nominal value and share premium. The nominal value is defined by law. The premium is any extra money received by the company when the shares were first issued.

Retained earnings consist of the brought forward accumulated retained profits, plus the net profit for the year, less dividends. The movement on retained earnings is reported in the statement of changes in equity.

2.2 Dividends

Dividends for limited companies are the equivalent of drawings for a sole trader. Dividends are reported in the statement of changes in equity (dealt with later). Dividends are recognised on a cash basis when they are paid. Dividends declared but not paid at the year-end are disclosed in the notes to the financial statements.

2.3 Taxation

Tax does not appear in a sole trader's statement of profit or loss. However, limited companies pay their own income tax, and this will be charged to the statement of profit or loss. The tax will not be paid until after the year-end, and so the charge for the year will be a liability at the year-end. The closing liability is an estimate, and any over or under estimate is reversed out through the following year's statement of profit or loss.

2.4 Cost of sales and other expenses

Cost of sales and other expenses can be reported in two ways.

The most common way is the **function of expenditure** method. This groups together expenses under three headings: cost of sales, distribution costs and administrative expenses.

Some manufacturing industries use the **nature of expenditure** method. This itemises out expenditure according to its nature, e.g. depreciation, staff costs.

2.5 Non-current assets

Non-current assets such as buildings, machinery or vehicles are analysed out in a note to the accounts. Only the total carrying amount appears in the statement of financial position.

2.6 Notes and workings

Notes are printed and published as part of the financial statements. Their contents are normally specified by an accounting standard.

Workings are confidential. They will not be published.

3 Introduction to company accounts

3.1 The content of company accounts

The financial statements of a company comprise the following elements.

- Statement of financial position and notes
- Statement of profit or loss and other comprehensive income and notes
- Statement of changes in equity
- Statement of cash flow and notes
- Accounting policies note
- Comparative figures.

3.2 Regulations governing company accounts

The main sources of regulations are the Companies Act 2006 (CA 06) and accounting standards.

IAS 1 (Revised) *(Presentation of Financial Statements)* is the main source for the required formats and disclosures in the published statement of profit or loss and other comprehensive income, statement of financial position and statement of changes in equity. IAS 7 provides guidance with regard to the statement of cash flows.

4 The statement of financial position for publication

Company statement of financial position as at 31 December 20XX

	£000
Non-current assets	
Goodwill	X
Other intangible assets	X
Investments	X
Property, plant and equipment	X
	X
Current assets	
Inventories	X
Trade and other receivables	X
Cash and cash equivalents	X
	X
Total assets	**X**
Equity and liabilities	
Equity	
Share capital	X
Share premium	X
Revaluation reserve	X
Retained earnings	X
Total equity	X
Non-current liabilities	
Bank loans	X
Long-term provisions	X
	X

Current liabilities	
Trade and other payables	X
Taxation payable	X
Bank overdrafts and loans	X
	X
Total liabilities	**X**
Total equity and liabilities	**X**

As well as the statement of financial position figures for this year, comparative figures as at the previous year-end must also be shown in a statutory statement of financial position.

Any line item with a nil value this year and the previous year need not be shown in the statement of financial position.

5 The statement of profit or loss and other comprehensive income for publication

Company statement of profit or loss and other comprehensive income for the year ended 31 December 20XX

	£000
Revenue	X
Cost of sales	(X)
Gross profit	X
Distribution costs	(X)
Administrative expense	(X)
Profit from operations	X
Finance costs	(X)
Profit before tax	X
Tax	(X)
Profit for the period	X
Other comprehensive income	
Gain/loss on property revaluation	X
Total comprehensive income for the year	X

6 Notes to the accounts

6.1 Accounting policies

The notes to the accounts must state the accounting policies adopted by the company for all material items in the financial statements, for example, depreciation of property, plant and equipment and valuation of inventories.

6.2 Notes to the statement of financial position – non-current assets

Classification of non-current assets

Assets are classified as non-current assets if they are intended for use on a continuing basis in the company's activities.

Non-current assets are subdivided as follows:

- **Intangible non-current assets** — These are assets that have no physical form, such as patents and goodwill.

  The notes to the accounts will detail the total intangible non-current assets in the statement of financial position.

	20XX
	£000
Development costs	X
Concessions, patents, licences and trade marks	X
Goodwill	X
	X

- **Tangible assets (property, plant and equipment)** — These assets have physical form, such as buildings.
- **Investments** — This relates to long-term investments in other companies. It includes shares and loans made to other companies.

- **Property, plant and equipment** The property, plant and equipment note analyses the total carrying amount shown in the statement of financial position by category, and by cost and cumulative depreciation.

  The movements for the year (by category, cost and depreciation) are disclosed as follows:

  - Opening balance
  - Additions/charges for the year
  - Effect of revaluations
  - Disposals
  - Closing balance.

An example of a property, plant and equipment note is shown below.

	Land and buildings	**Plant and machinery**	**Fixtures, fittings, tools and equipment**	**Payments on account and assets in course of construction**	**Total**
	£000	£000	£000	£000	£000
Cost or valuation:					
At 1 January 20XX	X	X	X	X	X
Additions	X	X	X	X	X
Disposals	–	(X)	(X)	–	(X)
At 31 December 20XX	X	X	X	X	X
Accumulated depreciation:					
At 1 January 20XX	X	X	X	–	X
Charge for year	X	X	X	X	X
Disposals	–	(X)	(X)	–	(X)
At 31 December 20XX	X	X	X	X	X
Carrying amount:					
At 1 January 20XX	X	X	X	X	X
At 31 December 20XX	X	X	X	X	X

6.3 Notes to the statement of financial position – current assets

Classification of current assets

Current assets are assets that are expected to be converted into cash within 12 months. For example, inventories will be sold and converted into cash or receivables. Receivables in turn will settle their debts in cash. If it becomes apparent that the amount of cash that will be received will be less than the book value of the asset, then the asset should be written down to its recoverable amount. This is the basis for valuing inventories at the lower of cost and net realisable value, and for making allowances for doubtful receivables.

Inventories

Inventories are stated at the lower of cost and net realisable value. They will be analysed as follows:

	20XX
	£000
Raw materials and consumables	X
Work in progress	X
Finished goods and goods for resale	X
	X

6.4 Notes to the statement of financial position – liabilities

Non-current liabilities do not have to be repaid within the next 12 months. Current liabilities are payable within the next 12 months.

Liabilities include provisions. Provisions are liabilities of uncertain timing or amount.

6.5 Notes to the statement of financial position – capital and reserves

Called up share capital

	20XX
	£000
Allotted and fully paid:	
Ordinary shares of £1 each	X
Ordinary shares of 50p each	X
	X

Any movement in the share capital of the company should be disclosed. This is done in the statement of changes in equity. The authorised share capital should also be disclosed.

Reserves

The movement in reserves is analysed out in the statement of changes in equity.

6.6 Notes to the statement of profit or loss and other comprehensive income

Operating costs and revenues

Disclose all material items of income and expense for example:

- Disposals of non-current assets
- Auditors' remuneration (all remuneration to the auditor, whether for audit or other services) – per CA06.

Example

Profit from operations

Profit is stated after charging the following

	£000	£000
Loss on sale of property plant and equipment		X
Auditors' remuneration		X
In capacity as auditor	X	
In other capacities	X	
		X
Exceptional write off of receivable		X

Tax on profit on ordinary activities

There are two elements to the tax charge, all of which are disclosed in the tax note:

Example

	20XX
	£000
Taxation on the profit for the year	
Income tax – estimate for the year	X
Under (over) provision in previous year	X/(X)
	X

Test your understanding 2

Florabundi, a limited liability company, shows an overprovision of £3,400 on its tax liability account at the end of the year ended 31 December 20X8 before accounting for that year's tax charge.

It estimates tax on profits for the year to be £67,900.

What amounts should be shown in the financial statements for the year ended 31 December 20X8 in respect of tax?

A £67,900 tax charge £67,900 tax payable

B £64,500 tax charge £64,500 tax payable

C £64,500 tax charge £67,900 tax payable

D £71,300 tax charge £67,900 tax payable

7 Statement of changes in equity

The statement of changes in equity brings together all the gains and losses for the period, including items which do not pass through the statement of profit or loss.

The most common example of an item which does not pass through the statement of profit or loss is a gain on the revaluation of a non-current asset. Revaluation gains cannot be taken to the statement or profit or loss because they are unrealised, but nevertheless, they may form an important part of a company's overall performance.

The statement of changes in equity highlights the effect of revaluations and other items such as prior period adjustments and helps users of the financial statements to appreciate their impact upon the company's overall financial performance.

Example plc

Statement of changes in equity

	Share capital	**Share premium**	**Revaluation**	**Retained earnings**	**Total**
	£000	£000	£000	£000	£000
At January 20X8	X	X	X	X	X
Total comprehensive income for the year			X	X	X
Dividends paid				(X)	(X)
At 31 December 20X8	X	X	X	X	X

Test your understanding 3

According to IAS 1 *Presentation of Financial statements* which of the following items should appear in the statement of changes in equity:

1 Total comprehensive income for the year

2 Dividends paid

3 Loss on sale of investments

4 Issue of share capital

A 1, 2 and 4 only

B 1, 3 and 4 only

C 1 and 3 only

D 1, 2, 3 and 4

8 Drafting financial statements

Now that you have studied all the necessary accounting concepts, standards and treatments it is important that you can bring all of this information together to enable you to prepare a complete set of company financial statements. The following example will guide you through this process.

Example

The following trial balance at 30 September 20X9 relates to Pattar Ltd.

	£000	£000
Revenue		103,500
Inventories at 1 October 20X8	5,460	
Purchases	67,206	
Distribution costs	8,000	
Sales staff's commission	2,920	
Administrative salaries	2,280	
Manufacturing wages	2,000	
Interest paid	540	
Administrative expenses	5,000	
3% debenture loans		18,000
Share capital		60,000
Retained earnings at 1 October 20X8		8,495
Cash and cash equivalents	2,685	
Dividends paid	2,820	
Revaluation reserve at 1 October 20X8		6,000
Trade and other payables		5,861
Land and Buildings – value/cost	92,578	
Accumulated depreciation		25,000
Plant and equipment at cost	35,000	
Accumulated depreciation		15,313
Trade and other receivables	16,395	
Accruals		715
	242,884	242,884

Further information:

(a) Inventories were valued at £7,850,000 on 30 September 20X9.

(b) Depreciation is to be provided for the year to 30 September 20X9 as follows:

Buildings	10% per annum straight line basis
Plant and equipment	25% per annum reducing balance basis

Depreciation is apportioned as follows:

Cost of sales	60%
Distribution costs	30%
Administrative expenses	10%

Land and Buildings in the trial balance includes a value for land at £42,578,000. It is to be revalued at £61,000,000 and this revaluation is to be included in the financial statements for 30 September 20X9.

(c) An irrecoverable debt of £21,000 which is included in trade receivables is to be written off.

(d) Administrative expenses of £85,000 owing at 30 September 20X9 are to be provided for.

(e) The corporation tax charge for the year has been calculated as £1,500,000.

All operations are continuing operations.

Required:

Prepare the statement of profit or loss and other comprehensive income for Pattar Ltd for the year ended 30 September 20X9 and a statement of financial position at that date.

Prepare the disclosure note for property, plant and equipment for the year ended 30 September 20X9.

Solution

Get yourself organised: you will need to prepare a sheet for the statement of profit or loss and other comprehensive income and a separate sheet for the statement of financial position.

Pattar Ltd

Statement of profit or loss and other comprehensive income for the year ended 30 September 20X9

Pattar Ltd

Statement of financial position as at 30 September 20X9

£ £

You will also need a sheet for notes to the accounts and a sheet for workings.

Pattar Ltd

Notes to the accounts

Pattar Ltd

Workings

Note: Some of the numbers you require for this answer will come straight out of the question. Some will require a working. We will go through the answer line by line and indicate how the amount is calculated.

You must let the statutory format dictate the order of working.

Below we show the answer as it will appear in the statutory format, and the workings and notes will follow.

Pattar Ltd – statement of profit or loss and other comprehensive income for the year ended 30 September 20X9

	Notes	£000
Revenue (Step 1)		103,500
Cost of sales (W1) (Step 2)		(72,769)
Gross profit		30,731
Distribution costs (W2) (Step 2)		(13,897)
Administrative expenses (W3) (Step 2)		(8,378)
Profit from operations		8,456
Finance costs (Step 3)		(540)
Profit before tax		7,916
Tax (Step 4)	1	(1,500)
Profit for the period from continuing operations		6,416
Other comprehensive income		
Revaluation gain (61,000 – 42,578)		18,422
Total comprehensive income		24,838

Step 1

The revenue figure is taken directly from the question. (**Note:** If there are sales returns listed in the TB this would reduce the value of reported revenue).

Step 2

Cost of sales, distribution costs and administrative expenses.

This is found by a working.

(**Note:** Remember that you have to identify cost of sales, distribution costs and administrative costs separately so you need three separate workings.)

In the exam you will need to select the account name and enter the amount in a table as below. (All workings in £000s).

(W1) Expenses – Cost of sales

Account name	
	£000
Opening inventories	5,460
Purchases	67,206
Manufacturing wages	2,000
Closing inventories	(7,850)
Depreciation – buildings(W4)	3,000
Depreciation – plant (W4)	2,953
	72,769

(W2) Expenses – Distribution costs

	£000
Distribution costs	8,000
Sales staff's commission	2,920
Depreciation – buildings (W4)	1,500
Depreciation – plant (W4)	1,477
	13,897

(W3) Expenses – Administrative expenses

	£000
Administrative salaries	2,280
Administrative expenses	5,000
Depreciation – buildings (W4)	500
Depreciation – plant (W4)	492
Administrative expenses accrued	85
Irrecoverable debt written off	21
	8,378

(W4) Deprecation is calculated as follows:

Buildings £50,000 × 10% = £5,000

The buildings value of £50,000 was calculated by subtracting the land value of £42,578 from the total land and buildings value of £92,578.

Attributable to:

Cost of sales £5,000 × 60% = £3,000

Distribution costs £5,000 × 30% = £1,500

Administrative expenses £5,000 × 10% = £500

Plant and equipment £35,000 – £15,313 = £19,687 × 25% = £4,922

Attributable to:

Cost of sales £4,922 × 60% = £2,953

Distribution costs £4,922 × 30% = £1,477

Administrative expenses £4,922 × 10% = £492

Step 3

Finance costs come straight from the question.

Interest paid = £540

Step 4

You are now in a position to prepare the statement of financial position using exactly the same approach. Allow the format to take you through the question.

As before we will show the answer below in the correct format and indicate where the numbers come from.

Pattar Ltd Statement of financial position as at 30 September 20X9

	£000
Non-current assets	
Property, plant and equipment (W5) (Step 5)	95,765
	95,765
Current assets	
Inventories (Step 6)	7,850
Trade and other receivables (Step 6)	16,374
Cash and cash equivalents (Step 6)	2,685
	26,909
Total assets	122,674
Equity	
Share capital	60,000
Retained earnings (Step 9)	12,091
Revaluation reserve (6,000 + 18,422)	24,422
Total equity	96,513
Non-current liabilities (Step 8)	
Debenture loans	18,000
	18,000
Current liabilities	
Trade and other payables (Step 7)	6,661
Tax liabilities (charge for the year)	1,500
	8,161
Total liabilities (18,000 + 8,161)	26,161
Total equity and liabilities	122,674

Step 5

We will now prepare the note for property, plant and equipment. This note will also form the working for the figure on the statement of financial position.

(W5) Property, plant and equipment

	Land and buildings	Plant and machinery	Total
	£000	£000	£000
Cost at 1 October 20X8	92,578	35,000	127,578
Revaluation	18,422		18,422
Cost at 30 September 20X9	111,000	35,000	146,000
Depreciation at 1 October 20X8	25,000	15,313	40,313
Charge for year	5,000	4,922	9,922
Depreciation at 30 September 20X9	30,000	20,235	50,235
CV at 1 October 20X8	67,578	19,687	87,265
CV at 30 September 20X9	81,000	14,765	**95,765**

This can then be taken to the statement of financial position and cross referenced to Note 2.

Step 6

(W6) Investments, inventories, and cash all come directly from the question.

Trade receivables are adjusted for the irrecoverable written off 16,395 – 21 = 16,374.

Step 7

(W7) Current liability workings

1 You will need a working for trade and other payables

Trade payables	5,861
Accruals	715
Administrative expenses accrued	85
	6,661

2 Working for tax

Tax estimate for year	1,500

In the exam the tax estimate for the year given in the question will be the current tax liability for the year.

Step 8

Debenture loans come directly from the question.

Step 9

(W8) You are now in a position to complete the equity section of the statement of financial position.

(a) The called up share capital comes directly from the question.

(b) The retained earnings figure comes from the retained earnings brought forward at 1/10/X8 of £8,495 and profit for the period of £6,416 from the statement of profit or loss less dividends paid of £2,820.

You should now have completed:

- a statement of profit or loss and other comprehensive income
- a statement of financial position
- the note for property, plant and equipment
- your working paper.

Required:

Prepare the statement of changes in equity for Pattar Ltd for the year ended 30 September 20X9.

Pattar Ltd

Statement of changes in equity

	Share capital	**Revaluation**	**Retained earnings**	**Total**
	£000	£000	£000	£000
At 31 October 20X8	60,000	6,000	8,495	74,495
Total comprehensive income for the year		18,422	6,416	24,838
Dividends paid			(2,820)	(2,820)
At 30 September 20X9	60,000	24,422	12,091	96,513

Exam focus

- Note that in the computer based assessment you will not be required to show all the workings above and tables will be provided in which you can select the account name from a list and enter the appropriate numerical amount.
- The approach above is given step by step so that you can consolidate your learning and are able to deal with exam type questions.

Test your understanding 4

The following is the trial balance of Transit Ltd at 31 March 20X8.

	£	£
Issued share capital (ordinary shares of £1 each)		42,000
Leasehold properties, at cost	75,000	
Motor vans, at cost (used for distribution)	2,500	
Accumulated depreciation on motor vans to 31 March 20X7		1,000
Administration expenses	7,650	
Distribution costs	10,000	
Inventories at 31 March 20X7	12,000	
Purchases	138,750	
Revenue		206,500
Directors' remuneration (administrative)	25,000	
Rents receivable		3,600
Investments at cost (short-term)	6,750	
Investment income		340
7% Debentures		15,000
Debenture interest	1,050	
Bank interest	162	
Bank overdraft		730
Trade receivables and payables	31,000	23,000
Sales tax control		1,100
Interim dividend paid	1,260	
Retained earnings, 31 March 20X7		17,852
	311,122	311,122

You are given the following additional information:

- All the motor vans were purchased on 1 April 20X5. Depreciation has been, and is to be, provided at the rate of 20% per annum on cost from the date of purchase.

  Depreciation is to be charged to distribution costs.
- On 31 March 20X8 one van, which had cost £900, was sold for £550, as part settlement of the price of £800 of a new van, but no entries with regard to these transactions were made in the books. The remaining balance due for the new van is payable in 30 days. Depreciation is charged on assets in the year of their disposal, no depreciation is to be charged on the new van.

- The estimated tax liability for the year to 31 March 20X8 is £12,700.
- It is proposed to pay a final dividend of 10% for the year to 31 March 20X8.
- Inventories valued at the lower of cost and net realisable value on 31 March 20X8 are £16,700.

Required:

Using the proformas given prepare:

(a) a statement of profit or loss for the year ended 31 March 20X8

(b) a statement of financial position at that date

(c) a statement of changes in equity.

Transit limited

Statement of profit or loss for the year ended 31 March 20X8

	£
Revenue	
Cost of sales (W1)	
Gross profit	
Investment income	
Rental income	
Distribution costs (W2)	
Administrative expenses (W3)	
Profit from operations	
Finance costs	
Profit before tax	
Tax	
Profit for the period	

Statement of financial position at 31 March 20X8

	£
Non-current assets	
Property, plant and equipment (W6)	
Current assets	
Inventories	
Trade and other receivables	
Investments held for resale	
Total assets	
Equity	
Share capital	
Retained earnings	
Non-current liabilities	
Debentures	
Current liabilities	
Trade and other payables (W7)	
Sales tax liability	
Corporation tax liability	
Bank overdraft and loans	
Total liabilities	
Total equity and liabilities	

Statement of changes in equity for the year ended 31 March 20X8

	Share capital	Retained earnings	Total
Balance at 31 March 20X7			
Profit for the period			
Dividends			
Balance at 31 March 20X8			

Workings

For (W1), (W2) and (W3) circle the appropriate account name and enter the amount.

(W1) Expenses – Cost of sales

Account name	**Cost of sales**
	£
Opening inventories/Depreciation	
Directors remuneration/Purchases	
Administrative expenses/Closing inventories	
	–––––
Total	
	–––––

(W2) Expenses – Distribution costs

Account name	Distribution costs
	£
Opening inventories/Distribution costs	
Depreciation/Distribution costs	
Administrative expenses/Profit from disposal of van	
	———
Total	
	———

(W3) Expenses – Administrative expenses

Account name	Administrative expenses
	£
Directors remuneration/Depreciation	
Administrative expenses/closing inventories	
	———
Total	
	———

(W4) Depreciation

(W5) Disposal account (complete the account name and amount)

Account name	£
	______
Profit on disposal	
	______

(W6) Property, plant and equipment

	Leasehold properties	**Motor vans**	**Total**
	£	£	£
Cost at 31 March X7			
Additions			
Disposals			
	______	______	______
At 31 March X8			
	______	______	______
Accumulated depreciation at 31 March 20X7			
Charge for year			
Disposals			
	______	______	______
	______	______	______
CV at 31 March 20X7			
CV at 31 March 20X8			

(W7) Trade payables

Account name	£
Trade payables	
Balance due on new motor vehicle	
	______
Total	
	______

Test your understanding 5

You have been asked to help prepare the financial statements of Laxdale Ltd for the year ended 31 October 20X8. The company's trial balance as at 31 October 20X8 is shown below.

Laxdale Ltd
Trial balance as at 31 October 20X8

	Debit	Credit
	£000	£000
Share capital		16,000
Trade and other payables		2,798
Property, plant and equipment – cost	47,652	
Property, plant and equipment – accumulated depreciation		23,415
Trade and other receivables	5,436	
Accruals		436
8% bank loan repayable 20Y2		15,000
Cash at bank	9,774	
Retained earnings		9,786
Interest paid	600	
Sales		58,975
Purchases	42,398	
Returns inwards	564	
Returns outwards		778
Distribution costs	5,443	
Administration expenses	4,789	
Inventories as at 1 November 20X7	9,032	
Final dividend for year ended 31 October 20X7	850	
Interim dividend for year ended 31 October 20X8	650	
	127,188	127,188

Further information:

- The share capital of the company consists of ordinary shares with a nominal value of £1.
- Inventories at the close of business on 31 October 20X8 were valued at £7,878,000.
- The corporation tax charge for the year has been calculated as £2,540,000.
- The company began a series of television adverts for the company's range of products on 1 October 20X8 at a cost of £45,000.
- The adverts were run for three months and were to be paid for in full at the end of December 20X8.
- Interest on the bank loan for the last six months of the year has not been included in the accounts in the trial balance.

Task 1

Using the proforma provided, and making any adjustments required as a result of the further information given above, draft the statement of profit or loss for Laxdale Ltd for the year ended 31 October 20X8.

Laxdale Ltd

Statement of profit or loss for the year ended 31 October 20X8

	£000
Revenue	
Cost of sales	
Gross profit	
Distribution costs	
Administrative expenses	
Profit from operations	
Finance costs	
Profit before tax	
Tax	
Profit for the period	

Task 2

Using the proforma provided, draft the statement of financial position for Laxdale Ltd as at 31 October 20X8.

Laxdale Ltd

Statement of financial position as at 31 October 20X8

	£000
Assets	
Non-current assets	
	______
Current assets	
	______
Total assets	______
Equity and liabilities	
Equity	
	______
	______
Non-current liabilities	
	______
	______
Current liabilities	
	______
Total equity and liabilities	______

Test your understanding 6

Data

You have been asked to help prepare the financial statements of Hightink Ltd for the year ended 31 March 20X2.

The trial balance of the company as at 31 March 20X2 is set out below.

Hightink Ltd

Trial balance as at 31 March 20X2

	£000	£000
Interest	240	
Distribution costs	6,852	
Administrative expenses	3,378	
Trade receivables	5,455	
Trade payables		2,363
Interim dividend	400	
Ordinary share capital		4,000
Revenue		31,710
Long term loan		6,000
Buildings – cost	3,832	
Fixtures and fittings – cost	2,057	
Motor vehicles – cost	3,524	
Office equipment – cost	2,228	
Land – cost	5,000	
Purchases	15,525	
Cash at bank	304	
Retained earnings at 1 April 20X1		6,217
Inventories as at 1 April 20X1	6,531	
Share premium		2,000
Buildings – accumulated depreciation		564
Fixtures and fittings – accumulated depreciation		726
Motor vehicles – accumulated depreciation		1,283
Office equipment – accumulated depreciation		463
	55,326	55,326

Further information:

- The authorised share capital of the company, all of which has been issued, consists of ordinary shares with a nominal value of £1.
- The company paid an interim dividend of 10p per share during the year. No final dividend has been proposed.
- Inventories at the close of business on 31 March 20X2 were valued at cost at £7,878,000.
- The tax charge for the year has been calculated as £1,920,000.
- Credit sales relating to April 20X2 amounting to £204,000 had been entered incorrectly into the accounts in March 20X2.
- Interest on the long term loan has been paid for six months of the year. No adjustment has been made for the interest due for the final six months of the year. Interest is charged on the loan at a rate of 8% per annum.
- The land has been revalued by professional valuers at £5,500,000. The revaluation is to be included in the financial statements for the year ended 31 March 20X2.
- On 21 April 20X2 there was a fire at the company's premises that destroyed non-current assets and inventory. The losses from the fire amounted to £487,000 and they were not covered by the company's insurance. This amount is considered by the directors to constitute a material loss to the company.

Required:

Using the proforma provided, and making any adjustments required as a result of the further information given above, draft a statement of profit or loss and other comprehensive income for the year ended 31 March 20X2, a statement of changes in equity and a statement of financial position for Hightink as at that date.

Note: You are NOT required to produce notes to the accounts.

Hightink Ltd

Statement of profit or loss and other comprehensive income for the year ended 31 March 20X2

	£000
Revenue	
Cost of sales	
Gross profit	
Distribution costs	
Administrative expenses	
Profit from operations	
Finance costs	
Profit before tax	
Tax	
Profit for the period	
Other comprehensive income	
Gain on revaluation	
Total comprehensive income for the year	

Statement of changes in equity for the year ended 31 March 20X2

	Share capital	Share premium	Revaluation reserve	Retained earnings	Total
Balance at 31 March 20X1					
Revaluation					
Profit for the year					
Dividends					
Balance at 31 March 20X2					

Hightink Ltd

Statement of financial position as at 31 March 20X2

	£000
Non-current assets	
Property, plant and equipment	
Current assets	
Inventories	
Trade and other receivables	
Cash and cash equivalents	
Total assets	
Equity	
Called-up share capital	
Share premium	
Revaluation reserve	
Retained earnings	
Non-current liabilities	
Long term loan	
Current liabilities	
Trade and other payables	
Taxation	
Bank overdraft and loans	
Total equity and liabilities	

Test your understanding 7

An extract from the accounts of Bay Ltd for the year ended 31 March 20X1 showed:

	£000
Revenue	9,320
Cost of sales	(5,120)
Gross profit	4,200
Distribution costs	(1,230)
Admin expenses	(940)
Profit from operations	2,030
Finance costs	(230)
Profit before taxation	1,800
Tax	(480)
Profit for the financial year	1,320

Extract from the statement of financial position

	£000
Equity:	
Share capital	3,500
Share premium	1,400
Revaluation reserve	600
Retained earnings	1,850
	7,350

The revaluation reserve arose in the year ended 31 March 20X1 as a result of land being revalued by a professional valuer. The revaluation is also reflected in the value of the tangible assets.

Dividends paid during the year totalled £420,000.

Task

Prepare a statement of changes in equity for the year ended 31 March 20X1.

Bay Ltd – Statement of changes in Equity for the year ended 31 March 20X1

All figures in £000

	Share capital	Share premium	Revaluation reserve	Retained earnings	Total
Balance at 31 March 20X0					
Total comprehensive income for the year					
Dividends					
	_____	_____	_____	_____	_____
Balance at 31 March 20X1					
	_____	_____	_____	_____	_____

9 Summary

In order to prepare limited company financial statements you need:

- a detailed knowledge of the disclosure requirements IAS 1
- the ability to get the knowledge onto paper quickly and neatly
- to apply a methodical approach and show workings.

Test your understanding answers

Test your understanding 1

There are two types of Limited company:

Public companies must include 'PLC' in its name.

PLC's are listed on the stock exchange and can sell shares to the public.

Private companies must include 'Ltd' or Limited after in their name and are not listed on the stock exchange therefore cannot offer their shares to the public.

Test your understanding 2

Answer is C

Over provision b/fwd	(3,400)
Current years estimated tax	67,900
Tax charge	64,500
Tax liability	67,900

Test your understanding 3

Answer is A

Test your understanding 4

Transit Limited

Statement of profit or loss for the year ended 31 March 20X8

	£
Revenue	206,500
Cost of sales (W1)	(134,050)
Gross profit	72,450
Investment income	340
Rental income	3,600
Distribution costs (W2)	(10,310)
Administrative expenses (W3)	(32,650)
Profit from operations	33,430
Finance costs (1,050 + 162)	(1,212)
Profit before tax	32,218
Tax	(12,700)
Profit for the period from continuing operations	19,518

Transit Ltd

Statement of financial position at 31 March 20X8

	£
Non-current assets	
Property, plant and equipment (W6)	76,440
	76,440
Current assets	
Inventories	16,700
Trade and other receivables	31,000
Investments held for re-sale	6,750
	54,450
Total assets	130,890
Capital and reserves	
Ordinary shares of £1 each	42,000
Retained earnings (see statement of changes in equity)	36,110
	78,110
Non-current liabilities	
7% Debentures	15,000
	15,000
Current liabilities	
Trade and other payables (W7)	23,250
Tax liabilities (12,700 + 1,100)	13,800
Bank overdraft	730
	37,780
Total liabilities	52,780
Total equity and liabilities	130,890

Statement of changes in equity for the year ended 31 March 20X8

	Share capital	Retained earnings	Total
Balance at 31 March 20X7	42,000	17,852	59,852
Profit for the period	–	19,518	19,518
Dividends	–	(1,260)	(1,260)
Balance at 31 March 20X8	42,000	36,110	78,110

Workings

(W1) Expenses – Cost of sales

Account name	Cost of sales
	£
Opening inventories	12,000
Purchases	138,750
Closing inventories	(16,700)
Total	134,050

(W2) Expenses – Distribution costs

Account name	Distribution costs
	£
Distribution costs	10,000
Depreciation (W4)	500
Profit from sale of van (W5)	(190)
Total	10,310

(W3) Expenses – Administrative expenses

Account name	Administrative expenses
	£
Director's remuneration	25,000
Administrative expenses	7,650
Total	32,650

(W4) Depreciation

£2,500 × 20% = £500

(W5) Disposal account

Account name	£
Motor vans cost	900
Accumulated depreciation on disposal (900 × 20% × 3 years)	(540)
Cash proceeds	(550)
	———
Profit on disposal	190
	———

(W6) Property, plant and equipment

	Leasehold properties	Motor vans	Total
	£	£	£
Cost at 31 March X7	75,000	2,500	77,500
Additions	–	800	800
Disposals	–	(900)	(900)
At 31 March X8	75,000	2,400	77,400
Accumulated depreciation at 31 March 20X7	–	1,000	1,000
Charge for year (W4)	–	500	500
Disposals	–	(540)	(540)
	–	960	960
CV at 31 March 20X7	75,000	1,500	76,500
CV at 31 March 20X8	75,000	1,440	76,440

(W7) Trade payables

Account name	£
Trade payables	23,000
Balance due on new motor vehicle	250
	———
Total charge for year	23,250
	———

Test your understanding 5

Task 1

Laxdale Ltd
Statement of profit or loss for the year ended 31 October 2008

	£000
Revenue (W1)	58,411
Cost of sales (W2)	(42,774)
Gross profit	15,637
Distribution costs (W3)	(5,458)
Administrative expenses	(4,789)
Profit from operations	5,390
Finance costs (W4)	(1,200)
Profit before tax	4,190
Tax	(2,540)
Profit for the period	1,650

Workings

(W1)	Sales		58,975
	Less: Returns in		(564)
			58,411
(W2)	Opening inventories		9,032
	Purchases	42,398	
	Less: Returns out	(778)	41,620
			50,652
	Less closing inventories		(7,878)
			42,774

(W3)	Distribution costs	5,443
	Accrual	15
		5,458
(W4)	Finance costs	600
	Accrual	600
		1,200

Task 2

Laxdale Ltd
Statement of financial position as at 31 October 20X8

	£000
Assets	
Non-current assets	
Property, plant and equipment (W1)	24,237
Current assets	
Inventories	7,878
Trade and other receivables	5,436
Cash and cash equivalents	9,774
Total assets	47,325
Equity and liabilities	
Equity	
Share capital	16,000
Retained earnings (W3)	9,936
	25,936
Non-current liabilities	
Bank loans	15,000
Current liabilities	
Trade and other payables (W2)	3,849
Tax payable	2,540
Total equity and liabilities	47,325

Workings

(W1)	Property, plant and equipment – Cost	47,652
	Property, plant and equipment – accumulated depreciation	(23,415)
		24,237
(W2)	Per TB	2,798
	Accruals	436
	Interest	600
	Distribution costs (advertising)	15
		3,849
(W3)	Per TB	9,786
	From statement of profit or loss	1,650
	Final dividend for year ended 31 October 2007	(850)
	Interim dividend for year ended 31 October 2008	(650)
		9,936

Test your understanding 6

Hightink Ltd
Statement of profit or loss for the year ended 31 March 20X2

	£000
Revenue (W1)	31,506
Cost of sales (W2)	(14,178)
Gross profit	17,328
Distribution costs	(6,852)
Administrative expenses	(3,378)
Profit from operations	7,098
Finance costs (W3)	(480)
Profit before tax	6,618
Tax	(1,920)
Profit for the period	4,698
Other comprehensive income	
Gain on revaluation	500
Total comprehensive income for the year	5,198

Statement of changes in equity for the year ended 31 March 20X2

	Share capital	Share premium	Revaluation reserve	Retained earnings	Total
Balance at 31 March 20X1	4,000	2,000	–	6,217	12,217
Total comprehensive income for the year			500	4,698	5,198
Dividends				(400)	(400)
Balance at 31 March 20X2	4,000	2,000	500	10,515	17,015

Hightink Ltd
Statement of financial position as at 31 March 20X2

	£000
Property, plant and equipment (W4)	14,105
Current assets	
Inventories	7,878
Trade receivables (5,455 – 204)	5,251
Cash and cash equivalents	304
	13,433
Total assets	27,538
Equity	
Called up share capital	4,000
Share premium	2,000
Revaluation reserve	500
Retained Earnings	10,515
	17,015
Non-current liabilities	
Long term loan	6,000
Current liabilities	
Trade and other payables (2,363 + 240)	2,603
Taxation	1,920
	4,523
Total liabilities	10,523
Total equity and liabilities	27,538

Workings (all figures in £000)

(W1) Revenue

Per TB	31,710
Adjustment for April 20X2 sales	(204)
	31,506

(W2) Cost of sales

Opening inventory	6,531
Purchases	15,525
Closing inventory	(7,878)
	14,178

(W3) Finance costs

Interest per TB	240
Interest accrued (6,000 × 8% – 240)	240
	480

(W4) Property, plant and equipment

	Cost or valuation	Accumulated depreciation	CV
Land	5,500	–	5,500*
Buildings	3,832	564	3,268
Fixtures and fittings	2,057	726	1,331
Motor vehicles	3,524	1,283	2,241
Office equipment	2,228	463	1,765
	17,141	3,036	14,105

*Land: 5,000 + 500 = £5,500

Test your understanding 7

Bay Ltd – Statement of changes in Equity for the year ended 31 March 20X1

All figures in £000

	Share capital	**Share premium**	**Revaluation reserve**	**Retained earnings**	**Total**
Balance at 31 March 20X0	3,500	1,400	–	950*	5,850
Total comprehensive income for the year			600	1,320	1,920
Dividends				(420)	(420)
Balance at 31 March 20X1	3,500	1,400	600	1,850	7,350

*Balancing figure

Property, plant and equipment

4

Introduction

For this unit you need to be able to draft limited company financial statements. This means that you need an awareness of the main requirements of relevant accounting standards.

In this chapter we will consider the detailed requirements of IAS 16 *Property, Plant and Equipment*.

ASSESSMENT CRITERIA

Examine the effect of international accounting standards on the preparation of financial statement (2.1)

Draft a statement of financial position (3.2)

CONTENTS

1 IAS 16 *Property, Plant and Equipment*

1.1 Introduction

IAS 16 *Property, Plant and Equipment* considers recognition of assets, determination of carrying amount and the depreciation charges to be recognised in relation to those assets.

Property, plant and equipment consist of assets used in the business over a number of accounting periods. Such assets are classified as non-current assets on the statement of financial position.

1.2 Initial measurement

Initial measurement of property, plant and equipment (whether acquired or self-constructed) should be at cost.

Cost should include all costs directly attributable to bringing the asset into working condition for its intended use, such as direct labour costs, delivery fees, legal fees and testing costs.

Example

AB plc incurs the following costs in constructing a new non-current asset which takes three months.

	£
Site clearance	2,000
Cost of materials used in asset	30,000
Legal fees to secure a license	1,000
Cost of materials wasted in a flood	500
Cost of labour used in asset	8,000
Cost of industrial dispute	1,500

Which of the above costs can be capitalised into the initial cost of the non-current asset?

Solution

The directly attributable costs are:

	£
Site clearance	2,000
Cost of materials in asset	30,000
Necessary legal fee	1,000
Cost of labour in asset	8,000
	41,000

The cost of the wasted materials and the industrial dispute are not direct costs and must be written off to the statement of profit or loss as incurred.

1.3 Subsequent expenditure

Subsequent expenditure should be capitalised if it enhances the economic benefits of the asset in excess of its previously assessed standard of performance. An example of this would be the cost of building an extension to a restaurant. As a result of the extension, more customers can be served and therefore more revenues can be earned.

Subsequent expenditure that solely maintains the standard of performance of the asset (e.g. routine repairs and maintenance) should be charged to the statement of profit or loss as it is incurred.

1.4 Depreciation

IAS 16 *Property, Plant and Equipment* says that **'the depreciable amount (cost less residual value) of a tangible non-current asset should be allocated on a systematic basis over its useful life.'** [IAS 16, para 50]. The following factors need to be considered when determining the useful life, residual value and depreciation method of an asset:

- Expected usage or idle (non-productive) time
- Expected physical wear and tear
- Economic or technological obsolescence
- Legal or similar limits on use, such as the expiry dates of leases.

Depreciation of an asset begins when it is available for use. Note that land is not depreciated. This is because it is not expected to have a finite life, whereas other assets such as buildings do have a finite life.

IAS 16 does not stipulate a particular method of depreciation. The directors of a company should decide upon the most appropriate depreciation method(s) to apply to each class or type of non-current asset.

1.5 Useful economic lives and residual values

The length of a non-current asset's life is clearly a very important number in a depreciation calculation. However, it is an estimate, as it is necessary to make predictions about the future.

Both the useful economic life and the residual value (if material) of a tangible non-current asset should be reviewed at the end of each reporting period. They should be revised 'if expectations are significantly different from previous estimates'.

2 Revaluation of property, plant and equipment

2.1 IAS 16 requirements

IAS 16 *Property, Plant and Equipment* permits (it is not compulsory) companies to revalue property, plant and equipment if a policy of revaluation is adopted, although in practice, this is only applied to land and buildings. If a company decides to revalue its land and buildings, it must then keep the valuation up to date by having periodic revaluations, perhaps at intervals between three and five years to ensure that amounts stated in the financial statements continue to be relevant and reliable for users of the financial statements.

All assets of the same class must be revalued. For example, if land and buildings were to be revalued, this would not require the revaluation of plant and machinery, but would require the revaluation of all (rather than some) land and buildings held.

If a revalued asset has a finite useful life, such as a building, it should continue to be depreciated over its remaining estimated useful life, based upon the new revalued amount and the remaining expected useful life. Following revaluation, the carrying amount at each reporting date will be the fair value from the latest valuation less any subsequent accumulated depreciation and any subsequent accumulated impairment losses.

2.2 Accounting for a revaluation

When accounting for revaluation of property, plant and equipment, the following procedure should be adopted:

- Restate the asset to the revalued amount (rather than at cost)
- Eliminate the accumulated depreciation to date on that asset
- Establish or update the revaluation surplus.

Example

A building was purchased at a cost of £200,000 on 1 January 20X8. It is depreciated over its useful life of 20 years on a straight line basis down to a nil residual value. At 31 December 20X8 the building was revalued at £247,000. The company does not make the annual transfer from revaluation surplus to retained earnings.

Show how this revaluation should be dealt with in the financial statements as at 31 December 20X8 and 20X9.

Solution

In the year ended 31 December 20X8, depreciation of $\frac{£200,000}{20}$ = £10,000 would be charged so the carrying amount at the date of revaluation is £190,000.

The revaluation surplus is £57,000 (from a carrying amount of £190,000 up to £247,000). This gain would be reported in other comprehensive income for the year and shown in the statement of financial position as a revaluation surplus within equity.

The revaluation is accounted for as follows:

	£	£
Dr Building (247 – 200)	47,000	
Dr Accumulated depreciation	10,000	
Cr Revaluation surplus		57,000

The revised depreciation charge for 20X9 would be £247,000/19 years = £13,000.

At 31 December 20X9, the amounts to be included in the statement of financial position would be:

Carrying amount of property (£247,000 – £13,000) = £234,000

Revaluation surplus £57,000

Test your understanding 1

At the end of its financial year, Tanner has the following non-current assets:

Land and buildings at cost	£10.4 million
Land and buildings: accumulated depreciation	£0.12 million

The company has decided to revalue its land and buildings at the year end to £15 million.

What will be the amount of the adjustment on revaluation?

A £4.48m

B £4.6m

C £4.72m

D £15.12m

A company which has revalued property, plant and equipment can choose whether or not to make an annual transfer from revaluation surplus to retained earnings for the amount of the 'excess depreciation' i.e. the increase in the depreciation charge as a result of the revaluation. In effect, this treats part of the revaluation surplus as being realised and can then be regarded as part of retained earnings from which dividends may be paid to shareholders.

If a company chooses to make this annual transfer, it must do so every year so that the financial statements are prepared using consistent accounting policies. The transfer is made within the statement of changes in equity as follows:

Dr: Revaluation surplus Cr: Retained earnings

Example

Continuing with information from the previous example when the building has been revalued to £247,000, calculate the amount of the 'excess depreciation' charged as a result of revaluing the building and state the accounting entries required to account for the transfer within the statement of changes in equity for the year ended 31 December 20X9.

Solution

The 'excess depreciation' is £3,000 (£13,000 – £10,000).

The accounting entries required are as follows:

	£	£
Dr Revaluation surplus	3,000	
Cr Retained earnings		3,000

Balance on revaluation surplus = £54,000 (£57,000 – £3,000)

2.3 Reporting valuation surpluses and decreases

Valuation surpluses are recorded in other comprehensive income for the year and held in a revaluation surplus within the equity section of the statement of financial position.

Decreases (losses) are recognised in the statement of profit or loss unless there is already a balance in the revaluation surplus for that asset. In this case, the decrease is taken first to other comprehensive income which will reduce the revaluation surplus in the statement of financial position. Any decrease in excess of the balance on revaluation surplus for that asset is taken to the statement of profit or loss.

3 Gains and losses on disposal

3.1 Gains and losses on disposal

Gains and losses on disposal of tangible non-current assets are shown in the statement of profit or loss and are calculated as the difference between disposal proceeds and carrying amount at the date of sale.

In addition, upon disposal of an asset that has previously been revalued, any remaining balance on revaluation surplus is transferred to retained earnings within the statement of changes in equity.

Test your understanding 2

Bill Ltd has provided the following information:

	£
List price of machinery	600,000
Transportation costs	3,500
Site preparation costs	1,500
Installation costs	3,800
Pre-production testing	5,300
Two year maintenance contract cost	15,000
Warranty cost	7,600
Annual insurance	3,200

The company received a 5% trade discount on the list price.

What is the initial measurement value (capitalised cost) of the machinery?

A £614,100

B £584,100

C £591,700

D £609,900

Test your understanding 3

The following is provided by Ivan Ltd:

	£
Land at cost	500,000
Buildings at cost	450,000
Buildings – accumulated depreciation	(180,000)
Carrying amount	770,000

Land was revalued to £600,000 and buildings to £600,000.

What is the correct double entry to record the revaluation of land and buildings?

		£
A	Dr Land	100,000
	Dr Buildings	150,000
	Cr Revaluation surplus	350,000
B	Dr Revaluation surplus	430,000
	Cr Land	100,000
	Cr Buildings	150,000
	Cr Building depreciation	180,000
C	Dr Buildings	270,000
	Dr Land	100,000
	Cr Revaluation surplus	370,000
D	Dr Land	100,000
	Dr Buildings	150,000
	Dr Buildings accumulated depreciation	180,000
	Cr Revaluation surplus	430,000

Test your understanding 4

Eyesore Ltd purchased a leasehold building 1 January 20X2 at a cost of £250,000 with an estimated useful life of twenty-five years with no estimated residual value.

On 1 January 20X4 the building was revalued to £253,000.

On 1 January 20X5 the building was sold for £245,000.

Eyesore Ltd's accounting policy is to make an annual transfer within the statement of changes in equity to account for the excess depreciation.

Required:

(a) Calculate the annual depreciation charge for the building and state the carrying amount of the building for each of the years ended 31 December 20X2 and 20X3.

(b) For the year ended 31 December 20X4:

  (i) state the accounting entries required to account for the revaluation on 1 January 20X4, and

  (ii) calculate the new annual depreciation charge and state the carrying amount of the building as at 31 December 20X4.

  (iii) Calculate the excess depreciation charge as a result of the revaluation and show the accounting entries required to account for the transfer within the statement of changes in equity.

(c) For the year ended 31 December 20X5, calculate the gain or loss on disposal of the building and state the final transfer required from revaluation surplus to retained earnings upon disposal of the building.

4 Summary

IAS 16 covers the accounting for property, plant and equipment. Property, plant and equipment should initially be shown at cost.

Subsequently they may either be shown at cost less depreciation, or revalued to fair value. If revalued, all similar items should be revalued and the revaluation must be kept up to date. If the revalued asset has a finite useful life, it should continue to be depreciated, with the depreciation charge recalculated based upon the revalued amount and the remaining expected useful life.

Test your understanding answers

Test your understanding 1

Answer is C

	£m	
Non-current assets at cost	10.40	
Accumulated depreciation	(0.12)	
Carrying amount	10.28	
Revaluation amount	15.00	
Surplus to revaluation surplus	4.72	

The accounting entry is:

Dr	Accumulated depreciation	0.12	
Dr	Land	4.6	
Cr	Revaluation surplus		4.72

Test your understanding 2

Answer B

	£
List price of machinery	600,000
Less: Trade discount (5% × £600,000)	(30,000)
Transportation costs	3,500
Site preparation costs	1,500
Installation costs	3,800
Pre-production testing	5,300
Initial measurement value (capitalised cost)	**584,100**

Two year maintenance contract cost, warranty cost and annual insurance should not be capitalised but treated as revenue expenditure.

Test your understanding 3

Answer D

	£
Land at CA	500,000
Revaluation surplus (gain)	**100,000**
Land valuation	600,000
Buildings at cost	450,000
Buildings – accumulated depreciation	(180,000)
Carrying amount	270,000
Revaluation surplus (gain)	**330,000**
Buildings valuation	600,000

Double entry:	£
Dr Land	100,000
Dr Buildings cost (600,000 – 450,000)	150,000
Dr Buildings depreciation	180,000
Cr Revaluation surplus (£330,000 + £100,000)	430,000

Test your understanding 4

(a) Year ended 31 December 20X2:

Annual depreciation charge = £250,000/25 years = £10,000

PPE carrying amount for SFP £250,000 – £10,000 = £240,000

Year ended 31 December 20X3:

Annual depreciation charge £10,000

Carrying amount £250,000 – (2 × £10,000) = £230,000

(b) Year ended 31 December 20X4:

(i) Account for the revaluation:

	£
Dr Buildings	3,000
Dr: Accumulated depreciation	20,000
Cr: Revaluation surplus	23,000

(ii) Calculate revised annual depreciation charge £253,000/23 years = £11,000 per annum

PPE carrying amount for SFP £253,000 – £11,000 = £242,000

(iii) Increase in depreciation charge due to revaluation £1,000 (£11,000 – £10,000)

Transfer from revaluation surplus to retained earnings within SOCIE:

Dr: Revaluation surplus £1,000 Cr: Retained earnings £1,000

Revaluation surplus on SFP = £23,000 – £1,000 = £22,000

(c) Year ended 31 December 20X5:

Disposal proceeds £245,000 – CA of PPE £242,000 = £3,000 gain on disposal

Transfer remaining balance on revaluation surplus to retained earnings in SOCIE = £22,000

Dr: Revaluation surplus £22,000 Cr: Retained earnings £22,000

Intangible assets

5

Introduction

For this unit you need knowledge of aspects of IAS 38 *Intangible assets*.

ASSESSMENT CRITERIA

Examine the effect of international accounting standards on the preparation of financial statements (2.1)

CONTENTS

1 IAS 38 *Intangible Assets*

1.1 Introduction

In the previous chapter you studied the accounting treatment of property, plant and equipment such as buildings, cars and computers. Items of property, plant and equipment have a physical form and can therefore be seen or touched. Sometimes companies will acquire assets with no physical form. These are known as intangible assets.

1.2 Criteria of an Intangible asset

IAS 38 says that an intangible asset is **'an identifiable, non-monetary asset without physical substance.'** [IAS 38, para 8].

To be identified as an intangible asset, an asset must either:

- be capable of being separated or divided from the entity and sold, transferred, licensed, rented or exchanged either individually or together with a related contract, asset or liability or
- arise from contractual or other legal rights.

Key examples of intangible assets are patents, copyrights and customer lists.

1.3 Recognition and measurement

IAS 38 requires an entity to recognise an intangible asset, whether purchased or self-created (at cost) if, and only if:

- **'it is probable that the expected future economic benefits that are attributable to the asset will flow to the entity; and**
- **the cost of the asset can be measured** reliably' [IAS 38, para 21].

Future economic benefits include revenue from sale of products or services, cost savings, or other benefits resulting from use of the asset by the entity.

It is not normally possible to measure the cost of an internally generated intangible asset, such as a brand name, and therefore these cannot be recognised. However, if a company purchases a brand name then the cost can be measured reliably and therefore an asset can be recognised.

An intangible asset shall initially be measured at cost.

1.4 Research and development

Internally generated intangible assets cannot normally be recognised because it is not possible to determine how much they cost. However, companies do normally carefully monitor their expenditure on research and develop activities. Therefore IAS 38 sets out a number of rules concerning the recognition of internally generated intangible assets arising from research and development.

Research involves uncovering new knowledge. This may have no commercial application and therefore might not give rise to future benefits. Therefore, no intangible asset arising from research shall be recognised. Expenditure on the research phase is recognised as an expense in the statement of profit or loss when it is incurred.

Development activities involve applying the findings of research activities and using this knowledge to develop something with a commercial use. This may be a new product, which can be sold for a profit, or new processes, which allow the company to operate more cheaply and efficiently. An intangible asset arising from development activities must be recognised if an entity can demonstrate all of the following:

(a) technical feasibility of completing the intangible asset so it is available for use or sale

(b) intention to complete the intangible asset and use or sell it

(c) ability to use or sell the intangible asset

(d) how the intangible asset will generate probable future economic benefits. E.g. how the entity can demonstrate the existence of a market for the output of the intangible asset or the intangible asset itself

(e) availability of adequate technical, financial and other resources to complete the development and to use or sell the intangible asset

(f) ability to measure reliably the expenditure attributable to the intangible asset during its development.

1.5 The cost of intangible assets

Cost comprises all directly attributable costs necessary to create, produce and prepare the asset for use. This will include the following:

- Costs of materials and services used or consumed in generating the intangible asset, such as materials used in the production of prototypes.
- Costs of employee benefits arising from the generation of the intangible asset.
- Fees to register a legal right.

The following are not components of cost:

- Selling, administrative, and other general overhead expenses.
- Identified inefficiencies and initial operating losses incurred before the asset achieves planned performance.
- The cost of training staff to operate the asset.

1.6 Measurement after recognition

Once an intangible asset has been recognised at cost, an entity shall choose either the cost model or revaluation model as its accounting policy.

Cost model: The asset is carried at cost less any accumulated amortisation and any accumulated impairment losses.

Revaluation model: The asset is carried at its revalued amount. This is its fair value at the date of revaluation less any subsequent accumulated amortisation and any subsequent impairment losses. The valuation must be reviewed regularly.

Intangible assets are usually not revalued as they are unique and therefore it is very difficult to reliably determine their market value.

1.7 Revaluation gains or losses

A revaluation gain should be credited other comprehensive income and held in a revaluation reserve within the equity section of the statement of financial position.

A revaluation loss will be debited to the statement of profit or loss (unless reversing a previous gain in which case the loss will be debited to other comprehensive income and deducted from the revaluation reserve).

1.8 Useful life

An entity needs to determine the useful life of its intangible assets.

Intangible assets are written down over their useful life. This process is called 'amortisation', although it is essentially the same as depreciation. Amortisation is charged to the statement of profit or loss.

Amortisation shall begin when the asset is available for use and cease when the asset is derecognised.

The amortisation method chosen should reflect the pattern in which the assets' benefits are expected to be consumed. If this cannot be reliably measured then the straight-line method shall be used. The amortisation charge for each period shall be recognised in the statement of profit or loss.

The residual value of an intangible asset shall normally be deemed to be zero unless:

- there is a commitment by a third party to purchase the asset at the end of its useful life or
- there is an active market for the asset and a residual value can be determined and the active market will still exist at the end of the assets useful life.

The amortisation period and method shall be reviewed at each financial year end.

If an asset has an indefinite life it shall not be amortised.

The asset must be tested annually for impairment in accordance with IAS 36 *Impairment of Assets.* Impairments are covered later in this text.

The useful life of intangible assets must be reviewed at the end of each accounting period.

Test your understanding 1

Explain the criteria in IAS 38 for capitalising research and development expenditure.

Test your understanding 2

Prepare brief notes for the directors of Harris plc in response to the following questions:

(a) What is meant by an intangible asset according to IAS 38?

(b) What would Harris plc have to demonstrate about development costs before these costs can be recognised as intangible assets in the financial statements according to IAS 38?

Test your understanding 3

Which of the following statements are true according to IAS 38?

(i) All development expenditure must be written off immediately to the statement of profit or loss as soon as the expenditure is incurred.

(ii) Amortisation of development costs can be based on the future sales revenue of the product.

(iii) All research expenditure should be capitalised as an intangible asset.

(iv) Development expenditure that is capitalised should be treated as a tangible non-current asset.

(v) One of the criteria to be met in considering whether or not development expenditure can be capitalised is whether the project is technically feasible.

A Only (ii) and (v)

B Only (i), (iii) and (v)

C Only (ii) and (iv)

D Only (iii) and (iv)

2 Summary

This chapter has covered IAS 38 *Intangible Assets.*

This requires purchased intangible assets to be capitalised and amortised over their useful economic lives.

It discusses the accounting treatment of research and development costs and lists the criteria to be fulfilled for an intangible asset to be recognised.

Test your understanding answers

Test your understanding 1

Expenditure on the research phase must be recognised as an expense in the statement of profit or loss when it is incurred and can never be capitalised.

An intangible arising from the development or development phase shall be recognised if an entity can demonstrate all of the following:

(a) technical feasibility of completing the intangible asset so it is available for use or sale

(b) the intention to complete the intangible asset and use or sell it

(c) the ability to use or sell the intangible asset

(d) how the intangible asset will generate probable future economic benefits e.g. how the entity can demonstrate the existence of a market for the output of the intangible asset or the intangible asset itself

(e) the availability of adequate technical, financial and other resources to complete the development and to use or sell the intangible asset

(f) the ability to measure reliably the expenditure attributable to the intangible asset during its development.

Test your understanding 2

(a) An intangible asset according to IAS 38?

"an identifiable, non-monetary asset without physical substance" [IAS 38, para 8].

(b) Harris would have to demonstrate:

- the technical feasibility of completing the intangible asset so that it will be available for use or sale
- its intention to complete the intangible asset and use or sell it
- its ability to use or sell the intangible asset
- how the intangible asset will generate future economic benefits
- the availability of adequate technical, financial and other resources to complete the development and to use or sell the intangible asset.

Test your understanding 3

Answer A

Development expenditure must be capitalised if it satisfies the criteria of IAS 38.

All research expenditure should be written off to the statement of profit or loss.

Development expenditure that is capitalised should be treated as intangible non-current asset.

Impairments

6

Introduction

For this unit you need knowledge of aspects of IAS 36 *Impairment of assets*.

ASSESSMENT CRITERIA

Examine the effect of international accounting standards on the preparation of financial statements (2.1)

Draft a statement of profit or loss and other comprehensive income (3.1)

CONTENTS

1 IAS 36 *Impairment of Assets*

1.1 Introduction

An impairment is the reduction in the recoverable amount of a non-current asset below its carrying amount.

Definition

Recoverable amount is the higher of the fair value less costs to sell and value in use.

Fair value less costs to sell is the amount at which an asset could be disposed of, less any direct selling costs.

Value in use is the total future cash flows (discounted to present value) arising from an asset's continued use, including those resulting from its ultimate disposal.

Example

A machine has a carrying amount of £5,000 in the draft statement of financial position as at 31 December 20X9. It could be sold now for £4,000, or retained in the business where its value in use is £4,476. Assess whether the machine is impaired at 31 December 20X9.

Solution

Current carrying amount = £5,000

Compare this with the recoverable amount:

higher of

Fair value less costs to sell	Value in use
£4,000	£4,476

Therefore recoverable amount = £4,476

The machine has a carrying amount of £5,000 but a recoverable amount of only £4,476. It is impaired and should be written down to £4,476 in the statement of financial position. An impairment loss of £5,000 – £4,476 = £524 must be recognised in the statement of profit or loss.

1.2 Identifying an asset that may be impaired

An entity shall assess at each reporting date whether there is any indication that an asset may be impaired.

Regardless of any indication an entity shall also:

- test an intangible asset with an indefinite useful economic life for impairment (this may be performed at any time during the year, provided it is performed at the same time each year)
- test goodwill acquired in a business combination for impairment annually.

1.3 Indicators of impairment

Examples of indications that impairment may have occurred are as follows.

External sources of information:

- a significant decline in a non-current asset's market value during the period
- a significant adverse change in the market in which the business operates
- changes in the economic environment, such as interest rates or inflation
- changes in the legal system.

Internal sources of information:

- evidence of physical damage to, or obsolescence of, the asset
- a current period operating loss
- net cash outflow from operating activities
- a management commitment to undertake a significant reorganisation
- a major loss of key employees.

1.4 Accounting for impairment losses

Impairment losses must be recognised in the statement of profit or loss, unless they arise on a previously revalued asset. Impairment losses on revalued assets are recognised in the revaluations reserve which is part of the statement of changes in equity.

After recognition of the impairment loss the depreciation (amortisation) charge for the asset shall be adjusted to allocate the asset's revised carrying amount over its remaining useful economic life.

1.5 Disclosure requirements

An entity shall disclose the amount of the impairment losses recognised during the period and the line item(s) of the statement of profit or loss in which those impairment losses are included.

Test your understanding 1

The directors of Smokey Ltd are carrying out a review of four assets which they consider may have become impaired.

	Carrying amount	Fair value less costs to sell	Value in use
	£	£	£
A	20,000	24,000	28,000
B	16,000	18,000	11,600
C	14,000	15,200	14,400
D	18,000	8,600	10,400

In accordance with IAS 36 *Impairment of assets*, which of the above assets will be impaired?

Test your understanding 2

Which of the following statements are true according to IAS 36?

(i) Impairment arises when the recoverable amount exceeds the carrying amount.

(ii) The recoverable amount is the higher of the fair value less costs to sell and the value in use.

(iii) The value in use is the net present value of future cash flows.

(iv) An impairment charge is recorded by debiting the asset account and crediting the statement of profit or loss.

(v) The value in use of an asset can be affected by both internal and external factors.

A Only (i), (ii) and (v)

B Only (ii), (iii) and (v)

C Only (ii), (iii) and (iv)

D Only (i), (iv) and (iv)

2 Summary

This chapter has covered IAS 36 *Impairment of Assets*.

IAS 36 requires impaired assets (those for which the carrying amount exceeds the recoverable amount) to be written down to their recoverable amount. The impairment loss is normally recognised in the statement of profit or loss.

Test your understanding answers

Test your understanding 1

Answer is D

According to IAS 36 an asset is impaired when its carrying amount exceeds its recoverable amount, where the recoverable amount of an asset is the higher of its fair value less costs to sell and its value in use.

Carrying amount = 18,000

The higher of recoverable amount is value in use = 10,400

Therefore only asset D is impaired by (18,000 – 10,400) = 7,600

Test your understanding 2

Answer B

Impairment arises when the carrying amount exceeds the recoverable amount.

An impairment charge is recorded by debiting the statement of profit or loss and crediting the asset account.

7 Inventories

Introduction

In order to prepare a set of limited company accounts you need to know how to deal with the valuation of inventories. This is covered by IAS 2 *Inventories*.

ASSESSMENT CRITERIA

Examine the effect of international accounting standards on the preparation of financial statements (2.1)

CONTENTS

1 Valuation of inventories

1.1 The basic rule

IAS 2 *Inventories* says that **'inventories are required to be stated at the lower of cost and net realisable value (NRV),'** [IAS 2, para 9] on an item by item basis.

1.2 Cost

IAS 2 *Inventories* defines cost as comprising: **'all costs of purchase, costs of conversion and other costs incurred in bringing the inventories to their present location and condition.'** [IAS 2, para 10].

Specifically excluded are:

(a) abnormal amounts of wasted materials, labour and other production costs

(b) storage costs, unless necessary in the production process before a further production stage

(c) administrative overheads that do not contribute to bringing inventories to their present location and condition

(d) selling costs.

This means that two identical items may have different costs if they are in different locations. For example, the cost of an item which has been shipped to a distribution centre in France will include the normal transport costs to France and hence will have a higher cost than a similar item held in the factory in England.

Note that only costs incurred in the normal course of business should be included. If the lorry taking items to France broke down, the costs of the breakdown would not be included as part of the transport costs since they are considered abnormal.

1.3 Net realisable value

This is the expected selling price in the ordinary course of business less any costs to complete and sell.

2 Methods of costing inventories

2.1 Acceptable inventory accounting methods

When a number of identical items of inventories have been purchased or made at different times, the actual cost of the items in inventories at the year end may not be known, so assumptions have to be made of the way in which the inventory items flowed through the business. Only methods that give the fairest practicable approximation to actual cost are acceptable.

2.2 Acceptable methods

IAS 2 accepts the use of any one of the following methods, consistently applied:

(i) **Unit cost** – The actual cost of purchasing or manufacturing identifiable units of inventory.

(ii) **Weighted average cost** – The calculation of the cost of inventories and work in progress on the basis of the application to the units of inventories on hand of an average price computed by dividing the total cost of units by the total number of such units (this average price may be arrived at by means of a continuous calculation, a periodic calculation or a moving periodic calculation).

(iii) **FIFO (first in, first out)** – The calculation of the cost of inventories and work in progress on the basis that the quantities in hand represent the latest purchases or production.

Example

RJ plc made the following purchases and sales of grommets in May 20X1:

1 May	Opening stock	Nil
8 May	Bought 200 units	@ £5 each
13 May	Bought 400 units	@ £5.60 each
20 May	Sold 300 units	@ £8 each

Determine the closing inventories valuation at 31 May using:

(a) FIFO

(b) Weighted average cost.

Solution

(a) There are 300 units in inventory and the FIFO method assumes that these consist of the purchases on 13 May as the earlier purchase has all been sold.

Closing inventories = 300 units @ £5.60 = £1,680

(b) The WAC method calculates an average price for the inventory purchases.

$$\text{Average price} = \frac{(200 \times £5) + (400 \times £5.60)}{600 \text{ units}} = £5.40$$

Closing inventories = 300 × £5.40 = £1,620

Test your understanding 1

S Ltd is a manufacturing company. It held its annual inventory count on 31 March 20X2, the company's year-end. The accounts department is currently working its way through the inventory sheets placing a value on the physical inventories. The company has had a difficult year and profits are likely to be lower than in the previous year.

Raw materials

Inventories of raw materials are valued at cost. The finance director has suggested that the cost has been understated in previous years because the company has not taken the costs of delivery into account. These can be substantial in the case of imported goods. It has been proposed that these costs be taken into account in the valuation of closing inventories of raw materials.

Finished goods

Finished goods have already been valued at £400,000. This figure includes some obsolete goods which cost £70,000 to produce, but which are likely to be sold at a scrap value of £500. There are also several batches of a new product which will be launched early in the new financial year. These cost £90,000 to manufacture. Independent market research suggests that it is very likely that the new product will be sold for considerably more than this. If, however, the launch is unsuccessful, the new product will have to be sold as scrap for £1,000. The finance director has said that the aggregate net realisable value of all closing inventories of finished goods is at least £500,000 and so there is no need to worry about the obsolete and new inventory products.

Required:

(a) Explain whether the costs of delivery should be included in the valuation of raw materials.

(b) (i) Explain whether the valuation of closing inventories at the lower of cost and net realisable value should be done on an item–by–item basis or on the basis of the aggregate cost of all items as compared with their aggregate net realisable value.

(ii) State how you would value the obsolete items and the new product line, giving reasons for your valuation in each case.

Test your understanding 2

(a) Why is an adjustment made for closing inventories in the financial statements?

(b) How should inventories be valued in the financial statements?

Test your understanding 3

1 A company has closing inventories of 100 items of Unit X. Each unit cost £4 but can only be sold for £3.50. What is the total closing inventories valuation?

2 State two circumstances when NRV is likely to be lower than cost.

3 What methods of cost measurement can be used per IAS 2?

4 Give two examples of items excluded from the cost of inventories.

Test your understanding 4

Tim's business sells two products A and B. The following information is available at the year end:

Product	**A**	**B**
	per unit	per unit
Purchase price	£10	£12
Carriage inwards costs	£2	£3
Estimated selling price	£15	£14
Estimated sales commission	£1	£6
Units of inventory	20	25

At what value should total inventory be stated in Tim's financial statements according to IAS 2 *Inventories*?

A £500

B £440

C £615

D £480

3 Summary

IAS 2 requires that inventories should be stated in the statement of financial position at the lower of cost and net realisable value.

Cost comprises all expenditure which has been incurred in the normal course of business in bringing the product or service to its present location and condition.

NRV is the expected selling price less the costs needed to complete and sell the item.

If the actual costs of the items in closing inventories are not known (since the items are interchangeable), an assumption has to be made of how the items physically flow through the business. The usual assumption is FIFO (First In First Out).

Test your understanding answers

Test your understanding 1

S Ltd

(a) Raw materials should be valued at the lower of cost and net realisable value, where cost includes all costs in bringing the items to their present location and condition.

Delivery costs could be included in this definition and so legitimately be added to the valuation, as long as they have been incurred in bringing the inventory items to their present location and condition.

(b) (i) Valuation at cost or net realisable value should be carried out on a product line-by-line basis. The value of assets and liabilities should be determined for individual items not in aggregate. The finance director's statement is therefore incorrect.

(ii) Obsolete items must be valued at £500, their net realisable value since this is lower than cost.

New product line. It seems likely from the initial market research that net realisable value will be considerably greater than the cost of £90,000. These items should thus be included at £90,000. If in a later period the launch proves unsuccessful the inventories will need to be written down to £1,000 and, if material, may be shown as an exceptional item.

Test your understanding 2

(a) We must match costs with related revenues. The cost of unsold inventories is therefore carried forward to be matched with revenue when it arises. So the cost of inventories is not shown in the year in which the cost is incurred but rather in the year the sale is made.

(b) Inventories should be valued at the lower of cost and net realisable value.

Test your understanding 3

1 100 × £3.50 = £350.

2 Physical deterioration, obsolescence.

3 Unit cost, FIFO, Weighted average cost.

4 Select from:

- abnormal amounts of wasted materials, labour and other production costs
- storage costs, unless necessary in the production process before a further production stage
- administrative overheads that do not contribute to bringing inventories to their present location and condition
- selling costs.

Test your understanding 4

Answer B

	A	B	Total
Purchase price	£10	£12	
Carriage inwards costs	£2	£3	
Total cost	**£12**	£15	
Estimated selling price	£15	£14	
Sales commission	£(1)	£(6)	
Net selling price	£14	**£8**	
Lower of: cost or net selling price	£12	£8	
× Number of units	× 20	× 25	
Valuation	£240	£200	**£440**

Taxation

8

Introduction

In order to prepare a set of limited company accounts you need to know how to deal with tax in the statement of profit or loss and the statement of financial position.

ASSESSMENT CRITERIA

Examine the effect of international accounting standards on the preparation of financial statements (2.1)

CONTENTS

1 IAS 12 *Income Taxes*

1.1 Introduction

Companies pay corporation tax on their profits.

In principle, the amount of current corporation tax should be calculated using the tax rates that the legislation has laid down for the company's financial year. In the exam you will normally be told the rate, and often the amount, of corporation tax.

When preparing a statement of financial position, current tax for current and prior periods is recognised as a liability. If the amount already paid in respect of current and prior periods exceeds the amount due for those periods, the excess shall be recognised as an asset.

1.2 Adjustments relating to prior years

When the provision for corporation tax is made in the accounts, it is only an estimate of the actual liability which will eventually be agreed with the HM Revenue and Customs (HMRC). Any difference between the original estimate and the actual figure will be adjusted in the next year's provision. If material this figure will be shown separately.

Example

A company makes an operating profit before taxation of £300,000. Tax on profits is estimated at £105,000. (The corporation tax charge is not 30% of the accounting profits before tax, since accounting profits are adjusted to calculate the taxable profit before tax.)

Solution

Statement of profit or loss (extract) for the year end 31 December 20X7

	£
Profit before taxation	300,000
Tax on profit	(105,000)
Profit after taxation	195,000

Tax liability account

	£		£
31 Dec X7 Balance c/d	105,000	Profit or loss charge	105,000
	105,000		105,000
		1 Jan X8 Balance b/d	105,000

The balance on the corporation tax account is carried forward and will appear on the statement of financial position under the 'current liabilities' heading.

Example

Continuing with the previous example, suppose that in 20X8 the company pays £99,000 corporation tax on the 20X7 profit, not the £105,000 as estimated.

The profit for the year 20X8 is £400,000 and corporation tax is estimated at £132,000.

Statement of profit or loss (extract) 20X8

	£	£
Profit before taxation		400,000
Tax		
Corporation tax	132,000	
Adjustment for over provision in previous year	(6,000)	(126,000)
Profit after taxation		274,000

Tax liability account

	£		£
01 Oct X8 Bank	99,000	01 Jan X8 Balance b/d	105,000
31 Dec X8 Over provision	6,000	31 Dec X8 Profit or loss	132,000
31 Dec X8 Balance c/d	132,000		
	237,000		237,000
		01 Jan X9 Balance b/d	132,000

The double entry for the over provision is:

Debit Tax liability £6,000

Credit Tax charge in the statement of profit or loss £6,000

This reduces both the liability and the charge.

Test your understanding 1

Rubislaw plc

Rubislaw was formed in 20X0. It has a 31 December year-end.

The balance on its tax liability account at 1 January 20X3 was £74,000. During 20X3 this liability was settled for £69,000. The taxable profits for 20X3 are estimated to be £150,000, and the tax due on the current year's profits is estimated at £45,000.

Required:

Show how the above should be presented in the statement of profit or loss for the year ended 31 December 20X3 and in the statement of financial position as at that date.

2 Summary

This chapter has summarised all the information regarding tax that you need for the preparation of a set of limited company financial statements.

The company's estimate of the tax due on the current year's profits is an expense in the statement of profit or loss and should also be shown as a current liability on the statement of financial position.

An opening balance in the tax payable account represents an under or over provision from the previous year. This is also included as part of the current year tax charge.

Test your understanding answers

Test your understanding 1

Rubislaw plc

Statement of profit or loss (extract) for the year ended 31 December 20X3

	£
Tax on profit (W1)	40,000

Statement of financial position (extract) at 31 December 20X4

	£
Current liabilities	
Tax liabilities	45,000

Workings

	£
Tax charge for the year	
Tax for year ended 31.12.X3	45,000
Overprovision for 31.12.X2 (£74,000 – £69,000)	(5,000)
	40,000

Leases

9

Introduction

Leases are covered by IFRS 16 *Leases*. For this unit you need an appreciation of the accounting treatment at the beginning and during the life of the lease. Both written and computational questions can be examined.

ASSESSMENT CRITERIA

Examine the effect of international accounting standards on the preparation of financial statements (2.1)

CONTENTS

1 Types of extended credit agreement

1.1 Introduction

A business may acquire the use of a non-current asset by outright purchase (cash or credit) or by some form of 'extended credit' agreement – credit sale, hire purchase or a lease.

If these 'extended credit' transactions were to be recorded according to their strict legal form, the picture presented by the statement of financial position and statement of profit or loss of the business using the asset could be quite misleading. This is because neither the asset used nor the liability for future payments would be recognised in the statement of financial position.

IFRS 16 *Leases* ensures that transactions that are in substance loans to acquire an asset, even if not in legal form, are treated as any other loan agreement or asset purchase.

1.2 Leases

Definitions

'A lease is a contract, or part of a contract, that conveys the right to use an asset (the underlying asset) for a period of time in exchange for consideration.'

The **lessor** is the **'entity that provides the right to use an underlying asset in exchange for consideration.'**

The **lessee** is the **'entity that obtains the right to use an underlying asset in exchange for consideration.'**

A **right-of-use asset 'represents the lessee's rights to use an underlying asset for the lease term.'**

[IFRS 16: Appendix A]

2 Accounting for leases

2.1 Capitalisation of leases in the lessee accounts

The basic principle is that at the commencement of the lease, the lessee should recognise a lease liability and a right-of-use asset.

2.2 Initial measurement

The liability

The lease liability is initially measured at the present value of the lease payments that have not yet been paid.

Lease payments should include the following:

- Fixed payments
- Amounts expected to be payable under residual value guarantees
- Options to purchase the asset that are reasonably certain to be exercised
- Termination penalties, if the lease term reflects the expectation that these will be incurred.

A residual value guarantee is when the lessor is guaranteed that the underlying asset at the end of the lease term will not be worth less than a specified amount.

The discount rate should be the rate implicit in the lease. If this cannot be determined, then the entity should use its incremental borrowing rate (the rate at which it could borrow funds to purchase a similar asset).

The right-of-use asset

The right-of-use asset is initially recognised at cost.

The initial cost of the right-of-use asset comprises:

- The amount of the initial measurement of the lease liability (see above)
- Lease payments made at or before the commencement date
- Any initial direct costs
- The estimated costs of removing or dismantling the underlying asset as per the conditions of the lease.

The lease term

To calculate the initial value of the liability and right-of-use asset, the lessee must consider the length of the lease term. The lease term comprises:

- Non-cancellable periods
- Periods covered by an option to extend the lease if reasonably certain to be exercised
- Periods covered by an option to terminate the lease if these are reasonably certain not to be exercised.

2.3 Subsequent measurement

The liability

The carrying amount of the lease liability is increased by the interest charge, calculated as the outstanding liability multiplied by the discount rate of interest. This interest is also recorded in the statement of profit or loss:

Dr Finance costs (SPL)	X
Cr Lease liability (SFP)	X

The carrying amount of the lease liability is reduced by cash repayments:

Dr Lease liability (SFP)	X
Cr Cash (SFP)	X

The right-of-use asset

The right-of-use asset is measured using the cost model (unless another measurement model is chosen). This means that the asset is measured at its initial cost less accumulated depreciation and impairment losses.

Depreciation is calculated as follows:

- If ownership of the asset transfers to the lessee at the end of the lease term then depreciation should be charged over the asset's useful life,
- Otherwise, depreciation is charged over the shorter of the useful life and the lease term (as defined previously).

Example

A lessee enters into a lease on 1 January 20X8 for an item of plant with an estimated useful life of five years. The present value of lease payments is £5,710. Under the terms of the lease there will be four annual payments of £2,000 paid in arrears with the first rental payable on 31.12.X8. The asset will not transfer to the lessee at the end of the lease.

The interest rate implicit in the lease is 15%.

Required:

Show how the lease liability would be recorded in the ledger accounts of the lessee for the first two years, and explain how the transaction would be reflected in the statement of profit or loss and statement of financial position over the four years.

Solution

When the lease starts, the right-of-use asset is capitalised at a value of £5,710 which is the present value of the lease payments not yet made.

The finance cost will be calculated as follows for each year:

Year	**Liability b/f**	**Interest @ 15%**	**Payment**	**Liability c/f**
	£	£	£	£
1	5,710	857	(2,000)	4,567
2	4,567	685	(2,000)	3,252
3	3,252	488	(2,000)	1,740
4	1,740	260	(2,000)	–
		2,290		

At the end of year 1 the total lease liability is £4,567, which can be split further into non-current and current liabilities as follows:

	£
Non-current liabilities	3,252
Current liabilities	1,315

The non-current liability is £3,252 as this is due after more than one year and the balance of £1,315 is the current liability.

The annual depreciation charge for each of the four years will be:

£5,710/4 years = £1,428 pa

The ledger entry at the beginning of the lease will be:

	£	£
Dr Right-of-use asset (SFP)	5,710	
Cr Lease liability (SFP)		5,710

Being the recording of the 'purchase' of an asset under a lease and the assumption of a liability.

The entries in the lease liability account will be as follows:

Lease liability account

	£		£
31.12.X8 Cash	2,000	1.1.X8 Leased asset	5,710
31.12.X8 Balance c/d	4,567	31.12.X8 Interest expense	857
	6,567		6,567
31.12.X9 Cash	2,000	1.1.X9 Balance b/d	4,567
31.12.X9 Balance c/d	3,252	31.12.X9 Interest expense	685
	5,252		5,252
		1.1.Y0 Balance b/d	3,252

The finance charges to the statement of profit or loss over the period of the lease are:

Year	**1**	**2**	**3**	**4**	**Total**
	£	£	£	£	£
Interest	857	685	488	260	2,290

At the end of the financial year the statement of financial position would reflect the carrying amount of the asset and the outstanding liability carried forward split between current liabilities and non-current liabilities.

Test your understanding 1

Finch

Finch Ltd entered into a leasing agreement with Tyrrell plc on 1 October 20X5.

The contract involves an annual payment in arrears of £1,200,000 for five years.

At the start of the lease with Tyrrell plc the present value of the lease payments was calculated to be £4,100,000.

The machinery would normally be expected to have a useful life of approximately seven years. The asset will not transfer to Finch Ltd at the end of the lease term.

The implied rate of interest is 14.2% per annum.

Required:

(a) Calculate the initial value of the right-of-use asset.

(b) Calculate the total lease liability as at the year-end 30 September 20X6.

(b) Calculate the carrying value of the right-of-use asset as at the year-end 30 September 20X6.

Test your understanding 2

MP Ltd entered into a four year lease agreement on 1 January 20X1 for a machine. The present value of the lease payments is £69,740. The lease rentals of £20,000 are payable in advance. The implicit interest rate is 10%. The machine has a useful life of four years.

What is the depreciation charge, finance charge, the carrying amount of the machine and total lease liability for the year ended 31 December 20X1?

	Depreciation charge	**Finance charge**	**Carrying amount**	**Total lease liability**
	£	£	£	£
A	17,435	4,974	52,305	54,714
B	17,435	6,974	52,305	56,714
C	20,000	4,974	39,740	74,714
D	20,000	6,974	52,305	56,714

3 Short-life and low value assets

If the lease is short-term (less than 12 months or equal to at the inception date) or of a low value then a simplified treatment is allowed.

In these cases, the lessee can choose to recognise the lease payments in profit or loss on a straight line basis. No lease liability or right-of-use asset would therefore be recognised.

Example

Danny Ltd needed a new computer. At 1 January 20X1, it entered into an agreement to lease a computer for 1 year at a cost of £1,000 which would be paid on 1 July 20X1. An up-front and non-refundable deposit of £500 was paid on 1 January 20X1.

Required:

Explain how to account for this transaction in accordance with IFRS 16 in the year ended 30 June 20X1.

Solution:

The simplified treatment of a short lease allows the lessee to choose to recognise the rental expense in the statement of profit or loss on a straight line basis.

The total rentals that Danny Ltd will pay for the computer are £1,500 (£1,000 + £500 deposit).

The expense in the statement of profit or loss for the year ended 30 June 20X1 should therefore be £750 (£1,500 × 6/12).

However, Danny Ltd has only made a cash payment of £500 at this date. Therefore, an accrual of £250 will also be recorded in current liabilities on the statement of financial position.

The double entry required is as follows:

Dr Lease rentals (SPL)	£750	
Cr Accruals (SFP)		£250
Cr Cash (SFP)		£500

4 Summary

It is important that you understand the following:

(a) the definitions under IFRS 16

(b) the initial accounting treatment of a lease in the lessee's accounts

(c) the subsequent accounting treatment of a lease in the lessee's accounts

(d) the accounting treatment of short-life and low value assets.

Test your understanding answers

Test your understanding 1

Finch

(a) Under IFRS 16 the right-of-use asset will be initially recognised at the present value of the lease payments which is £4,100,000.

(b) A lease liability table will be used to calculate the total lease liability

Year	Liability b/f	Interest @ 14.2%	Payment	Liability c/f
	£	£	£	£
1	4,100,000	582,200	(1,200,000)	**3,482,200**

As at the year-end 30 September 20X6 the total lease liability is £3,482,200.

(a) The right-of-use asset will be depreciated over the shorter of the useful life of the asset and the lease term. Therefore, the annual depreciation charge will be £4,100,000/5 years = **£820,000**

The carrying value of the right-of-use asset as at 30 September 20X6 is £4,100,000 – £820,000 = £3,280,000.

Test your understanding 2

Answer A

The annual **depreciation charge** will be **£17,435** (£69,740/4 years)

The **carrying amount** will be **£52,305** (£69,740 – £17,435)

Year ended 31 December	Opening balance	Lease payment	Total	Finance charge 10%	Closing balance
	£	£	£	£	£
20X1	69,740	(20,000)	49,740	**4,974**	**54,714** Total liability

10 Events after the reporting period, provisions and contingencies

Introduction

For this unit you need to know all aspects of IAS 10 *Events after the Reporting* period and almost all aspects of IAS 37 *Provisions, Contingent Liabilities and Contingent Assets.*

ASSESSMENT CRITERIA

Examine the effect of international accounting standards on the preparation of financial statements (2.1)

CONTENTS

1 IAS 10 *Events after the Reporting Period*

1.1 Introduction

'An event, which could be favourable or unfavourable, that occurs between the end of the reporting period and the date that the financial statements are authorised for issue.' [IAS 10, para 3]. There are two types of event:

(a) adjusting events, which require the accounts to be adjusted to reflect their impact, and

(b) non-adjusting events, which are merely noted in the accounts if material.

1.2 Adjusting events

These are events which **'provides additional evidence of conditions that existed at the end of the reporting period.'** [IAS 10, para 3] Such events are relevant because they relate to items appearing in the accounts or transactions reported in them. Examples of adjusting events are:

(a) The settlement post year end of a court case that confirms that the entity had a present obligation at the reporting date. The entity must adjust any previously recognised provisions related to the court case in accordance with IAS 37 *Provisions, Contingent Liabilities and Contingent Assets* or recognise a new provision.

(b) The receipt of information post year end indicating an asset was impaired at the reporting date, or the amount of a previously recognised impairment loss for that asset needs to be adjusted. For example:

  (i) the bankruptcy of a customer usually confirms that a loss existed at the reporting date on a trade receivable and the entity needs to adjust the carrying amount of the trade receivable

  (ii) the sale of inventories after the end of the reporting period may give evidence about their net realisable value at the reporting date.

(c) The subsequent determination of the purchase price or of the proceeds of sale of assets purchased or sold before the year-end.

(d) The determination after the reporting period of the amount of profit-sharing or bonus payments, if the entity had a present legal or constructive obligation at the statement of financial position date to make such payments as a result of events before that date.

(e) The discovery of errors or frauds which show that the financial statements were incorrect.

1.3 Non-adjusting events

These events concern conditions which did not exist at the reporting date. These events therefore shall not be adjusted for in the financial statements. Some examples of non-adjusting events are:

(a) issues of shares and debentures

(b) purchases and sales of non-current assets and investments

(c) losses of non-current assets or inventories as a result of a catastrophe, such as a fire or flood

(d) declines in the value of property and investments held as non-current assets, if it can be demonstrated that the decline occurred after the year end.

1.4 Dividends

If an entity declares dividends after the reporting date, the entity shall not recognise those dividends as a liability at the reporting date.

1.5 Going concern

The financial statements should not be prepared on a going concern basis if management determines after the statement of financial position date that it intends to liquidate or cease trading.

1.6 Disclosure

The notes to the financial statements must disclose the date the financial statements were authorised for issue and who gave that authorisation.

The following disclosures are also required for material non-adjusting events:

(i) the nature of the event, and

(ii) an estimate of the financial effect, or a statement it is not possible to reasonably estimate the financial effect.

Example

How would the following events be accounted for in the financial statements for the year to 31 December 20X7?

Assume that each event is material in size in the context of the accounts as a whole.

(a) On 5 January 20X8 a large credit customer went into liquidation owing £100,000 as at the reporting date. It is unlikely that this balance will be paid.

(b) On 10 January 20X8 all the inventories in the Dudley warehouse were destroyed by fire. They had a cost at that date of £50,000 and a net realisable value of £70,000. Although this loss is serious, it is not so serious that the company is no longer able to continue as a going concern.

Solution

(a) This is an adjusting event giving additional information on the receivables figure at the year end. The £100,000 irrecoverable debt must be written off in the 20X7 accounts.

(b) This is a non-adjusting event as the fire occurred after the statement of financial position date. The damage to the inventory occurred post year end so the year end position is not affected. This should be described in a note to the accounts.

Test your understanding 1

Ribblesdale prepares its accounts to a 30 September year end. Its accounts for the year ended 30 September 20X8 are approved on 12 January 20X9 and issued on 20 February 20X9.

Which of the following is an adjusting event after the reporting period?

A A flood destroys inventory which cost £1,700 on 3 December 20X8

B A credit customer with an outstanding balance at the year end was declared bankrupt on 20 January 20X9

C Inventory valued at a cost of £800 in the year end accounts was sold for £650 on 11 January 20X9

D An ordinary dividend of 4p per share was declared on 1 December 20X8

2 IAS 37 *Provisions, Contingent Liabilities and Contingent Assets*

2.1 Introduction

The objective of IAS 37 is to ensure that:

- provisions and contingencies are recognised and measured consistently
- sufficient information is disclosed to enable a user of the accounts to understand the nature, timing and amount of any provisions and contingencies included in the accounts.

Definition

Provision – liability of uncertain timing or amount.

Liability – present obligation of the entity arising from past events, the settlement of which is expected to result in an outflow from the entity of resources embodying economic benefits.

Obligating event – an event that creates a legal or constructive obligation that results in the entity having no realistic alternative to settling the obligation.

Constructive obligation – A constructive obligation arises from the entity's past actions, where there is a pattern of past practice that indicates that an entity will behave in a certain way, for example:

- A retail store that habitually refunds purchases for dissatisfied customers and could not change its policy without damaging its reputation.
- An entity that has caused environmental damage and is obliged to rectify this because of its published policies and previous actions, even though there may be no legal obligation for it to do so.

Contingent liability – a possible obligation from a past event whose existence will be confirmed only by the occurrence or non-occurrence of one or more uncertain future events not wholly within the control of the entity; or a present obligation that arises from past events that is not recognised because the outflow required to settle the obligation is not probable or the amount of the obligation cannot be measured with sufficient reliability.

Contingent asset – a possible asset that arises from past events and whose existence will be confirmed only by the occurrence or non-occurrence of one or more uncertain future events not wholly within the control.

2.2 Provisions versus other liabilities versus contingent liabilities

A provision is a liability of uncertain timing or amount. This means that a provision can only be recognised if it meets the definition and recognition criteria of a liability. These are as follows:

1 A present obligation must exist at the statement of financial position date as a result of a past transaction or event, and

2 It is probable that an outflow of economic resources will be required to settle the obligation, and

3 A reliable estimate can be made of the amount of the obligation.

Other liabilities such as trade payables, are liabilities to pay for goods that have been received and invoiced, therefore there is no uncertainty over their timing or amount. This makes them different.

Contingent liabilities are never recognised in the financial statements because their existence will be confirmed only by the occurrence or non-occurrence of one or more uncertain future events not wholly within the control of the entity.

2.3 Recognition

The amount recognised as a provision shall be the best estimate of the expenditure required to settle the present obligation at the statement of financial position date.

Where the time value of money is material, the amount of the provision shall be the present value of the expenditures expected to be required to settle the obligation.

The provisions must be reviewed at each statement of financial position date and adjusted to reflect the current best estimate. If it is no longer probable an outflow of resources will be required to settle the obligation then the provision shall be reversed.

The provision must only be used for expenditures for which the provision was originally recognised.

- Contingent assets are never recognised.
- Contingent liabilities are never recognised.

2.4 Future operating losses

No provision can be made for future operating losses as they arise on a day-by-day basis and are therefore regarded as avoidable. There is no obligation to incur such losses and a provision cannot be recognised for such losses.

For example, if a company is in the process of closing down a loss-making activity over a three month time period, by closing it down immediately, rather than over the next three months, operating losses will be avoided.

2.5 Disclosure of contingent liabilities and contingent assets

The accounts should give the following disclosures for each material class of contingent liability and asset that are not recognised in the statement of financial position, unless the possibility of transfer of economic benefits is remote:

- The nature of the contingency
- The uncertainties expected to affect the ultimate outcome
- An estimate of the potential financial effect.

Test your understanding 2

Hill plc

The year end of Hill plc is 31 March 20X0. Hill plc is a very diverse group. One of its consistent features is that it has a reputation as an ethical organisation. Much is made of the company's policies with regard to recycling, controls over emission of noxious substances and making use of renewable resources.

Many of its goods in its beauty and cosmetic range (Sophie Beauty Products) use ingredients that are sourced overseas and the company publishes full details of its environmental policies as part of its annual report.

You are the chief accountant of the group and your assistant has prepared draft accounts for the year ended 31 March 20X0. Your assistant, however, is uncertain as to the application of IAS 37 *Provisions, Contingent Liabilities and Contingent Assets* to the two material items described below and has requested your advice.

Required:

(a) Explain the circumstances under which a provision should be recognised in the financial statements according to IAS 37.

(b) Explain how the following issues should be treated in the consolidated financial statements for the year ended 31 March 20X0.

(i) During the year to 31 March 20X0, a customer started legal proceedings claiming one of the products from the 'Sophie Beauty' range had caused a skin complaint. The group's lawyers have advised that the chances of this action succeeding are remote.

(ii) The group has an overseas subsidiary 'Melinat' that is involved in mining certain minerals. These activities cause significant damage to the environment, including deforestation. The company expects to abandon the mine in eight years' time. The country where the subsidiary is based has no environmental legislation obligating companies to rectify environmental damage and it is unlikely that such legislation will be enacted within the next eight years. It has been estimated that the cost of putting right the site will be £10 million if the tree re-planting were successful at the first attempt, but it will probably be necessary to have a further attempt costing an additional £5 million.

Test your understanding 3

1 A receivable goes into liquidation on 12 January 20X8, owing £300,000 to the company on its statement of financial position date of 31 December 20X7. Is this an adjusting or a non-adjusting event?

2 A company issues new shares soon after its statement of financial position date. Is this an adjusting or a non-adjusting event?

3 Should contingent assets be shown on the statement of financial position?

Test your understanding 4

Caroline Ltd has a year end of 30 September 20X9. The accounts are anticipated to be approved in a couple of months' time.

How would the following events be accounted for in the Financial Statements?

(Assume all amounts are material to the organisation.)

(i) On 2 October 20X9 a fire completely destroyed the entire inventory in one of its warehouses. The total cost of the inventory was £10 million. The company unfortunately did not update its insurance cover for fire and consequential damages.

The directors still believe that Caroline Ltd is a going concern.

(ii) On 20 October 20X9 the directors proposed a dividend amounting to £120,000.

Test your understanding 5

John Ltd is currently being sued by an ex-employee for £45,000. The company's solicitors have stated that the claim may possibly succeed. The company's solicitor's fees will amount to £3,000. This fee will have to be paid whether the ex-employee's claim is successful or not.

What should be the treatment of the above in the John Ltd's financial statements?

A Provide a liability for £48,000 comprising the £45,000 claim by the ex-employee and the solicitor's fees

B Provide for £45,000

C Disclose a total of £48,000 comprising the £45,000 claim by the ex-employee and the solicitor's fees

D Provide a liability for £3,000 for the solicitor's fees and disclose £45,000 for the claim by the ex-employee

3 Summary

You need to be able to recognise both adjusting and non-adjusting events. You should also ensure that you understand what is meant by a provision and when provisions should be shown as a liability in the statement of financial position. You should be able to distinguish a provision from a contingent liability and understand the different treatment of contingent liabilities and contingent assets. The key in deciding whether a provision should be recognised is to ask whether:

1. A present **obligation** must exist at the statement of financial position date as a result of a past transaction or event, and
2. It is **probable** that an outflow of economic resources will be required to settle the obligation, and
3. A **reliable estimate** can be made of the amount of the obligation.

If these factors can be satisfied then a provision should be made in the financial statements otherwise it is a contingent liability which should just be disclosed.

Test your understanding answers

Test your understanding 1

Answer is C

- A flood does not provide additional information to conditions existing at the year end and therefore is non adjusting.
- The credit customer's bankruptcy occurs after the accounts are approved.
- The declaration of an ordinary dividend is a non-adjusting event.

Test your understanding 2

Hill plc

(a) A provision should be recognised when, and only when:

1 A present **obligation** must exist at the statement of financial position date as a result of a past transaction or event, and

2 It is **probable** that an outflow of economic resources will be required to settle the obligation; and

3 A **reliable estimate** can be made of the amount of the obligation.

An obligation exists when the entity has no realistic alternative to making a transfer of economic benefits. This is the case only where the obligation can be enforced by law or in the case of constructive obligation (see below).

(b) (i) **Legal proceedings**

It is unlikely the group has a present obligation to compensate the customer and therefore no provision should be recognised.

There may be a contingent liability but as the possibility of a transfer of economic benefit is remote we can ignore this in the accounts.

(ii) **Environmental damage**

The company has no legal obligation to rectify this damage, but through its published policies it has created expectation on the part of those affected that it will take action to do so. There is therefore a constructive obligation to rectify the damage. It is probable that a transfer of economic benefits will take place and an estimate of the amount involved can be made.

A provision should be made of the best estimate of the cost involved, i.e. the full amount of £15 million should be provided for.

Test your understanding 3

1 Adjusting event.

2 Non-adjusting event.

3 No. Contingent assets should be disclosed in a note to the accounts.

Test your understanding 4

(i) **Outline answer**

- The fire took place after the year end therefore it is an event after the reporting period.
- According to IAS 10 this is an example of a non-adjusting event because it does not provide evidence about the valuation of inventory at the end of the reporting period (30 September 20X9).
- The loss of £10 million is material so, per IAS 10, it should be disclosed in the notes to the financial statements.

(ii) **Outline answer**

- The dividend is proposed after the year end therefore it should be treated as a non-adjusting event.
- This should be disclosed in the notes to the financial statements.

Test your understanding 5

Answer D

The company's solicitor's fees amounting to £3,000 is to be provided for in full.

The claim by the ex-employee of £45,000 may possibly succeed therefore it should be disclosed.

Revenue

11

Introduction

In this chapter we will consider IFRS 15 *Revenue from Contracts with Customers*.

ASSESSMENT CRITERIA

Examine the effect of international accounting standards on the preparation of financial statements (2.1)

CONTENTS

1 IFRS 15 *Revenue from Contracts with Customers*

1.1 Scope and definitions

IFRS 15 looks at how and when revenue will be recognised. The standard provides a single, principles-based model to be applied to all contracts with customers.

Definitions

Revenue	**'income arising in the course of an entity's ordinary activities.'**
Customer	**'a party that has contracted with an entity to obtain goods or services that are an output of the entity's ordinary activities in exchange for consideration.'**
Income	**'increases in economic benefits during the accounting period in the form of inflows or enhancements of assets or decreases of liabilities that result in an increase in equity, other than those relating to contributions from equity participants.'**

[IFRS 15: Appendix A]

1.2 5-step approach

An entity recognises revenue by applying the following five steps (COPAR!):

1 Identify the **c**ontract

2 Identify the separate performance **o**bligations within a contract

3 Determine the transaction **p**rice

4 **A**llocate the transaction price to the performance obligations in the contract

5 **R**ecognise revenue when (or as) a performance obligation is satisfied

The five steps will now be considered in more detail.

Step 1: Identify the contract

A contract can be agreed in writing, orally, or through other customary business practices.

IFRS 15 says that an entity can only account for revenue from a contract if it meets the following criteria:

(a) **'the contract has been approved by the parties to the contract**

(b) **each party's rights in relation to the goods or services to be transferred can be identified**

(c) **the payment terms for the goods or services to be transferred can be identified**

(d) **the contract has commercial substance; and**

(e) **it is probable that the consideration to which the entity is entitled to in exchange for the goods or services will be collected.'** [IFRS 15: 9].

Step 2: Identify the separate performance obligations

Performance obligations are promises to transfer distinct goods or services to a customer.

Some contracts contain more than one performance obligation. For example:

- An entity may enter into a contract with a customer to sell a car, which includes one year's free servicing and maintenance
- An entity might enter into a contract with a customer to provide 5 lectures, as well as to provide a textbook on the first day of the course.

The distinct performance obligations within a contract must be identified.

Step 3: Determine the transaction price

The **transaction price** is the consideration that the selling entity will be entitled to once it has fulfilled the performance obligations in the contract.

Amounts collected on behalf of third parties (such as sales tax) are excluded.

A contract may include an element of variable consideration, for example a discount or a performance bonus. IFRS 15 says that if a contract includes variable consideration then the entity must estimate the amount it expects to receive, but only include such value within the transaction price if the likelihood of payment is highly probable.

Example

Heart enters into a contract with a customer on 1 January 20X1 to sell products for £50 per unit. The terms of the contract state that the price is retrospectively reduced to £40 per unit if the customer buys more than 2,000 units in a calendar year.

By the reporting date of 31 March 20X1, the customer has purchased 300 units. Based on extensive experience, Heart estimates that the customer's purchases will not exceed 2,000 units within the calendar year.

How much revenue should Heart recognise from the contract in the year ended 31 March 20X1?

Solution

The consideration in the contract is variable because Heart might receive £40 or £50 per unit. Heart will recognise revenue at £50 per unit because it is highly probable that this is the amount that will be received.

The revenue to be recognised from the contract in the year ended 31 March 20X1 is £15,000 (£50 × 300 units).

Step 4: Allocate the transaction price

The total transaction price should be allocated to each performance obligation in proportion to stand-alone selling prices.

The best evidence of a stand-alone selling price is the observable price of a good or service when the entity sells that good or service separately in similar circumstances and to similar customers.

In relation to a bundled sale, any discount should generally be allocated across each component in the transaction.

If a stand-alone selling price is not directly observable, then the entity **estimates** the stand-alone selling price.

Test your understanding 1

Tance sells a machine and one year's free technical support for £100,000. It usually sells the machine for £95,000 but does not sell technical support for this machine as a stand-alone product. Other support services offered by Tance attract a mark-up of 50%. It is expected that the technical support will cost Tance £20,000.

How much of the transaction price should be allocated to the machine and to the technical support?

Step 5: Recognise revenue when or as a performance obligation is satisfied

Revenue is recognised '**when (or as) the entity satisfies a performance obligation by transferring a promised good or service to a customer**' (IFRS 15: 31).

For each performance obligation identified, an entity must determine whether it satisfies the performance obligation over time, or satisfies the performance obligation at a point in time.

IFRS 15 states that an entity only satisfies a performance obligation over time if **one** of the following criteria is met:

(a) the customer simultaneously receives and consumes the benefits from the entity's performance

(b) the entity is creating or enhancing an asset controlled by the customer

(c) the entity cannot use the asset 'for an alternative use' and the entity can demand payment for its performance to date.

If a performance obligation is satisfied over time, then revenue is recognised based on the progress towards completion.

If an entity does not satisfy its performance obligation over time, it satisfies it at a point in time. Revenue will be recognised when control is passed at a certain point in time. An entity controls an asset if it can direct its use and obtain its remaining benefits.

Some indicators that control has passed to the customer include:

(a) the customer has physical possession of the asset

(b) the customer has the significant risks and rewards of ownership

(c) the customer has legal title

(d) the seller has a right to payment.

Test your understanding 2

On 1 January 20X1, Evans enters into a contract with a customer to provide monthly payroll services. Evans charges £120,000 per year.

What is the accounting treatment of the above in the financial statements of Evans for the year ended 30 June 20X1?

Test your understanding 3

Glover sells residential properties in the ordinary course of business. Glover purchased a luxury apartment block many years ago for £1.2 million. On 31 December 20X1 it sold the block to a customer for £2 million and transferred legal title. Glover has retained an option to repurchase the building for £3 million in 3 years' time.

Should Glover recognise revenue from the above transaction in the year ended 31 December 20X1?

The following example applies the five-step model:

Example

On 1 October 20X2, Welland receives an order from a customer for a computer as well as 12 months of technical support. Welland delivers the computer (and transfers its legal title) to the customer on the same day.

The customer paid £550 upfront. The computer sells for £390 and the technical support sells for £160.

Welland's accounting year-end is 31 December.

This is how the five steps would be applied to this example:

Step 1 – Identify the contract

There is an agreement between Welland and its customer for the provision of goods and services.

Step 2 – Identify the separate performance obligations

There are two performance obligations (promises) within the contract:

1 The supply of a computer

2 The supply of technical support

Step 3 – Determine the transaction price

The total transaction price is £550.

Step 4 – Allocate the transaction price to the performance obligations in the contract

Based on standalone sales prices, £390 should be allocated to the sale of the computer and £160 should be allocated to the technical support.

Step 5 – Recognise revenue when (or as) a performance obligation is satisfied

Control over the computer has been passed to the customer so the full revenue of £390 should be recognised on 1 October 20X2.

The technical support is provided over time, so revenue from this should be recognised over time. In the year ended 31 December 20X2, revenue of £40 (3/12 × £160) should be recognised from the provision of technical support.

Test your understanding 4

Place the following steps for recognising revenue in the correct order in accordance with IFRS 15.

Step	Correct order
Identify the separate performance obligations within a contract	
Identify the contract	
Determine the transaction price	
Recognise revenue when (or as) a performance obligation is satisfied	
Allocate the transaction price to the performance obligations in the contract	

Test your understanding 5

Cameron sells computers, and also offers installation and technical support services. The individual selling prices of each product are shown below:

Computer hardware	£700
Installation	£60
One year technical support service	£110

Company X bought a computer on 1 June 20X2, and was charged a reduced price of £810, including installation and one year's technical support. Cameron only offers discounts when customers purchase a package of products together.

According to IFRS 15, how much should Cameron record in revenue for the year ended 31 December 20X2? Workings should be rounded to the nearest £.

2 Summary

IFRS 15 looks at how and when revenue is recognised. The standard provides a principles-based model to be applied to all contracts with customers. An entity recognises revenue by applying the following five steps:

1 Identify the contract

2 Identify the separate performance obligations within a contract

3 Determine the transaction price

4 Allocate the transaction price to the performance obligations in the contract

5 Recognise revenue when or as a performance obligation is satisfied.

When applying step five of the model, a performance obligation can be satisfied either; at a point in time or over time.

Test your understanding answers

Test your understanding 1

The selling price of the machine is £95,000.

There is no stand-alone selling price for the technical support. Therefore, the stand-alone selling price needs to be estimated. An approach for doing this is the expected costs plus a mark-up approach. Based on this, the selling price of the service could be estimated as £30,000 (£20,000 × 150%).

The total standalone selling prices of the machine and support are £125,000 (£95,000 + £30,000). However, total consideration receivable is only £100,000. This means that the customer is receiving a discount for purchasing a bundle of goods and services of £25,000.

The transaction price allocated to the machine is £76,000 (£95,000 × £100,000/£125,000).

The transaction price allocated to the technical support is £24,000 (£30,000 × £100,000/£125,000).

The revenue will be recognised when (or as) the performance obligations are satisfied.

Test your understanding 2

The payroll services are a single performance obligation.

This performance obligation is satisfied over time because the customer simultaneously receives and consumes the benefits of the payroll processing. This is evidenced by the fact that the payroll services would not need to be re-performed if the customer changed its payroll service provider.

Evans must therefore recognise revenue from the service over time.

In the year ended 30 June 20X1, they would recognise revenue of £60,000 (6/12 × £120,000).

Test your understanding 3

If revenue is recognised at a point in time, the entity must determine the point in time at which the customer obtains control over the promised asset. Control refers to the ability to direct the use of the asset and to obtain substantially all of the remaining benefits.

Due to the repurchase agreement, the customer has not obtained substantially all of the remaining benefits of the asset. Control of the asset has not passed to the customer and so revenue should not be recognised.

In substance this is a financing arrangement because the repurchase amount exceeds the original selling price. A loan liability for £2 million should be recognised.

Test your understanding 4

Place the following steps for recognising revenue in the correct order in accordance with IFRS 15.

Correct order
Identify the contract
Identify the separate performance obligations within a contract
Determine the transaction price
Allocate the transaction price to the performance obligations in the contract
Recognise revenue when (or as) a performance obligation is satisfied

Test your understanding 5

The discount should be allocated to each part of the bundled sale. Applying the discount across each part gives revenue as follows:

Computer hardware	£652	(£700 × £810/£870)
Installation	£56	(£60 × £810/£870)
Service	£102	(£110 × £810/£870)

The revenue in relation to the computer hardware and installation should be recognised on 1 June 20X2 because control has been passed to the customer. The performance obligation to provide the support service is satisfied over time. As 7 months of the service has been performed (from 1 June to 31 December 20X2), then £60 should be recognised (£102 × 7/12). This gives a total revenue for the year of 652 + 56 + 60 = **£768**.

Company finance

12

Introduction

This chapter provides additional detail with regards to share issues, debt and different types of reserves.

ASSESSMENT CRITERIA

Explain the regulatory framework that underpins financial reporting (1.1)

Examine the effect of international accounting standards on the preparation of financial statements (2.1)

CONTENTS

1 Share capital

1.1 Introduction

The way in which the assets of a company (non-current assets, inventories, receivables and cash) are financed will vary from one company to another. Part of the finance may be provided by the owners or proprietors of the company (referred to as shareholders), while part may be provided by outsiders including suppliers, banks and other lenders of funds. Companies will also normally be partly financed by their own accumulated profits known as retained earnings.

1.2 The nature and purpose of share capital and reserves

Definition

Share capital represents the capital invested in the company by its shareholders by the purchase of shares.

Definition

Reserves represent the balance of net assets belonging to the shareholders. These may include part of past issues of share capital (known as share premium), retained trading profits and revaluation gains on the revaluation of non-current assets.

The total of share capital and reserves represents the book value of the net assets of the company.

1.3 Distinction between nominal value and market value of share capital

Definition

The nominal value of a share is its face value e.g. £1 ordinary shares or 50p ordinary share.

Each share has a stated nominal (or par) value. This has little practical significance except as a base line price below which further shares may not generally be issued. The nominal value is also used as a means of calculating dividends to shareholders.

Definition

The market value of a share is the price at which that share could be bought or sold.

The market value of a share is not fixed at any particular date. The market value is related to the market value of the business of the company. For example, if a business is worth £100,000 and there are 1,000 £1 shares in issue in the company, the market value of each share is £100 whereas the nominal value is £1.

If the company is listed on a stock exchange then a price will be quoted for the shares based upon recent transactions between purchasers and sellers of shares.

This is also referred to as the market value of a share, but this may not be the same value that would apply if the entire business was sold and thus all the shares were sold as one transaction.

1.4 Why companies are concerned with the value of their shares

Companies are concerned with the value the stock market places on the shares for two main reasons:

(a) Shareholders will look at a steadily rising price of the shares as evidence of sound management of the company by the directors. It would indicate additional profits being made every year.

(b) If the company wishes to raise further finance through the issue of shares, the current market price will be used as a basis for issuing more shares.

The higher the price, the fewer shares will need to be issued and the less dilution there will be of the existing shareholders' effective interest in the company.

It is important to appreciate that the market value of a share quoted on the stock exchange has no direct relationship to the nominal value.

1.5 Share capital

The share capital of a company may be divided into various classes. The company's internal regulations (the articles of association) define the respective rights attached to the various shares e.g. as regards dividend entitlement or voting at company meetings. The various classes of share capital are dealt with below. In practice it is usually only larger companies which have different classes of share capital.

1.6 Ordinary shares

Definition

Ordinary shares are the normal shares issued by a company. The normal rights of ordinary shareholders are to vote at company meetings and to receive dividends from profits.

Ordinary shares are often referred to as equity shares. A special class of ordinary share is the redeemable ordinary share where the terms of issue specify that it is repayable by the company.

There are various accounting terms to describe share capital: authorised, issued, called up and paid up.

(a) When a company is first established it must prepare a Memorandum of Association which will state the maximum amount of shares which the company is allowed to issue to its shareholders. This is the **authorised share capital** of the company.

(b) There is nothing to compel the company to issue to shareholders all of the shares which it is authorised to issue. The number of shares actually issued is known as the **issued share capital**.

(c) Once the company has asked its shareholders to pay for the shares it has issued to them, the shares are said to be **called up**.

(d) Once those shareholders have paid the company for the shares. The shares are said to be **paid up**.

1.7 Share premium account

Each share in the UK has a nominal value, e.g. a company might have in issue 1,000 £1 shares. The share premium is the amount for which a share is issued over and above its nominal value. Thus if a share has a nominal value of £1 and it is issued for £1.50, 50p will be the share premium.

The amounts of share premium received by a company must be credited to a share premium account on the statement of financial position.

Example

Enterprise Limited makes an issue of 10,000 £1 ordinary shares for £1.60 each. What are the accounting entries?

Solution

Debit	Cash account £16,000 (10,000 × £1.60)
Credit	Share capital account £10,000 (10,000 × £1)
Credit	Share premium account £6,000 (10,000 × £0.60)

The share capital account is only ever credited with the nominal value of the shares issued. Any excess over this nominal value must be credited to the share premium account.

Test your understanding 1

What are the accounting entries for an issue of 1,000 ordinary £1 shares for £3 each?

Dr

Cr

Cr

1.8 Preference shares

Definition

Preference shares are shares carrying a fixed rate of dividend, the holders of which have a prior claim to any company profits available for distribution.

The rights and advantages of the shares will be specified in the articles of association.

1.9 Ordinary and preference shares compared

Aspect	Ordinary shares	Preference shares
Voting power	Carry a vote	Do not carry a vote
Distribution of profits (dividends)	A dividend which may vary from one year to the next after the preference shareholders have received their dividend.	A fixed dividend (fixed percentage of nominal value) in priority to ordinary dividend.
Liquidation of the company	Entitled to surplus assets on liquidation after liabilities and preference shares have been repaid.	Priority of repayment over ordinary shares but not usually entitled to surplus assets on liquidation.

1.10 Rights issues

A rights issue is the offer of new shares to existing shareholders, usually in proportion to their existing shareholding at a price (the offer price is normally below market value). A rights issue is the cheapest way for a company to raise finance through the issuing of further shares.

A rights issue is accounted for in the same way as a normal share issue and therefore has exactly the same impact on the statement of financial position as an issue at full price.

1.11 Bonus issues

A bonus issue is the issue of new shares to existing shareholders, usually in proportion to their existing shareholding. No consideration is exchanged for the share issue. Issued share capital is divided into a larger number of shares, thus making the market value of each one less, and so more marketable.

As no cash is received from a bonus issue, the issue must be funded from reserves. Any reserve can be used (other than the share capital account), but it is usual that retained earnings or the share premium account would be used in your assessment.

Accounting for a bonus issue:

Dr Share premium/retained earnings (Nominal value per share)

Cr Share capital (Nominal value per share)

Test your understanding 2

BLC Co is a limited liability company with 200,000 ordinary £1 shares in issue. At 1 April 20X8 the balance on the share premium account is £75,000. The following transactions occur in the year ended 31 March 20X9:

30 April There is a fully taken-up 2 for 5 rights issue. The issue price is £1.80.

11 Dec There is a 1 for 10 bonus issue made using the share premium account.

Required:

(a) What accounting entries are required in the year ended 31 March 20X9?

(b) What are the balances on the share capital and share premium accounts of BLC Co at 31 March 20X9?

1.12 Debentures or loan stock

A debenture is a written acknowledgement of a loan to a company, given under the company's seal, which carries a fixed rate of interest.

A debenture may relate to a loan from one person. Debenture stock, on the other hand, rather like shares, may be held by a large number of individuals. The conditions and regulations are set out in a debenture trust deed.

Debentures are not part of a company's share capital – they are third party liabilities. Debenture interest is therefore a charge against profit and must be paid whether or not the company makes a profit.

Debentures are shown as liabilities in the statement of financial position, just like any other loan.

1.13 Gearing and risk

Companies with borrowings (such as long-term loans or debentures) or preference shares in their capital structure are said to have 'gearing'. This means that they have raised loans (i.e. borrowed money or raised capital from preference shares) and thereby taken on a degree of financial risk.

The risk comes from the fact that even if the company's financial performance deteriorated badly, the company would still have to pay the annual interest charge and the preference dividend each year.

There is less risk associated with ordinary share capital, since there are no penalties directly associated with not paying an ordinary dividend in one year.

Gearing is looked at in more detail in the next chapter covering the interpretation of financial statements.

2 Types of reserve

2.1 Introduction

Having looked at share capital we will now consider the different types of reserves a company might have.

2.2 Reserves

The non-current assets and current assets are shown on the top half of a statement of financial position; the non-current liabilities, current liabilities and equity and reserves are shown on the bottom half.

Equity and reserves comprise of:

- Share capital
- Retained earnings
- Capital reserves.

2.3 Retained earnings

These comprise the cumulative total of the company's retained profits.

In respect of each accounting period the profit attributable to equity holders will be added to retained earnings.

When a dividend is paid to the equity holders, this is deducted from retained earnings.

2.4 Capital reserves

The balance on capital reserves cannot legally be paid to the equity holders as a dividend. Common capital reserves include:

(a) the share premium account

(b) the revaluation reserve.

3 Finance costs and dividends

3.1 Finance costs

If a company has debentures in issue then the company usually must pay interest to the debenture holder. Effectively the company is paying interest on the money it has borrowed. Usually the rate is fixed when the debenture is purchased e.g. 10% debentures. This means the company must pay 10% of the issued debentures as interest.

The accounting entries are as follows:

Dr Interest charges (finance costs)

Cr Trade and other payables (current liabilities)

When the interest is paid

Dr Trade and other payables

Cr Cash

3.2 Dividends

When a sole trader withdraws money from their business for personal use it is referred to as drawings and accounted for as follows:

Debit	Drawings account
Credit	Cash

However for a company, where there may be many hundreds of shareholders, it would be far from practical for each one of them to have a drawings account. A system of dividend payments is therefore used. The actual amount of dividend to be paid by a company will be determined by many factors, the main one being the need to retain sufficient profits to provide for the future working capital and fixed assets requirements of the company.

3.3 Interim dividend

Some companies pay an amount on account of the total dividend before the end of the year. This is known as an interim dividend. The bookkeeping entry is as follows:

Debit	Retained earnings
Credit	Cash

3.4 Final dividend

It will only be at the end of the year, when the company's results for the whole accounting period are known, that the directors can declare ('propose') a final dividend. The dividend is usually declared after the year end and therefore is not a liability at the statement of financial position date and so cannot be accounted for until the next period. Any dividends that are proposed but not approved by the year end are disclosed in the financial statements.

Example

A Ltd pays an interim dividend of £50,000 and proposes to pay a final dividend of £75,000.

Profit for the year before any entries for the dividends was £300,000.

Retained earnings at the start of the accounting period were £500,000.

Calculate retained earnings at the end of the accounting period.

Solution:

	Retained earnings
B/f	500,000
Profit for period	300,000
Dividend paid	(50,000)
C/f	750,000

The financial statements would disclose the fact that a final dividend of £75,000 has been proposed.

4 Summary

You need to understand how to calculate finance costs, debenture interest and dividends in order to make adjustments to company account questions.

You need to have a basic understanding of shares and debentures.

Test your understanding answers

Test your understanding 1

Debit	Cash	£3,000
Credit	Share capital	£1,000
Credit	Share premium	£2,000

The share capital account is only ever credited with the nominal value of the shares issued. Any excess over this nominal value must be credited to the share premium account.

Test your understanding 2

(a) **Rights issue:**

Debit	Cash	£144,000	(80,000 × £1.80)
Credit	Share capital	£80,000	(80,000 × £1)
Credit	Share premium	£64,000	(80,000 × £0.80)

Bonus issue:

Debit	Share premium	£28,000	(1/10 × 280,000) × £1
Credit	Share capital	£28,000	(1/10 × 280,000) × £1

(b) Share capital account: £308,000 (£200,000 + £80,000 + £28,000)

Share premium account: £111,000 (£75,000 + £64,000 – £28,000)

Interpretation of financial statements

13

Introduction

Every exam will include tasks which ask you to apply ratio analysis to company financial statements and to analyse and interpret the results.

ASSESSMENT CRITERIA

Calculate ratios with regard to profitability, liquidity, efficient use of resources and financial position (5.1)

Appraise the relationship between elements of the financial statements with regard to profitability, liquidity, efficient use of resources and financial position, by means of ratio analysis (5.2)

Effectively present an analysis with recommendations (5.3)

CONTENTS

1 Profitability ratios

1.1 Introduction

Ratios calculated from financial statements help to interpret the information they present. Various users may use these ratios to analyse financial statements.

We can break down the ratios into categories to make our discussion more structured. To begin with we look at ratios relating to profitability.

1.2 Return on capital employed (ROCE)

Return on capital employed is frequently regarded as the best measure of profitability, indicating how successful a business is in utilising the funding it has received.

$$\text{Return on capital employed} = \frac{\text{Profit from operations}}{\text{Capital employed}} \times 100$$

Capital employed = working capital + non-current assets

Working capital = current assets – current liabilities

A low return on capital employed is caused by either a low profit margin or a low asset turnover or both.

1.3 Return on shareholders' funds

$$\text{Return on shareholders' funds} = \frac{\text{Profit after tax}}{\text{Total equity}} \times 100\%$$

This looks at the return earned for ordinary shareholders. We use the profit after preference dividends and interest (i.e. the amounts that have to be paid before ordinary shareholders can be rewarded).

1.4 Gross profit percentage

$$\text{Gross profit percentage} = \frac{\text{Gross profit}}{\text{Revenue}} \times 100\%$$

The gross profit percentage focuses on the trading account. A low margin could indicate selling prices are too low or cost of sales is too high.

1.5 Expense/revenue percentage

$$\text{Expense/revenue percentage} = \frac{\text{Specified expense}}{\text{Revenue}} \times 100$$

The expenses/revenue percentage focuses on individual expenses in relation to revenue.

1.6 Operating profit percentage

$$\text{Operating profit percentage} = \frac{\text{Profit from operations}}{\text{Revenue}} \times 100$$

A low margin indicates low selling prices or high costs or both. Comparative analysis will reveal the level of prices and costs in relation to competitors.

2 Liquidity ratios

2.1 Current ratio

This is a common method of analysing working capital (net current assets) and is generally accepted as a good measure of short-term solvency. It indicates the extent to which the claims of short-term payables are covered by assets that are expected to be converted to cash in a period roughly corresponding to the maturity of the claims.

$$\text{Current ratio} = \frac{\text{Current assets}}{\text{Current liabilities}}$$

The current ratio should ideally fall between 1:1 and 2:1.

2.2 Acid test ratio (quick ratio)

This is calculated in the same way as the current ratio except that inventories are excluded from current assets.

$$\text{Acid test ratio} = \frac{\text{Current assets} - \text{Inventories}}{\text{Current liabilities}}$$

This ratio is a much better test of the immediate solvency of a business because of the length of time necessary to convert inventories into cash (via revenue and receivables).

Contrary to what might be expected, this ratio may fall in a time of prosperity since increased activity may lead to larger inventories but less cash; conversely, when trade slows down inventories may be disposed of without renewal and the ratio will rise.

Although increased liquid resources more usually indicate favourable trading, it could be that funds are not being used to their best advantage (e.g. large cash balance).

3 Use of resources

3.1 Inventory turnover

This ratio indicates whether inventory levels are justified in relation to cost of sales. The higher the ratio, the healthier the cash flow position, but with the qualification that the profit margin must also be acceptable.

$$\text{Inventory turnover} = \frac{\text{Cost of sales}}{\text{Inventories}}$$

It is usual to calculate this ratio using the closing inventories. A limitation on this ratio is that in a seasonal business inventories may fluctuate considerably during the year. The level of inventory turnover will vary between businesses. A retailer will have a fairly fast inventory turnover as goods are bought and sold fairly quickly. A manufacturing company will have a much slower inventory turnover as inventory is held in the business much longer as it goes through the production process.

3.2 Inventory holding period in days

Inventory turnover can also be calculated in terms of days. This is calculated as follows:

$$\text{Inventory turnover period} = \frac{\text{Inventories}}{\text{Cost of sales}} \times 365 \text{ days}$$

3.3 Trade receivables collection period

This is computed by dividing the trade receivables by the average daily sales to determine the number of days sales held in receivables. It is usually calculated as:

$$\text{Average collection period} = \frac{\text{Trade receivables}}{\text{Revenue}} \times 365 \text{ days}$$

A long average collection period probably indicates poor credit control, but it may be due to other factors such as overseas sales where the collection period will be much longer, or a deliberate decision to extend the credit period to attract new customers.

3.4 Trade payables payment period

This is computed by dividing the trade payables by the average daily purchases to determine the number of days purchases held in payables.

$$\text{Average payment period} = \frac{\text{Trade payable}}{\text{Cost of sales}} \times 365 \text{ days}$$

If only cost of sales rather than purchases is available in the information given this can be used as an approximation to purchases. If the payables period is very low, then the business might not be making the best use of its cash by paying suppliers early. If the period is very long then this is a free source of credit but the business must be careful not to harm relations with suppliers.

3.5 Working capital cycle

Inventory days + Receivable days – Payable days

This is the length of time between paying out cash for inventory and receiving the cash for goods or services supplied.

3.6 Asset turnover

$$\text{Asset turnover (non-current assets)} = \frac{\text{Revenue}}{\text{Non-current assets}}$$

OR

$$\text{Asset turnover (net assets)} = \frac{\text{Revenue}}{\text{Total assets} - \text{Current liabilities}}$$

This is a measure of how fully a company is utilising its assets.

A low turnover shows that a company is not generating a sufficient volume of business for the size of the asset base. This may be remedied by increasing sales or by disposing of some of the assets or both.

4 Financial position

4.1 Gearing

Gearing measures the extent to which a business is dependent on non-equity funds, as opposed to equity funding. A high gearing ratio means that the business has a high proportion of borrowed funds in its total capital.

Gearing gives an indication of long-term liquidity and the financial risk inherent within the business. Highly geared companies have to meet large interest commitments before paying dividends and may have problems raising further finance if expansion is necessary.

$$\text{Gearing} = \frac{\text{Non-current liabilities}}{\text{Total equity} + \text{Non-current liabilities}} \times 100$$

4.2 Interest cover

$$\text{Interest cover} = \frac{\text{Profit from operations}}{\text{Finance costs}}$$

Interest on debt has to be paid before shareholders can receive dividends. Therefore a good measure of risk is to compare available profit with the amount of interest to be paid.

Example

Fieldsomer Ltd

Data

Maurice Sun plans to invest in Fieldsomer Ltd.

This is a chain of shops. He is to meet his consultants to discuss the profitability of the company.

To prepare for the meeting he has asked you to comment on the change in profitability and the return on capital of the company.

He also has some questions about the company's statement of financial position.

He has given you Fieldsomer's statement of profit or loss and the summarised statement of financial position for the past two years prepared for internal purposes. These are set out below.

Fieldsomer Ltd
Summary statement of profit or loss for the year ended 31 March

	20X4	**20X3**
	£000	£000
Revenue	8,420	7,595
Cost of sales	(3,536)	(3,418)
Gross profit	4,884	4,177
Distribution costs	(1,471)	(1,016)
Administrative expenses	(1,224)	(731)
Profit from operations	2,189	2,430
Finance costs	(400)	(480)
Profit before tax	1,789	1,950
Tax	(465)	(569)
Profit for the period	1,324	1,381

Fieldsomer Ltd

Summary statement of financial position as at 31 March

	20X4	20X3
	£000	£000
ASSETS		
Non-current assets		
Property, plant and equipment	15,132	13,880
Current assets	4,624	3,912
Total assets	**19,756**	**17,792**
EQUITY AND LIABILITIES		
Equity		
Ordinary shares of £1 each	6,000	5,000
Share premium	2,000	1,000
Retained earnings	4,541	3,937
Total equity	12,541	9,937
Non-current liabilities		
Long term loan	5,000	6,000
Current liabilities	2,215	1,855
Total liabilities	7,215	7,855
Total equity and liabilities	**19,756**	**17,792**

Prepare a report for Maurice Sun that includes:

(a) a calculation of the following ratios of Fieldsomer Ltd for each of the two years:

(i) return on capital employed

(ii) operating profit percentage

(iii) gross profit percentage

(iv) asset turnover (based on net assets).

(b) an explanation of the meaning of each ratio and a comment on the performance of Fieldsomer Ltd as shown by each of the ratios.

(c) a conclusion on how the overall performance has changed over the two years.

Solution

REPORT

To: Maurice Sun **Subject:** Interpretation of financial statements

From: A Student **Date:** June 20X4

This report has been prepared to assist in the interpretation of the financial statements of Fieldsomer Ltd. It considers the profitability and return on capital of the business over 20X3 and 20X4.

(a) Calculation of the ratios

	20X4	**20X3**
Return on capital employed	$\frac{2,189}{17,541} \times 100 = 12.5\%$	$\frac{2,430}{15,937} \times 100 = 15.2\%$
Operating profit percentage	$\frac{2,189}{8,420} \times 100 = 26\%$	$\frac{2,430}{7,595} \times 100 = 32\%$
Gross profit percentage	$\frac{4,884}{8,420} \times 100 = 58\%$	$\frac{4,177}{7,595} \times 100 = 55\%$
Asset turnover	$\frac{8,420}{17,541} = 0.48$	$\frac{7,595}{15,937} = 0.48$

(b) Explanation and comment

Return on capital employed

- This ratio shows in percentage terms how much profit is being generated by the capital employed in the company.
- The company is showing a lower return on capital employed in 20X4 compared to 20X3 and hence is generating less profit per £ of capital employed in the business.

Operating profit percentage

- This ratio shows in percentage terms how much net profit is being generated from revenues.
- The ratio has decreased over the two years.
- This could be explained either by a decrease in the gross profit margin or by an increase in expenses, or both.
- In fact, the ratio of distribution costs and admin expenses as a percentage of revenue has increased from 23% in 20X3 to 32% in 20X4.

20X4:	20X3:
(1,471 + 1,224)/8,420 × 100	(1,016 + 731)/7,595 × 100
= 32%	= 23%

Gross profit percentage

- This ratio shows in percentage terms how much gross profit is being generated from the company's revenues and thus indicates the gross profit margin on sales.
- The ratio has improved over the two years with an increase in the percentage from 55% to 58%.
- The company is increasing its revenue without significantly cutting its margins.
- This may be due to increasing its sales price or reducing the cost of sales or both.

Asset turnover

- This ratio shows how efficient the company is in generating revenue from the available capital employed/net assets.
- The ratio has stayed the same between the two years and so a similar level of revenue has been generated from the available capital employed/net assets in 20X4 than in 20X3.
- The new investment that has been made in property, plant and equipment and current assets in 20X4 has generated a proportional increase in sales.

(c) Overall

The ratios show that the return on capital employed has deteriorated in 20X4 and that the company is thus generating less profit from the capital employed/net assets. Although there are increased margins there is less control over expenses and this has contributed to the deteriorating position. Control of expenses needs to be addressed by management. The efficiency in the use of assets has remained the same in 20X4 and the increased investment in assets that has taken place in 20X4 has yielded benefits in terms of increased sales.

Regards

AAT Student

5 General points about financial ratios

There are some more points on ratio analysis which should be particularly noted.

5.1 Caution in interpretation

Dogmatic conclusions should be avoided. For example, a reduction in the inventory holding period may be a good thing, but if it is likely to cause loss of customer goodwill or production dislocations due to inventory shortages, it may not be such an advantage. Ratios rarely answer questions but they can highlight areas where questions might usefully be asked.

5.2 Statement of financial position figures

Many of the ratios considered in this chapter involve the use of statement of financial position figures. These ratios should be interpreted with caution since the statement of financial position shows the position at a specific moment only and this may not be typical of the general position.

This point is particularly important where the ratio is derived from a statement of financial position figure in conjunction with a figure from the statement of profit or loss and other comprehensive income.

This is because the first figure relates to a moment in time whereas the second is a total for a period. A sensible way to try to avoid possible distortions here is to use the average figure for the statement of financial position figure. So, for example, the receivables collection period would relate credit sales to the average of the trade receivables figures at the beginning and at the end of the year.

However in many industries the existence of recurrent seasonal factors may mean that averaging beginning and end of year figures will not solve the problem.

It may be for example, that the date up to which a business draws up its final accounts has been selected because it is a time when inventory levels are always low, so that inventory is relatively easy to value.

In such cases, averaging the inventory figures for two consecutive year end dates would simply be averaging two figures which were totally untypical of inventory levels throughout the rest of the year. Averaging monthly figures would usually be the solution to this problem. However, outsiders would not typically have access to such information.

5.3 Other financial ratios

There are an almost infinite number of ratios which can be calculated from a set of final accounts. The ones shown above are those most commonly used in practice and include those which have been specifically identified by the FNST study guide. It should be noted, however, that there are many other ratios which could be useful in particular contexts.

5.4 Partial sightedness of ratios

It is usually unwise to limit analysis and interpretation only to information revealed by ratios. For example, revenue for a business could double from one year to the next.

This would be a dramatic and important development, yet none of the ratios whose use is advocated in most textbooks would reveal this, at least not directly.

However, this significant increase in turnover would be fairly obvious from even a superficial glance at the final accounts. There is the danger that excessive reliance on ratios in interpretation and analysis can lead to a 'blinkered' approach.

6 The working capital cycle

6.1 Introduction

The working capital cycle can be illustrated by the following set of activities which underpin the process of manufacture and trade:

- a company acquires inventories on credit
- inventories are held until sold (or used in production)
- the sale is usually made on credit
- trade payables need to be paid and cash needs to be collected from trade receivables
- more inventories are then acquired and the cycle starts again.

The working capital cycle

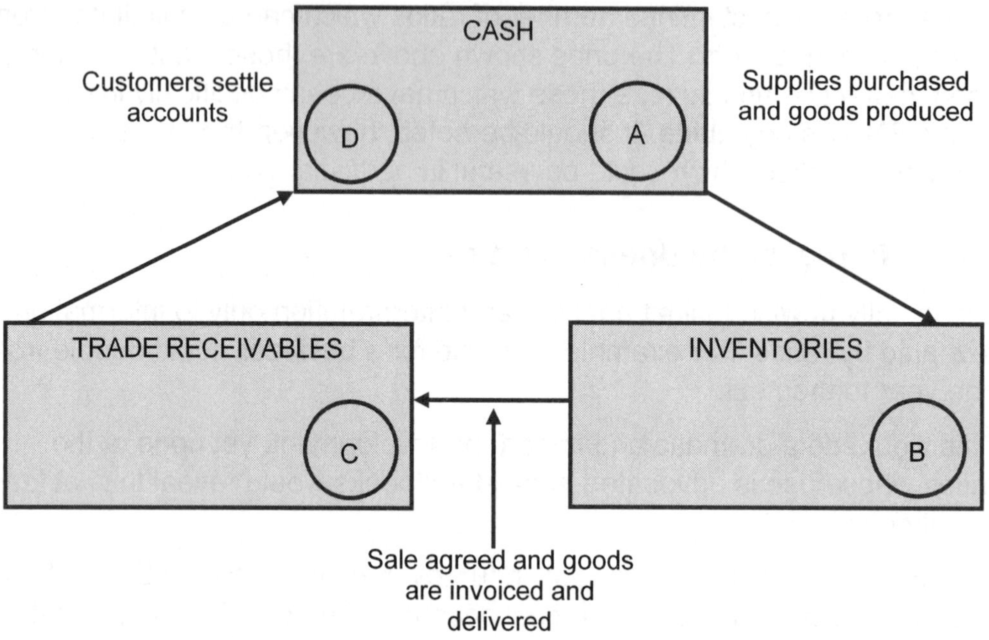

6.2 Effect on cash flows

All of these activities affect cash flows:

- acquisition of inventories on credit helps cash flow temporarily
- when trade payables are paid cash flows out
- while inventories are held, and until customers settle, cash is 'tied up', i.e. cash inflow is deferred
- when customers settle, cash flows in.

The longer the period over which cash is tied up, the greater is the exposure of the firm to exceptional demands for cash. In terms of cash management:

- a working cash balance must be retained at the bank to avoid the bank imposing bank interest and charges
- any surplus cash in excess of the working balance could be invested in higher interest earning accounts.

The longer the period of time that cash is tied up in working capital the more cost that is incurred by companies either directly, by virtue of bank interest, or indirectly, as a result of the inability to invest cash surpluses into higher interest yielding accounts.

6.3 Working capital management

The company must therefore ensure that inventory levels are watched very carefully and that trade receivables are collected on a timely basis whilst simultaneously monitoring the cash balance to ensure that sufficient funds are held for short-term requirements. Any genuinely surplus funds in excess of a working cash balance should be reinvested in higher interest accounts.

Test your understanding 1

Falcon Ltd

The draft accounts of Falcon Ltd for the years ended 30 June 20X8 and 30 June 20X7 are as follows.

Summary statement of financial position

	20X8		20X7	
	£	£	£	£
ASSETS				
Non-current assets				
Freehold premises at cost		125,000		75,000
Plant at cost		130,000		70,000
		255,000		145,000
Current assets				
Inventories		120,000		100,000
Trade receivables		80,000		60,000
		200,000		160,000
Total assets		455,000		305,000

EQUITY AND LIABILITIES		
Equity		
£1 ordinary shares	100,000	50,000
Retained earnings	135,000	120,000
Share premium account	90,000	35,000
Total equity	325,000	205,000
Non-current liabilities		
7% debentures	50,000	50,000
	50,000	50,000
Current liabilities		
Trade payables	45,000	30,000
Bank overdraft	15,000	5,000
Current taxation	20,000	15,000
	80,000	50,000
Total liabilities	130,000	100,000
Total equity and liabilities	455,000	305,000

Extracts from the statement of profit or loss

	20X8	**20X7**
	£	£
Revenue	525,000	425,000
Cost of sales	(446,500)	(364,000)
Gross profit	78,500	61,000
Administration expenses	(25,000)	(20,000)
Profit from operations	53,500	41,000
Finance costs	(3,500)	(3,500)
Profit before tax	50,000	37,500
Tax	(20,000)	(15,000)
Profit after tax	30,000	22,500
Note:		
Dividends paid (shown in SOCIE)	15,000	10,000

Required:

Calculate the following ratios:

- Return on capital employed
- Operating profit percentage
- Asset turnover (net assets)
- Inventory turnover
- Current ratio
- Acid test ratio
- Trade receivables collection period.

Comment upon on the relative performance of the company for the two years based on the ratios calculated and what this tells you about the company.

Test your understanding 2

1 What is the formula for return on capital employed?

2 What is the formula for return on shareholders' funds?

3 What is the difference between the current ratio and the acid test ratio?

4 What does interest cover measure?

Test your understanding 3

Fylingdales Quarries Ltd is a medium sized business which supplies a variety of products to the civil engineering sector of industry.

The following is an extract from its accounts for the year ended 31 December 20X1. The company contributes to an inter-firm comparison scheme through the Quarrying Trade Association and a summary of performance indicators are also shown below.

Statement of profit or loss	£m
Revenue	6.90
Cost of sales	(6.08)
Operating profit before tax	0.82
Taxation	(0.24)
Profit after tax	0.58
Statement of financial position	
Assets	£m
Property, plant and equipment	2.90
Current assets	
Inventories	0.60
Trade receivables	1.84
Bank	0.05
Total assets	5.39
Equity and liabilities	
Equity	3.49
Current liabilities	1.90
Total equity and liabilities	5.39

Note: The finished goods valuation included in inventories was £0.40m. Distribution and administration costs included in cost of sales were £0.88m.

Quarrying Trade Association performance indicators – year ended 31 December 20X1

Return on capital employed	25.60%
Asset turnover (net assets)	1.80
Net profit before tax to sales	14.22%
Current ratio	1.50 : 1
Liquidity ratio (acid test)	1.02 : 1
Receivables collection period	82 days
Cost of sales to finished goods	8.10
Operating costs % of sales	72.1%
Distribution and admin costs as % of sales	14.12%

NB: Operating costs are defined as cost of sales excluding distribution and administration costs.

Task

(a) Calculate for Fylingdales Quarries Ltd the ratios listed in the Trade Association data based on the accounts for the year ended 31 December 20X1.

(b) Compare the performance of Fylingdales Quarries with the performance for the sector as a whole based on the data from the Trade Association.

Test your understanding 4

Wodehouse

Your firm has been asked by Wodehouse plc, a company owning a chain of hardware shops, to carry out a preliminary investigation with a view to the possible acquisition of two smaller companies in the same trade, Pelham Ltd and Grenville Ltd.

You are not yet able to visit either of the companies' premises, but have obtained copies of their latest accounts, both for the year ended 31 March 20X8. The statements of profit or loss and statements of financial position are set out below.

Statements of profit or loss

	Pelham Ltd	Grenville Ltd
	£000	£000
Revenue	840	762
Cost of sales	(610)	(505)
Gross profit	230	257
Distribution costs	(115)	(56)
Administrative expenses	(30)	(57)
Profit from operations	85	144
Finance costs	(10)	(6)
Net profit before taxation	75	138
Taxation	(30)	(40)
Profit for the financial year	45	98

Statement of financial positions

	Pelham Ltd	Grenville Ltd
	£000	£000
ASSETS		
Non-current assets	216	268
Current assets		
Inventories	104	80
Trade receivables	38	86
Cash at bank	205	3
Total assets	563	437
EQUITY AND LIABILITIES		
Equity		
Share capital – £1 ordinary shares	100	100
Retained earnings	182	149
Total equity	282	249
Non-current liabilities		
10% debentures	150	–
Bank loan (secured)	–	56
Current liabilities		
Trade and other payables	101	92
Taxation payable	30	40
Total equity and liabilities	563	437

Task

Write notes for a meeting with the directors of Wodehouse plc to discuss your findings.

Include in your notes the following:

(a) Appropriate accounting ratios indicating the profitability and liquidity of the two companies.

(b) Brief comments on these ratios.

(c) An indication of the reasons for which one company might be preferable to the other as an investment.

Test your understanding 5

Data

Magnus Carter has recently inherited a majority shareholding in a company, Baron Ltd. The company supplies camping equipment to retail outlets. Magnus wishes to get involved in the management of the business, but until now he has only worked in not-for-profit organisations.

He would like to understand how the company has performed over the past two years and how efficient it is in using its resources. He has asked you to help him to interpret the financial statements of the company which are set out below.

Baron Ltd – Summary statement of profit or loss for the year ended 31 March

	20X1	20X0
	£000	£000
Revenue	1,852	1,691
Cost of sales	(648)	(575)
Gross profit	1,204	1,116
Expenses	(685)	(524)
Profit from operations	519	592
Tax	(125)	(147)
Profit for the period	394	445

Baron Ltd – Summary statement of financial positions as at 31 March

	20X1	20X0
Assets	£000	£000
Non-current assets	1,431	1,393
Current assets		
Inventories	217	159
Trade receivables	319	236
Cash	36	147
Total assets	2,003	1,935
Equity and liabilities		
Equity		
Share capital	500	500
Retained earnings	1,330	1,261
	1,830	1,761
Current liabilities		
Trade payables	48	44
Taxation	125	130
	173	174
Total equity and liabilities	2,003	1,935

Task 1

Prepare a report for Magnus Carter that includes:

(a) A calculation of the following ratios for the two years:

- (i) gross profit percentage
- (ii) net profit percentage
- (iii) receivable turnover in days
- (iv) payable turnover in days (based on cost of sales)
- (v) inventory turnover in days (based on cost of sales).

(b) For each ratio calculated:

- (i) a brief explanation in general terms of the meaning of the ratio
- (ii) comments on how the performance or efficiency in the use of resources has changed over the two years.

Task 2

Prepare brief notes to answer the following questions asked by Magnus:

(a) How can the accounting equation in a company balance, when, unlike a not-for-profit organisation, there are no funds to balance with net assets on its statement of financial position?

(b) Can you give me two examples of users outside of the company, other than myself and the other shareholders, who may be interested in the financial statements of Baron Ltd. For each user can you tell me for what purpose they would use them?

(c) A statement, with reasons, identifying the areas that could be improved over the next year as indicated by the ratios and analysis performed.

Test your understanding 6

Data

Jonathan Fisher is intending to invest a substantial sum of money in a company. A colleague has suggested to him that he might want to invest in a private company called Carp Ltd which supplies pond equipment to retail outlets. You have been asked to assist him in interpreting the financial statements of the company which are set out below.

Carp Ltd – Summary statement of profit or loss for the year ended 30 September 20X9

	20X9	**20X8**
	£000	£000
Revenue	3,183	2,756
Cost of sales	(1,337)	(1,020)
Gross profit	1,846	1,736
Expenses	(1,178)	(1,047)
Profit from operations	668	689
Finance costs	(225)	(92)
Profit before tax	443	597
Taxation	(87)	(126)
Profit for the period	356	471

Carp Ltd – Summary statement of financial positions at 30 September

	20X9	20X8
	£000	£000
Assets		
Non-current assets	4,214	2,030
Current assets		
Inventories	795	689
Trade receivables	531	459
Cash	15	136
Total assets	5,555	3,314
Equity and liabilities		
Equity		
Share capital	700	500
Retained earnings	1,517	1,203
Total equity	2,217	1,703
Non-current liabilities		
Long term loan	2,500	1,000
Current liabilities		
Trade payables	751	485
Taxation	87	126
Total liabilities	3,338	1,611
Total equity and liabilities	5,555	3,314

Task

Prepare notes for Jonathan Fisher covering the following points:

(a) Explain what a 'statement of financial position' is and what a 'statement of profit or loss' is and identify the elements that appear in each statement.

(b) Explain the 'accounting equation' and demonstrate that the statement of financial position at 30 September of Carp Ltd as at 30 September 20X9 confirms it.

(c) Calculate the following ratios for the two years:
   (i) gearing
   (ii) net profit percentage
   (iii) current ratio
   (iv) return on shareholders' funds (after tax).

(d) Using the ratios calculated, comment on the company's profitability, liquidity and financial position and consider how these have changed over the two years.

(e) Using only the calculation of the ratios and the analysis of the changes over the two years, state whether the company is a better prospect for investment in 20X9 than it was in 20X8. Give reasons for your answer.

Test your understanding 7

Bimbridge Hospitals Trust has just lost its supplier of bandages. The company that has been supplying it for the last five years has gone into liquidation.

The Trust is concerned to select a new supplier which it can rely on to supply it with its needs for the foreseeable future. You have been asked by the Trust managers to analyse the financial statements of a potential supplier of bandages.

You have obtained the latest financial statements of the company, in summary form, which are set out below.

Patch Ltd – Summary statement of profit or loss for the year ended 30 September 20X8

	20X8	**20X7**
	£000	£000
Revenue	2,300	2,100
Cost of sales	(1,035)	(945)
Gross profit	1,265	1,155
Expenses	(713)	(693)
Net profit from operations	552	462

Patch Ltd – Summary statement of financial positions at 30 September

	20X8	20X7
	£000	£000
Assets		
Non-current assets	4,764	5,418
Current assets		
Inventories	522	419
Trade receivables	406	356
Cash	117	62
Total assets	5,809	6,255
Equity and Liabilities		
Equity		
Share capital	1,100	1,000
Share premium	282	227
Retained earnings	2,298	2,073
	3,680	3,300
Non-current liabilities		
Long-term loan	1,654	2,490
Current liabilities		
Trade payables	305	254
Taxation	170	211
Total liabilities	2,129	2,955
Total equity and liabilities	5,809	6,255

You have also obtained the relevant industry average ratios which are as follows:

	20X8	20X7
Return on capital employed	9.6%	9.4%
Net profit percentage	21.4%	21.3%
Quick ratio/acid test	1.0 : 1	0.9 : 1
Gearing (debt/capital employed)	36%	37%

Task

Prepare a report for the managers of Bimbridge Hospitals Trust recommending whether or not to use Patch Ltd as a supplier of bandages. Use the information contained in the financial statements of Patch Ltd and the industry averages supplied.

Your answer should:

- Comment on the company's profitability, liquidity and financial position.
- Consider how the company has changed over the two years.

Include a comparison with the industry as a whole.

The report should include calculation of the following ratios for the two years:

(i) Return on capital employed.

(ii) Net profit percentage.

(iii) Quick ratio/acid test.

(iv) Gearing.

Test your understanding 8

Youngernst Ltd

Data

A colleague has asked you to take over an assignment. He has been helping a shareholder of Youngernst Ltd to understand the financial statements of the company for the past two years.

The shareholder is interested in finding out how well the company has managed working capital.

Your colleague has obtained the financial statements of Youngernst Ltd for the past two years and has calculated the following ratios:

Ratio	20X3	20X2
Current ratio	2.8 : 1	2.3 : 1
Quick ratio	0.6 : 1	1.1 : 1
Receivables turnover in days	48 days	32 days
Payables turnover in days	27 days	30 days
Inventory turnover in days (inventory turnover period based on cost of sales)	84 days	67 days

Task

Prepare notes for a meeting with the shareholder that includes the following:

(a) the formulas used to calculate each of the ratios

(b) an explanation of the meaning of each of the ratios

(c) your comments on the change in the ratios of Youngernst Ltd over the two years, including an analysis of whether the change in each of the ratios shows that the management of the components of working capital has improved or deteriorated.

7 Summary

By comparing the ratios of different companies, or of one company year-on-year, users of the financial statements will develop a more thorough understanding of a particular company and will therefore be able to make better decisions.

In this chapter we have covered the following categories of ratios:

- profitability
- liquidity
- use of resources
- financial position.

Test your understanding answers

Test your understanding 1

Falcon Ltd

As a first step, produce a table which shows your ratio calculations.

	20X8	20X7
Return on capital employed	$\frac{53,500}{375,000} \times 100 = 14.27\%$	$\frac{41,000}{255,000} \times 100 = 16.08\%$
Operating profit percentage	$\frac{53,500}{525,000} \times 100 = 10.19\%$	$\frac{41,000}{425,000} \times 100 = 9.65\%$
Asset turnover	$\frac{525,000}{375,000} = 1.4$	$\frac{425,000}{255,000} = 1.67$
Inventory turnover rate	$\frac{446,500}{120,000} = 3.72$	$\frac{364,000}{100,000} = 3.64$
Current ratio	$\frac{200,000}{80,000} = 2.5$	$\frac{160,000}{50,000} = 3.2$
Acid test ratio	$\frac{80,000}{80,000} = 1.0$	$\frac{60,000}{50,000} = 1.2$
Trade receivables collection period	$\frac{80,000}{525,000} \times 365 = 56 \text{ days}$	$\frac{60,000}{425,000} \times 365 = 52 \text{ days}$

Comments

Profitability

The return on capital employed has worsened and this is as a result of less efficient use of assets. (The asset turnover has deteriorated whereas the operating profit percentage has improved.)

If we look at the assets individually the inventory turnover and the trade receivables collection period should not have caused any substantial reduction of the asset turnover.

The major change appears to have occurred in the non-current assets where at some point during the year, extra capital has been raised for a major investment in non-current assets.

If these assets were purchased towards the end of the year then this would have made the figure for assets at the year-end unrepresentative of the assets used throughout the year. If we take the average of the beginning and year end assets, the return on capital employed is 16.98%.

Therefore, before we can draw any firm conclusions about the performance of the company, we need further information about the purchase of the non-current assets.

Liquidity

The ratios used to measure liquidity have also worsened during the year.

This is mostly due to a large increase in the overdraft, perhaps to part finance the purchase of the non-current assets.

Once again, it is necessary to establish whether the year-end picture is really representative of the year as a whole before coming to any firm conclusions.

Inventory turnover has remained fairly stable which is good. The receivables collection period has worsened slightly so this is an area the company need to keep under control. This is likely to lead to a further increase in the overdraft if the collection period is allowed to get longer.

Test your understanding 2

1 Return on capital employed =

$$\frac{\text{Profit from operations}}{\text{Working capital + non-current assets}} \times 100$$

2 Return on shareholders' funds =

$$\frac{\text{Profit after tax}}{\text{Total equity}} \times 100$$

3 The current ratio includes inventories while the acid test ratio excludes inventories.

4 The risk that profits might be insufficient to pay the interest payments due.

Test your understanding 3

(a) Return on capital employed

$$\frac{\text{Profit from operations}}{\text{Working capital} + \text{non-current assets}} \times 100\%$$

$\frac{0.82}{3.49} \times 100$ = 23.50%

Asset turnover (net assets)

$$\frac{\text{Revenues}}{\text{Total assets less current liabilities}}$$

$\frac{6.90}{3.49}$ = 1.98 times

% net profit before tax to revenue

$\frac{0.82}{6.90} \times 100$ = 11.88%

Current ratio

Current assets : current liabilities

2.49 : 1.90 = 1.31 : 1

Liquidity ratio/acid test

Current assets less inventories : current liabilities

1.89 : 1.90 = 0.99 : 1

Receivables collection period

$$\frac{\text{Receivables}}{\text{Revenues}} \times 365$$

$\frac{1.84}{6.90} \times 365$ = 97 days

Cost of sales to finished goods

6.08 : 0.40 = 15.2

Operation costs as % of revenue

$$\frac{6.08 - 0.88}{6.90} \times 100 \quad = \quad 75.36\%$$

Distribution and admin costs % of revenue

$$\frac{0.88}{6.90} \times 100 \quad = \quad 12.75\%$$

(b) Comparison of Flyingdales Quarries Ltd with sector as a whole

Ratio	Flyingdales	Sector	Comment
Return on capital employed	23.50%	25.60%	Marginally less than sector as a whole but still giving a more than adequate return on investment.
Asset turnover	1.98	1.80	The company is generating more volume of output per '£' worth of investment than its competitors.
% net profit to revenue	11.88%	14.22%	The company is less profitable than the sector as a whole. It seems to be achieving volume at the expense of profitability.
Current ratio	1.31 : 1	1.50 : 1	The company has a sound level of liquidity, but marginally less than the sector.
Acid test	0.99 : 1	1.02 : 1	An ideal ratio here would be 1 : 1, the company has almost achieved this desired level of liquidity; again marginally less than the sector.
Trade receivables collection period	97 days	82 days	Tighter controls are required here. The collection period is typically high for the sector but the company needs to review is position. There is always the danger of the incidence of irrecoverable debts.

Cost of sales to finished goods	15.2	8.10	The company is turning over its finished goods inventories faster than the industry as a whole. It is holding approx 0.8 months compared with 1.48 month for the sector.
Operating costs % of revenue	75.36%	72.10%	The lack of profitability is highlighted here. Costs may need review and control or selling prices may need revising.
Distribution and admin cost % of revenue	12.75%	14.12%	More favourable than the sector as a whole.

Overall the company performance is marginally worse than the average performance for the sector.

The lack of profitability as highlighted in the % of operating costs to revenue is the significant factor which affects the return on capital. The company is achieving a good level of activity but is marginally less profitable.

Test your understanding 4

Wodehouse

(a) Accounting

Profitability

Ratios			**Pelham Ltd**	**Grenville Ltd**
(i)	Gross profit margin	$\frac{\text{GP}}{\text{Revenues}}$	$\frac{230}{840} \times 100 = 27.4\%$	$\frac{257}{762} \times 100 = 33.7\%$
(ii)	Operating profit margin	$\frac{\text{Op profit}}{\text{Revenues}}$	$\frac{85}{840} \times 100 = 10.1\%$	$\frac{144}{762} \times 100 = 18.9\%$
(iii)	ROCE	$\frac{\text{Op profit}}{\text{Cap employed}}$	$\frac{85}{432} \times 100 = 19.7\%$	$\frac{144}{305} \times 100 = 47.2\%$
(iv)	Asset turnover	$\frac{\text{Revenue}}{\text{Cap employed}}$	$\frac{840}{432} = 1.9$	$\frac{762}{305} = 2.5$
(v)	Inventory turnover	$\frac{\text{Cost of sales}}{\text{Inventory}}$	$\frac{610}{104} = 5.9$	$\frac{505}{80} = 6.3$

Liquidity

(i)	Current ratio	$\frac{CA}{CL}$	$\frac{347}{131} = 2.65$	$\frac{169}{132} = 1.28$
(ii)	Quick ratio	$\frac{CA - Inventory}{CL}$	$\frac{243}{131} = 1.85$	$\frac{89}{132} = 0.67$
(iii)	Receivables collection period (days)	$\frac{Receivables}{Revenues} \times 365$	$\frac{38}{840} \times 365 = 16½$	$\frac{86}{762} \times 365 = 41.2$

(b) Comments

Profitability

1 There are large difference in both gross profit and operating profit margins between two companies in same retailing sector. Grenville is performing much better than Pelham.

Possible reasons:

Grenville may have shops in better positions than Pelham.

Pelham may have a higher proportion of cash sales or prompt payment discounts.

Grenville may simply be more effective in its control of costs.

Pelham's comparatively low CV of non-current assets could indicate a need for high maintenance costs.

2 ROCE is much lower for Pelham: high cash balance may point to under-use of resources. With a lower gross margin, Pelham's asset turnover should be considerably higher than Grenville's to compensate. This is not the case so more revenue volume is needed by Pelham.

Liquidity

1 Pelham's large cash balance makes its current ratio unnecessarily high: it could afford an increase in capital expenditure, leading potentially to increased production and revenue.

2 Grenville's liquidity looks alarming but may not be if the amount of the bank loan can be increased and if trade receivables will pay promptly. Its credit period of 41 days is somewhat high, and there could be a problem here. Further information needed as to the ageing of receivables and the terms of the bank loan.

(c) Comparison of two companies as investments

Pelham: could be said to be ripe for a takeover as it appears to be under-using its assets. A safe but unexciting performance which could be improved with more dynamic management.

Grenville: more of a risk. Needs an injection of cash for security, but given a state of continued solvency it has the potential to make high profits and a good return on investment.

Test your understanding 5

Task 1

REPORT

To: Magnus Carter

From: A Student

Subject: Interpretation of financial statements

Date: 23 June 20X1

This report has been prepared to support the interpretation of the financial statements of Baron Ltd and to compare and contrast the company performance over the two year period.

(a) Calculation of the ratios

	20X1		*20X0*	
Gross profit percentage	$\frac{1,204}{1,852}$	= 65%	$\frac{1,116}{1,691}$	= 66%
Net profit percentage	$\frac{519}{1,852}$	= 28%	$\frac{592}{1,691}$	= 35%
Receivables collection period in days	$\frac{319}{1,852} \times 365$	= 63 days	$\frac{236}{1,691} \times 365$	= 51 days
Payables payment period in days	$\frac{48}{648} \times 365$	= 27 days	$\frac{44}{575} \times 365$	= 28 days
Inventory turnover in days	$\frac{217}{648} \times 365$	= 122 days	$\frac{159}{575} \times 365$	= 101 days

(b) Explanation and comment

- *Gross profit percentage*

  This measure of profitability shows the percentage of gross profit in relation to revenue, it is often termed the gross margin.

  The ratio has remained fairly constant over the two year period with only a marginal decrease from 66% to 65%. It is expressed as:

  $$\frac{\text{Gross profit}}{\text{Revenues}} \times 100\%$$

  The company has achieved a greater volume of business without having to reduce its margins.

- *Net profit percentage*

  This measure of profitability shows the percentage of net profit in relation to revenue. It is influenced by the gross margin and the level of other costs in relation to revenue. There has been a significant fall in the net return over the period. The gross margin has only fallen marginally, however the expenses in relation to revenue have increased from 31% to 37% over the period and this has had an adverse effect on the performance.

  This indicates that the company is generating less net profit per '£' of revenue than previously achieved.

- *Receivables collection period*

  This is a measure of management control as it relates to the effectiveness of the credit control policy.

  The ratio shows the average number of days it takes to collect debts. It is expressed as:

  $$\frac{\text{Receivables}}{\text{Revenues}} \times 365 \text{ days}$$

  The collection period has increased over the two year period and it is taking 12 days longer to collect debts than previously experienced. This may be due to either customer cash flow problems or poor and less effective credit control.

- *Payables payment period*

  This ratio shows the average days it takes for the company to pay its suppliers. This period has remained similar over the two years. It indicates that the company can meet its demands from trade payables on a timely and regular basis.

- *Inventory turnover*

  This is a measure of the effectiveness of the inventory control policy. It shows the average number of days it takes to turn over inventories.

  There has been a deterioration in this control over the two years as it is taking a further 21 days to turn over inventories than previously experienced.

Task 2

(a) The accounting equation is:

Assets = Equity + Liabilities

In a not-for-profit entity, funds given to the organisation by donors and those generated from within are utilised to meet the entity's objective. Such funds are equivalent to the equity interest element of the accounting equation.

In a company's statement of financial position the equity interest of the shareholders is represented by the share capital and reserves of the company.

(b) Examples of outside users and uses (only two required):

User	**Uses**
Potential investors	To decide whether to invest in the company.
Bank	To decide whether to grant a loan to the company.
Payables	To decide whether to supply goods or services to the company.

Other reasonable examples of outside users are also acceptable.

(c) **Areas for improvement**

The measures of performance and other ratios indicate that Baron Ltd should focus on the control of expenses, trade receivables and inventories.

The gross margin and payables payment periods have remained similar to the previous year, but there has been a decline in the net profit percentage due to a more than proportional increase in the level of expenses to revenue, which suggests controls are needed.

The credit control policy and procedures need review and there is also the danger of irrecoverable debts occurring. The inventory holding policy needs considering with a full analysis of both moving and slow moving inventories.

Test your understanding 6

Notes to Jonathan Fisher

(a) A statement of financial position shows the financial position of an entity at a point in time. It lists the assets, liabilities and equity interest at the statement of financial position date.

An statement of profit or loss shows the financial performance of an entity over a specific period of time. It shows income and expenditure, the difference between these elements being profit over the accounting period.

(b) The accounting equation is:

Assets = Equity + Liabilities

Figures in £000 at 30 September 20X9

The accounting equation is: £5,555 = £2,217 + £3,338

(c) **Calculation of ratios**

The following ratios for the company have been computed:

	20X9		20X8	
(i) Gearing Debt/cap. employed	2,500 / 4,717	× 100 = 53%	1,000 / 2,703	× 100 = 37%
or				
Debt/equity	2,500 / 2,217	× 100 = 113%	1,000 / 1,703	× 100 = 59%
(ii) Net profit percentage	668 / 3,183	× 100 = 21%	689 / 2,756	× 100 = 25%
(iii) Current ratio	1,341 / 838	= 1.6:1	1,284 / 611	= 2.1:1
(iv) Return on shareholders' funds	356 / 2,217	× 100 = 16%	471 / 1,703	× 100 = 28%

(d)
- Gearing ratio: This measure represents the company's reliance on debt in relation to total equity. The gearing has increased over the two years and the company is now a 'high geared' organisation. There is a greater reliance on borrowed funds in the second year. This increases shareholder risk as when profits reduce, interest payments must still be met.

- Net profit percentage: The net return to revenue has fallen over the period. This is a result of a fall in the gross margin from 63% to 58%, the level of expenses to revenue remaining fairly constant.
- Current ratio: There has been a reduction in this measure of liquidity over the period, there has been a deterioration in the cash position and the acid test ratio has fallen significantly from 0.97 to 0.65. The business now has less current assets per '£' of current liabilities than previously.
- Return on shareholders' funds: The return has fallen over the two year period which has been influenced by the overall reduction in profitability as shown in the net profit percentage to revenue.

  The company is not generating as much profit for each '£' worth of equity investment as it did in the previous year.

(e) The decrease in both profitability and liquidity indicates that the company is a worse prospect for investment than it was in the previous year.

Test your understanding 7

To: Managers of Bimbridge Hospitals Trust

From: AAT Student

Date: 3 December 20X8

Re: Analysis of Patch Ltd's financial statements

Introduction

The purpose of this report is to analyse the financial performance of Patch Ltd for 20X8 and 20X7 to consider it as a major supplier of bandages and dressings to the Trust.

The following are key financial ratios together with industry benchmarks.

	Patch Ltd	**Industry average**	**Patch Ltd**	**Industry average**
	20X8	*20X8*	*20X7*	*20X7*
Return on capital employed	$\frac{552}{5,334}$ = 10.3%	9.6%	$\frac{462}{5,790}$ = 8.0%	9.4%
Net profit percentage	$\frac{552}{2,300}$ = 24%	21.4%	$\frac{462}{2,100}$ = 22%	21.3%

Quick ratio/acid test	$\frac{523}{475}$ = 1.1:1	1.0:1	$\frac{418}{465}$ = 0.9:1	0.9:1
Gearing: Debt/capital employed	$\frac{1,654}{5,334}$ = 31%	36%	$\frac{2,490}{5,790}$ = 43%	37%

Comment and analysis

Overall company profitability has improved over the two years with return on capital employed strengthening from 8% to 10.3%.

The company is generating more net profit per '£' of investment in 20X8 than in the previous year.

Compared with the sector average their performance was adverse in 20X7 but more favourable in 20X8.

The percentage of net profit to revenue also increased over the period increasing from 22% to 24%.

The company is therefore more profitable in the current year and is performing more favourably than the sector as a whole and a good indicator for the future.

Company liquidity has shown an improvement with a slightly stronger acid test ratio than the sector as a whole.

The company currently has £1.10 worth of liquid assets for each '£' worth of current liabilities. This appears to be a sound liquidity position.

There has been a reduction in gearing over the two year period, with a much less reliance on debt than previously experienced.

High geared companies increase shareholder risk in times of profit decline. The company is moving to a 'lower' geared structure and to a position less than the industry average.

The company is considered to be a lower risk than previously.

Conclusion

Based on this assessment of the financial statements provided, it is recommended that Patch Ltd can be used as a supplier to the Trust.

Its profitability, liquidity and gearing suggest that the company is financially sound.

Test your understanding 8

Youngernst Ltd

Notes for a meeting

(a) Formulas used in calculating the ratios:

Current ratio $= \dfrac{\text{Current assets}}{\text{Current liabilities}}$

Quick ratio $= \dfrac{\text{Current assets less inventories}}{\text{Current liabilities}}$

Receivables turnover $= \dfrac{\text{Trade receivables}}{\text{Revenue}} \times 365$

Payables turnover $= \dfrac{\text{Trade payables}}{\text{Cost of sales (or purchases)}} \times 365$

Inventories turnover $= \dfrac{\text{Inventories}}{\text{Cost of sales}} \times 365$

(b) Explanation of the meaning of the ratios

Current ratio:

- this ratio measures the extent to which the company has sufficient current assets to meet its current liabilities
- it gives an indication of the liquidity of the company, but can also show that too much is invested in current assets such as inventories and trade receivables and cash in relation to current liabilities.

Quick ratio/Acid test:

- this ratio measures the extent to which the company has sufficient current assets that are quickly convertible into cash to meet its current liabilities
- it also gives an indication of the liquidity of the company, but can also indicate whether too much is invested in trade receivables and cash in relation to current liabilities.

Receivable turnover:

- this ratio shows the average number of days it takes to collect trade receivables.

Payable turnover:

- this ratio shows the average number of days it takes for the company to pay its trade payables.

Inventory turnover

- this ratio shows the average number of days that it takes to sell the inventories of the company.

(c) Comment on change in ratios

Current ratio:

- this ratio has increased during the year suggesting that the company has more current assets to meet its current liabilities than in previous years and hence better liquidity
- however, this might be because inventories or trade receivable balances have increased rather than cash balances and these may not be readily convertible to cash to pay off trade payables and so does not necessarily mean more liquidity and may indicate problems in selling inventories or collecting trade receivables.

Quick ratio/Acid test:

- this ratio has deteriorated during the year which means that there are less current assets that are quickly convertible into cash to meet its current liabilities which suggests decreased liquidity
- the fact that this ratio has decreased even though the current ratio has increased suggests that the reason why the current ratio has increased is due to increases in the amount of inventories held in relation to current liabilities rather than any genuine improvement in liquidity
- because the quick assets include trade receivables, this ratio might conceal further liquidity problems since a failure to collect trade receivable balances may also result in a higher ratio.

Receivables turnover:

- the ratio has deteriorated over the two years as it now takes, on average, 16 more days to collect debts than last year
- the fact that it takes longer this year to collect debts than last year may be due to liquidity problems of customers, an increase in irrecoverable debts or a failure to chase up overdue debts which might point to failures of management of working capital.

Payables turnover:

- the number of days taken to pay trade payables has fallen a little over the two years
- this does not suggest that the company has had difficulty in finding funds to pay trade payables and, therefore, does not appear to have liquidity problems that have forced the business to pay trade payables more slowly
- the decrease may be due to inefficiencies in management and the failure to make full use of credit terms, but it is possible that trade payables have tightened up on the period of credit allowed which might indicate suspicions about the liquidity of the company.

Inventory turnover:

- this ratio has deteriorated over the two years as it now takes 17 days longer to sell inventories than it did last year
- this shows that there may be problems with inventory control which may point to overstocking or to increasing amounts of old inventories being included against which provisions may be required to be made.

Statement of cash flows

Introduction

A typical task in the exam might be to draft a statement of cash flows from information provided in the statement of financial position, statement of profit or loss and other comprehensive income and additional information.

ASSESSMENT CRITERIA

Explain the regulatory framework that underpins financial reporting (1.1)

Examine the effect of international accounting standards on the preparation of financial statements (2.1)

Draft a statement of cash flows (3.4)

CONTENTS

1 IAS 7 *Statement of cash flows*

1.1 The need for a statement of cash flows

IAS 7 requires all financial statements (except those of small companies as defined in the CA 06) to include a statement of cash flow, showing the generation of cash and cash equivalents and the uses of cash and cash equivalents in the period.

One reason why a statement of cash flows is considered necessary is that final profit figures are relatively easy to make different assumptions or estimates. There are many items in a statement of profit or loss involving judgement, including:

- Valuation of inventories
- Depreciation policy
- Allowance for doubtful debts.

This makes it difficult to interpret a company's results with confidence. A statement of cash flows showing merely inflows and outflows of cash and cash equivalents is easier to understand and more difficult to manipulate.

Cash flows, including net present value calculations, have always been a popular management accounting tool and the requirement to produce a statement of cash flows as part of the financial statements helps to form a basis for any future decision making process.

1.2 Benefits of cash flow information

As outlined above in section 1.1, a statement of cash flow shows solely inflows and outflows of cash and cash equivalents. Cash flow information is useful in assessing the ability of the entity to generate cash and cash equivalents.

It also assists with comparing the performance made by different entities because it eliminates the effects of using different accounting treatments for similar transactions and events.

1.3 The IAS 7 proforma

The standard headings shown in the IAS 7 *Statement of cash* flows are as follows.

- Cash flows from operating activities
- Cash flows from investing activities

- Cash flows from financing activities
- Net increase or decrease in cash and cash equivalents
- Cash and cash equivalents at beginning of period
- Cash and cash equivalents at end of the period.

The key to producing an accurate statement of cash flows in the examination is to know which cash flows go under which heading. Below is a typical IAS 7 statement showing many of the cash flows one would normally expect to see.

Proforma statement of cash flow for the year ended 31 December 20X9

Cash flows from operating activities	£000	£000
Profit before tax	X	
Adjustments for:		
Depreciation/amortisation	X	
(Gain)/loss on disposal of PPE	(X)/X	
Finance costs	X	
Investment income	(X)	
Operating profit before working capital changes	X	
(Increase)/decrease in inventories	(X)/X	
(Increase)/decrease in trade and other receivables	(X)/X	
Increase/(decrease) in trade payables	X/(X)	
Cash generated from operations	X	
Interest paid	(X)	
Tax paid	(X)	
Net cash from operating activities		X
Cash flows from investing activities		
Purchase of property plant and equipment	(X)	
Purchase of intangibles	(X)	
Purchase of investments	(X)	
Proceeds from sale of property plant and equipment	X	
Proceeds from sale of intangibles	X	
Proceeds from sale of investments	X	
Interest received	X	
Dividends received	X	
Net cash from investing activities		X/(X)

Cash flows from financing activities		
Proceeds from issue of ordinary shares	X	
Proceeds from issue of preference shares	X	
Proceeds from long-term borrowing	X	
Redemption of long-term borrowings	(X)	
Dividends paid	(X)	
Net cash used in financing activities		(X)
Net increase or decrease in cash and cash equivalents		X/(X)
Cash and cash equivalents at beginning of period		X
Cash and cash equivalents at end of period		X

The above proforma can also start with profit from operations rather than profit before tax. If this is the case then the statement of profit or loss finance cost will not be required to be added back.

2 The elements of a statement of cash flows

2.1 Net cash flow from operating activities

This is the first heading of the statement of cash flows in the proforma shown above. It can be derived by adjusting the profit before tax figure shown in the statement of profit or loss.

The profit figure is adjusted for any transactions not involving the movement of cash, e.g. depreciation or profit/loss on disposal of non-current assets. The statement of profit or loss finance costs are added back to profit because it is not part of cash from operations and may include accrued (i.e. non cash) amounts (interest is dealt with later in the statement of cash flows). Investment income is deducted as it is not part of cash from operations (belongs in cash flows from investing activities).

Note the increase/decrease in inventories, trade receivables and trade payables. An increase in inventories involves an outflow of cash and is, hence, a negative figure. Likewise, if the payables balance has reduced then cash has been spent paying our suppliers and hence this is also a cash outflow which is a negative figure.

The main issue is to understand the impact on cash, i.e. is it a cash outflow or inflow?

Interest paid and tax paid also appear here. This is the amount paid during the year, not the amount charged in the statement of profit or loss.

2.2 Direct and indirect methods

There are two methods of preparing the figure for cash flows from operating activities. These are the indirect method and the direct method.

You will only be asked to use the indirect method when drafting a statement of cash flows in the exam. However, you are required to demonstrate an understanding of the direct method.

Proforma statement of cash flow for the year ended 31 December 20X9 – Direct method for calculating cash generated from operations

Cash flows from operating activities	£000
Cash receipts from customers	X
Cash payments to suppliers	(X)
Cash payments to employees	(X)
Cash payments for expenses	(X)
Cash generated from operations	X

Proforma statement of cash flow for the year ended 31 December 20X9 – Indirect method for calculating cash generated from operations

Cash flows from operating activities	£000	£000
Profit before tax	X	
Adjustments for:		
Depreciation/amortisation	X	
(Gain)/loss on disposal of PPE	(X)/X	
Finance costs	X	
Investment income	(X)	
Operating before working capital changes	X	
(Increase)/decrease in inventories	(X)/X	
(Increase)/decrease in trade and other receivables	(X)/X	
Increase/(decrease) in trade payables	X/(X)	
Cash generated from operations	X	

2.3 Cash flows from investing activities

This shows the extent to which the business has spent cash investing in the future of the business. An example is the purchase of non-current assets such as plant and machinery which will be used to generate cash and profits in the future.

2.4 Cash flows from financing activities

This includes any or all of the following elements.

- Proceeds of share issues
- Proceeds of taking out a new loan or debenture
- Payments to redeem a loan or debenture
- Dividends paid.

2.5 Increase/decrease in cash and cash equivalents

This is the net amount of the cash flows from operating, investing and financing activities. It reconciles the opening and closing balances for cash and cash equivalents from the statements of financial position. The composition of cash and cash equivalents is analysed in a note as below.

Proforma note to the statement of cash flow	£
Cash and cash equivalents	
Cash on hand and balances with banks	X
Short term investments	X
Cash and cash equivalents as previously reported	X

3 Preparing a statement of cash flows

Example – Indirect method

The following information relates to X plc. The company's accounting year ends on 30 September. Note that 20X9 is on the right.

Statements of financial position

	30 September 20X8		30 September 20X9	
ASSETS	£000	£000	£000	£000
Non-current assets				
Plant property and equipment (Note 1)		945		1,662
Current assets				
Inventories	1,225		1,488	
Trade receivables	700		787	
Short-term liquid investments	175		262	
Cash at bank	184		186	
		2,284		2,723
Total assets		3,229		4,385
EQUITY AND LIABILITIES				
Equity				
Share capital		1,225		1,400
Share premium		–		87
Retained earnings		613		945
		1,838		2,432
Non-current liabilities				
Long-term loan		525		700
Current liabilities				
Trade and other payables	534		745	
Taxation	280		403	
Bank overdraft	52		105	
		866		1,253
Total liabilities		1,391		1,953
Total equity and liabilities		3,229		4,385

Summary statement of profit or loss for the year ended 30 September 20X9

	£000
Profit before tax	735
Tax	(403)
Profit for the period	332

Note 1 Plant, property and equipment

	20X8		*20X9*	
	Freehold premises	**Plant and machinery**	**Freehold premises**	**Plant and machinery**
	£000	£000	£000	£000
At cost	560	455	560	718
Additions during the year	–	263	280	700
	560	718	840	1,418
Less accumulated depreciation	(35)	(298)	(53)	(543)
Carrying amount	525	420	787	875

Prepare a statement of cash flows (using the indirect method) for the year ended 30 September 20X9, conforming to the requirements of IAS 7, in so far as this is possible from the information given.

Solution

Step 1

We start by producing the statement of cash flows and calculating the increase in cash and cash equivalents.

Step 2

Start to work down the proforma statement of cash flows. Only the headings required are used in the answer below.

Remember to tick the numbers you have used in the question as you work through.

Cash flows from operating activities	£000	£000
Profit before tax	735	
Adjustments for:		
Depreciation charges (W1)	263	
	998	
Increase in inventories (1,488 – 1,225) (W2)	(263)	
Increase in trade and other receivables (787 – 700) (W2)	(87)	
Increase in trade payables (745 – 534) (W2)	211	
Cash generated from operations	859	
Tax paid (W3)	(280)	
Net cash from operating activities		579
Cash flows from investing activities		
Purchase of property plant and equipment (W4)	(980)	
Net cash used in investing activities		(980)
Cash flows from financing activities		
Proceeds from issue of shares (W5)	262	
Proceeds from long-term borrowing (W6)	175	
Net cash used in financing activities		437
Net increase in cash and cash equivalents (W7)		36
Cash and cash equivalents at beginning of period		307
Cash and cash equivalents at end of period		343

Note 1

Cash and cash equivalents	*X8*	*X9*
Cash on hand and balances with banks	132	81
Short-term investments	175	262
	307	343

Workings

(W1) Depreciation

You have to go to the note to the statement of financial position to calculate the depreciation charge as we are not given a detailed statement of profit or loss. The easiest way of calculating the depreciation charge for the year would be to set up an accumulated depreciation ledger account.

You need to calculate the difference between the accumulated depreciation at the end of the current year and at the end of the previous year.

Freehold premises (53 – 35)	18
Plant and machinery (543 – 298)	245

(W2) Changes in working capital

The other figures are calculated by simply comparing the two statements of financial position and calculating the increase or decrease in the relevant items.

Inventories have increased in the second year compared to the first year, this means that extra cash has been spent, i.e. a decrease in cash.

Trade receivables have increased, this means that more credit has been offered to customers and therefore cash has not been received.

Trade payables have increased, this means that cash has been conserved so that cash has increased.

(W3) Taxation

The 20X9 tax charge of £403,000 in the summary statement of profit or loss has not been paid and is a payable in the statement of financial position.

The 20X8 tax charge of £280,000 has been paid and that is the cash that is entered in the statement of cash flows.

(W4) Payments to acquire plant property and equipment

You have to go to Note 1 in the statement of financial position to find the information for this. In the line 'additions during the year' the amounts are given (280 + 700) = 980.

(W5) Issue of ordinary share capital

Ordinary share capital has increased, as has the share premium account. Clearly shares have been issued at a premium. The total amount issued = (£1,400 + £87 – £1,225) = £262.

(W6) Loans

Long-term loans have increased. New loans raised = £700 – £525 = £175.

(W7) Increase in cash and cash equivalents

We can use the note required to produce this. Short-term investments plus cash less overdrafts.

(£262 + £186 – £105) – (£175 + £184 – £52) = (£343 – £307) = £36

Example – Direct method

The following information relates to Y plc.

Statement of profit or loss for the year ended 30 September 20X9

	£000
Revenue	444
Cost of sales	(269)
Gross profit	175
Distribution costs	(35)
Administrative expenses	(8)
Profit from operations	132
Finance costs	(18)
Profit before tax	114
Income tax expense	(42)
Profit after tax	72

The expenses can be analysed as follows:

	£000
Wages	72
Auditors remuneration	12
Depreciation	84
Cost of materials used	222
Profit on disposal of non-current assets	(60)
Rental income	(18)
	312

The following information is also available:

	30/09/X9	**30/09/X8**
	£000	£000
Inventories	42	24
Receivables	48	42
Payables	(30)	(18)

Required:

Prepare the cash generated from operations using the direct method for the year ended 30 September 20X9, conforming to the requirements of IAS 7, in so far as this is possible from the information given.

Solution

Y plc Statement of cash flows for the year ended 30 September 20X9.

Cash flows from operating activities	£000
Cash receipts from customers (W1)	438
Rental income	18
Cash payments to suppliers (W2)	(228)
Cash payments to employees	(72)
Cash payments for expenses	(12)
Cash generated from operations	144

Workings

(W1) Cash receipts from customers

Opening receivables	42
Revenue	444
Closing receivables	(48)
Cash received from customers	438

(W2) Cash payments to suppliers

Opening inventories	24
Purchases (bal figure)	240
Closing inventories	(42)
Cost of materials used	222
Opening payables	18
Purchases (above)	240
Closing payables	(30)
Payments to suppliers	228

The remaining parts of the cash flow will be the produced in the same way as shown in the previous example.

Test your understanding 1

Extracts from the accounts of Deuce showed balances as follows:

	20X9	20X8
Share capital £1	300,000	120,000
Share premium	260,000	100,000

During 20X9 loan notes of £300,000 were issued at par. Interest of £12,000 was also paid during the year. What is the net cash inflow from financing activities?

A £480,000

B £605,000

C £617,000

D £640,000

Test your understanding 2

A draft statement of cash flows contains the following:	£m
Profit before tax	22
Depreciation	8
Increase in inventories	(4)
Decrease in receivables	(3)
Increase in payables	(2)
Net cash inflow from operating activities	21

Which of the following corrections needs to be made to the calculations?

1 Depreciation should be deducted, not added.

2 Increase in inventories should be added, not deducted.

3 Decrease in receivables should be added, not deducted.

4 Increase in payables should be added, not deducted.

A 1 and 2

B 1 and 3

C 2 and 4

D 3 and 4

4 More complex areas

4.1 Introduction

In many cases the figures for the statement of cash flows can be found simply by comparing the opening and closing statements of financial position. However in other instances a slightly more involved approach is required.

4.2 Interest paid

Care must be taken as the interest charge in the statement of profit or loss may not always be the amount of cash paid in interest. If there are accruals for interest payable in the statement of financial position then either a ledger account working will be required in order to determine the interest paid or the alternative working shown.

Example

The interest charge in a company's statement of profit or loss is £300. The statement of financial position shows the following figures under current liabilities.

	Opening statement of financial position	Closing statement of financial position
	£	£
Interest payable	120	150

What is the amount of interest paid in the year?

Solution

	£
Opening liability	120
Statement of profit or loss charge	300
Closing liability	(150)
Interest paid (bal fig)	270

4.3 Tax paid

A similar method is used in order to determine the amount of tax paid during a year.

A ledger account is opened for tax. The opening and closing payables for tax and are entered together with the relevant statement of profit or loss figures and the amount of cash paid is the balancing figure.

Example

Given below are extracts from the statement of profit or loss and statements of financial position for a business.

Statement of profit or loss

	£000
Profit before tax	1,300
Tax	(400)
Profit after tax	900

	Opening statement of financial position	**Closing statement of financial positions**
	£	£
Current liabilities		
Taxation	360	500

What figures should appear in the statement of cash flows for tax paid?

Tax payable

	£
Opening liability	360
Statement of profit or loss charge	400
Closing liability	(500)
Tax paid (bal fig)	260

4.4 Non-current assets and depreciation

Further calculation problems can arise when trying to find the relevant figures for non-current assets and depreciation.

The depreciation charge for the year is required in order to add back to operating profit. Any additions to non-current assets are also cash outflows and they may also have to be calculated.

Again the technique is to use either a ledger account for non-current assets at cost and for accumulated depreciation and to enter into these accounts all of the relevant figures from the question or to use the alternative working shown.

Example

Given below are extracts from the opening and closing statement of financial positions for a company.

	Opening statement of financial position	**Closing statement of financial position**
	£000	£000
Non-current assets at cost	1,000	1,100
Accumulated depreciation	(400)	(480)
Carrying amount	600	620

You are also told that an asset which had cost £150,000 and on which £90,000 of accumulated depreciation had been charged was sold during the year for £50,000.

What are the figures for depreciation, profit or loss on disposal and additions to non-current assets for the statement of cash flow?

Solution

Purchase of PPE

	£000
PPE at start	1,000
Less disposal	(150)
PPE at end	(1,100)
PPE additions	250

Now we need to find the depreciation charge for the year by using the same technique.

Depreciation charge

	£000
Accumulated depreciation at start	400
Less depreciation on disposal	(90)
Accumulated depreciation at end	(480)
Charge in the year	170

Therefore the depreciation charge for the year is £170,000 to be added back to operating profit.

Finally any profit or loss on disposal can be found as follows:

Loss on disposal

	£000
Proceeds	50
Less carrying amount (150 – 90)	(60)
Loss on disposal	(10)

4.5 Non-current assets at carrying amount

In some tasks you are only given the carrying amount of the non-current assets rather than separate cost and accumulated depreciation information.

In such questions you may need to find either the depreciation charge for the year or the additions. Again this is done in a similar fashion to before but you must now combine the cost and accumulated depreciation workings, as follows:

	£
PPE CA at start	X
Revaluations during year	X
CA of disposals	(X)
Depreciation charge	(X)
PPE CA at end	(X)
PPE additions	X

Example

Given below is an extract from the opening and closing statements of financial position of a company.

	Opening statement of financial position	**Closing statement of financial position**
	£000	£000
Non-current assets carrying amount	3,000	3,200

During the year assets with a carrying amount of £100,000 were sold and assets costing £650,000 were purchased. What is the depreciation charge for the year?

Solution

Purchase of PPE

	£000
PPE at start	3,000
Additions	650
Less disposal	(100)
PPE at end	(3,200)
PPE depreciation charge	350

4.6 Provisions

In some tasks you may find a provision in the statement of financial position. Any increase or decrease in a provision is not a cash flow and therefore the increase or decrease should be dealt with by adjusting the operating profit. An increase in provision will be added back to profit and a decrease will be deducted.

Test your understanding 3

Fallen plc

Fallen plc has prepared the following draft accounts for the year ended 31 December 20X8.

Statement of profit or loss	£000
Revenue	11,019
Cost of sales	(5,502)
Gross profit	5,517
Distribution costs	(402)
Administrative expenses	(882)
Profit from operations	4,233
Finance costs	(152)
Profit before tax	4,081
Taxation	(1,531)
Profit after tax	2,550

Statement of financial positions	*31 December*	
	20X8	**20X7**
	£000	£000
ASSETS		
Non-current assets		
Property plant and equipment (CA)	11,640	9,480
Current assets		
Inventories	2,880	1,986
Trade receivables	2,586	1,992
Short-term investments at cost	2,406	2,208
Bank	–	576
	7,872	6,762
Total assets	**19,512**	**16,242**
EQUITY AND LIABILITIES		
Equity		
Share capital (25p ordinary)	2,280	1,800
Share premium	2,112	1,800
Retained earnings	9,498	6,948
Total equity	13,890	10,548
Non-current liabilities		
Debentures (10%)	1,240	1,800
	1,240	1,800
Current liabilities		
Trade and other payables	2,228	1,718
Overdraft	222	0
Taxation	1,932	2,176
	4,382	3,894
Total liabilities	5,622	5,694
Total equity and liabilities	**19,512**	**16,242**

The following data is relevant.

1 The 10% debentures redeemed during the year were redeemed at par.

2 Plant and equipment with a carrying amount of £276,000 was sold for £168,000 giving a loss on disposal of £108,000. New plant was purchased for £2,500,000.

3 Depreciation charged for the year was £1,364,000.

4 Leasehold premises costing £1,300,000 were acquired during the year.

Required:

Prepare the statement of cash flow for 20X8 in accordance with IAS 7.

5 Interpretation of a statement of cash flows

5.1 Introduction

Users of the financial statements can learn a lot about a company from analysing the statement of cash flows.

The best approach to take when interpreting a statement of cash flows is to work through each of the headings in the statement of cash flows in turn. You need to look for large changes in the balances compared to the previous year or any figure that seems to stand out.

5.2 Net cash from operating activities

Operating cash flow is very important to a business as this reflects how well it is generating cash from its day to day activities. A negative operating cash flow is not good and would suggest that the business is not operating efficiently. This would lead you to look at the cash flow from working capital – inventories, receivables and payables.

Also, compare the operating cash flow to the profit from operations to establish the quality of profits. The higher the cash from operations in relation to profit from operations, the better quality of profits as most of it is being converted into cash.

5.3 Working capital

Another easy comment to make is the effect of working capital on the company's cash position. If a company has moved from having net cash balances in the previous period to having a net overdraft in the current period then look at the movements on working capital.

For example, you may see that inventories have risen as the company has increased inventory levels, thus spending cash. It may be that receivables have increased which suggests potential inefficiency in credit control procedures. If trade payables have increased then this suggests that the company has not paid its suppliers which is good for cash flow but potentially harmful for supplier relations.

5.4 Purchase of non-current assets

Within the cash flows from investing activities section of the statement of cash flows, it deals with the company's investments for the long term. A cash outflow now may bring benefits in the future.

If a company has made an investment in non-current assets, then they are obviously planning for the future which is a positive move. You must also comment on how they have financed this investment. If they are cash rich they may manage to purchase the assets out of cash. Watch out for an increasing overdraft as this is an expensive form of finance and should not be used in the long term.

Other methods of financing the purchase could be an issue of share capital which is a cheap method of raising finance and encourages new investors into the business. Alternatively, the business may take out a loan. This is a common method of financing assets, but the business will now need to pay the interest on the loan.

5.5 Sale of non-current assets

A company may sell non-current assets because they are old or obsolete. Often the cash flow will show the sale of assets and the purchase of new assets as the business is updating its facilities.

However, if the company's cash flow is looking severely depleted, the sale of non-current assets may be a desperate measure to raise cash. Whilst this will get cash into the business it is not a good idea in the long term as the business will not have the assets to continue operating.

5.6 Financing

In the financing section you can comment on issues of new shares and loan transactions. A share issue is a means of raising finance for expansion of the business. You may be able to relate this to non-current asset purchases in the investing section.

As with the share issue, if you see that there has been increased loan finance, then try and establish why the loan has been taken out. This may point you in the direction of non-current asset purchases or perhaps to fund the expansion of the business. You can also look at the level of interest payable to see the effect of an increase in the statement of profit or loss.

If debt has decreased then the business may have had surplus cash and decided to reduce interest payments by repaying the debt. This is a strong position to be in.

Dividend payments will also be seen in the financing section of the statement of cash flows. You must ensure that there is sufficient cash available to pay the dividend without the company having to rely on overdrafts. Many companies are not keen on reducing dividend payments to shareholders as it sends a sign that the business is not performing well.

Test your understanding 4

The financial statements of Flyingdales Ltd for the year ended 31 March 20X1 include:

Statement of profit or loss

	£000
Revenue	205,000
Cost of sales	(191,250)
Profit from operations	13,750
Finance costs	(2,150)
Profit before taxation	11,600
Taxation	(2,850)
Profit after tax	8,750

Note: The depreciation charge for the year was £6.5m. There had been no disposals of non-current assets in the year.

Statement of financial position at 31 March

	20X1	20X0
ASSETS	£000	£000
Property, plant and equipment	73,000	70,500
Current assets		
Inventories	27,500	25,500
Trade receivables	37,500	33,000
Cash and cash equivalents	4,250	1,250
	69,250	59,750
Total assets	142,250	130,250
EQUITY AND LIABILITIES		
Equity:		
Share capital	11,610	10,000
Retained earnings	74,790	66,040
	86,400	76,040
Non-current liabilities		
10% debenture	21,500	20,000
	21,500	20,000
Current liabilities		
Trade payables	31,500	31,950
Taxation	2,850	2,260
	34,350	34,210
Total liabilities	55,850	54,210
Total equity and liabilities	142,250	130,250

Task 1

Provide a reconciliation of profit before tax to net cash from operating activities for Flyingdales Ltd for the year ended 31 March 20X1.

Task 2

Using the proforma below prepare the statement of cash flow for Flyingdales Ltd for the year ended 31 March 20X1.

Flyingdales Ltd

Company statement of cash flows for the year ended 31 March 20X1.

	£000
Net cash from operating activities	
Investing activities	
Net cash used in investing activities	
Financing activities	
Net cash from financing activities	
Net increase/(decrease) in cash and cash equivalents	
Cash and cash equivalents at beginning of year	
Cash and cash equivalents at end of year	

Workings

(W1) Purchase of property, plant and equipment:

	£000

Test your understanding 5

Data

You have been asked to prepare the statement of cash flows for Eigg Ltd for the year ended 31 March 2008.

The most recent statement of profit or loss and statements of financial position of Eigg Ltd for the past two years are set out below.

Eigg Ltd – Statement of profit or loss for the year ended 31 March 2008

	£000
Revenue	44,800
Cost of sales	(24,640)
Gross profit	20,160
Dividends received	120
Gain on the disposal of plant and equipment	448
Distribution costs	(9,408)
Administrative expenses	(4,480)
Profit from operations	6,840
Finance costs	(105)
Profit before taxation	6,735
Tax	(2,884)
Profit for the period	3,851

Eigg Ltd – Statement of financial position at 31 March

	2008	2007
	£000	£000
ASSETS		
Non-current assets		
Property, plant and equipment	27,890	21,340
Current assets		
Inventories	5,914	4,928
Trade and other receivables	4,480	5,376
Cash and cash equivalents	280	
Total assets	38,564	31,644
Equity and liabilities		
Equity		
Share capital	4,500	3,000
Share premium	3,000	2,000
Retained earnings	24,216	20,642
Total equity	31,716	25,642
Non-current liabilities		
Bank loans	1,500	500
Current liabilities		
Trade and other payables	2,464	4,435
Tax liability	2,884	887
Bank overdraft	0	180
Total equity and liabilities	38,564	31,644

You have been given the following further information:

- The total depreciation charge for the year was £4,458,000.
- Property, plant and equipment costing £878,000 with accumulated depreciation of £334,000 was sold in the year.
- All sales and purchases were on credit. Other expenses were paid for in cash.
- A dividend of £277,000 was paid during the year.

Task 1

Prepare a reconciliation of profit before tax to net cash from operating activities for Eigg Ltd for the year ended 31 March 2008.

Task 2

Using the proforma below prepare the statement of cash flows for Eigg Ltd for the year ended 31 March 2008.

Eigg Ltd

Company statement of cash flows for the year ended 31 March 2008.

	£000
Net cash from operating activities	
Investing activities	
Net cash used in investing activities	
Financing activities	
Net cash (used in)/from financing activities	
Net increase/(decrease) in cash and cash equivalents	
Cash and cash equivalents at beginning of year	
Cash and cash equivalents at end of year	

Workings

(W1) Proceeds of property, plant and equipment:

	£000
	———
Proceeds	

(W2) Purchase of property, plant and equipment:

	£000
	———
PPE additions	

Test your understanding 6

Data

You have been asked to prepare a statement of cash flows for Adlington Ltd for the year ended 31 October 20X9.

The most recent statement of profit or loss and statements of financial position of the company for the past two years are set out below.

Adlington Ltd
Statement of profit or loss for the year ended 31 October 20X9

	£000
Revenue	45,500
Cost of sales	(27,300)
Gross profit	18,200
Gain on disposal of property, plant and equipment	455
Distribution costs	(6,825)
Administrative expenses	(5,005)
Profit from operations	6,825
Finance costs	(595)
Profit before tax	6,230
Tax	(1,757)
Profit for the period	4,473

Adlington Ltd

Statement of financial position at 31 October

	20X9	**20X8**
	£000	£000
ASSETS		
Non-current assets		
Property, plant and equipment	31,989	22,246
Current assets		
Inventories	6,552	4,914
Trade and other receivables	4,550	4,641
Cash and cash equivalents	450	0
Total assets	43,541	31,801
EQUITY AND LIABILITIES		
Equity		
Share capital	10,000	8,000
Share premium	4,000	3,000
Retained earnings	15,462	10,989
Total equity	29,462	21,989
Non-current liabilities		
Bank loans	8,500	3,500
Current liabilities		
Trade and other payables	3,822	4,368
Tax liability	1,757	658
Bank overdraft	0	1,286
Total liabilities	14,079	9,812
Total equity and liabilities	43,541	31,801

Further information:

- The total depreciation charge for the year was £4,398,000.
- Property, plant and equipment costing £568,000 with accumulated depreciation of £226,000 was sold in the year.
- All sales and purchases were on credit. Other expenses were paid for in cash.

Task 1

Prepare a reconciliation of profit before tax to net cash from operating activities for Adlington Ltd for the year ended 31 October 20X9.

Task 2

Using the proforma below prepare the statement of cash flows for Adlington Ltd for the year ended 31 October 20X9.

Adlington Ltd

Company statement of cash flows for the year ended 31 October 20X9.

	£000
Net cash from operating activities	
Investing activities	
Net cash used in investing activities	
Financing activities	
Net cash (used in)/from financing activities	
Net increase/(decrease) in cash and cash equivalents	
Cash and cash equivalents at beginning of year	
Cash and cash equivalents at end of year	

Workings

(W1) Proceeds of property, plant and equipment:

	£000
	——
Proceeds	

(W2) Purchase of property, plant and equipment:

	£000
	——
PPE additions	

6 Summary

A statement of cash flows provides information additional to that contained in the statement of profit or loss and other comprehensive income and statement of financial position. It is an obligatory disclosure for all except small companies.

The format of the statement of cash flows is specified by IAS 7.

Test your understanding answers

Test your understanding 1

Answer is D

	£
Issue of shares (560,000 – 220,000)	340,000
Issue of loan notes	300,000
	640,000

Interest paid is included within the 'operating activities' heading of the statement of cash flows.

Test your understanding 2

Answer is D

Depreciation is a non-cash expense and should therefore be added back to profit.

An increase in assets (inventory and receivables) means that less cash is available (as it has been used to fund assets), hence an increase in assets is shown as a deduction in the statement of cash flow.

An increase in liabilities (payables) means that more cash is available (i.e. it has not been used to pay liabilities), hence an increase in liabilities is shown as an addition in the statement of cash flow.

Test your understanding 3

Fallen plc

Statement of cash flows for the year ended 31 December 20X8

	£000	£000
Cash from operating activities		
Profit before tax	4,081	
Adjustments for:		
Depreciation charges (note 3 from question)	1,364	
Finance costs	152	
Loss on disposal (note 2 from question)	108	
	5,705	
Increase in inventories (2,880 – 1,986)	(894)	
Increase in trade receivables (2,586 – 1,992)	(594)	
Increase in trade payables (2,228 – 1,718)	510	
Cash generated from operations	4,727	
Interest paid	(152)	
Tax paid (W1)	(1,775)	
Net cash from operating activities		2,800
Cash flows from investing activities		
Purchase of property, plant and equipment (note 2 and 4 from question)	(3,800)	
Proceeds from sale of equipment (note 2 from question)	168	
Net cash used in investing activities		(3,632)
Cash flows from financing activities		
Proceeds from issue of shares (4,392 – 3,600)	792	
Redemption of loan (1,240 – 1,800)	(560)	
Net cash used in financing activities		232
Net decrease in cash and cash equivalents		(600)
Cash and cash equivalents at beginning of period		2,784
Cash and cash equivalents at end of period		2,184

	£
Opening liability	2,176
Statement of profit or loss charge	1,531
Closing liability	(1,932)
Tax paid (bal fig)	1,775

Test your understanding 4

Task 1

Flyingdales Ltd
Reconciliation of profit before tax to net cash from operating activities

	£000
Profit before tax	11,600
Depreciation charges	6,500
Finance costs	2,150
Operating cash flows before working capital changes	20,250
Increase in inventories (27,500 – 25,500)	(2,000)
Increase in trade and other receivables (37,500 – 33,000)	(4,500)
Decrease in trade, and other payables (31,500 – 31,950)	(450)
Cash generated from operations	13,300
Interest paid	(2,150)
Tax paid	(2,260)
	8,890

Task 2

Flyingdales Ltd
Statement of cash flows for the year ended 31 March 20X1

	£000
Net cash from operating activities	8,890
Investing activities	
Purchase of property plant and equipment (W1)	(9,000)
Net cash used in investing activities	(9,000)
Financing activities	
Proceeds from issue of shares (11,610 – 10,000)	1,610
Proceeds from long-term borrowing (21,500 – 20,000)	1,500
Net cash from financing activities	3,110
Net increase in cash and cash equivalents	3,000
Cash and cash equivalents at beginning of period	1,250
Cash and cash equivalents at end of period	4,250

Working

(W1) Purchase of property, plant and equipment:

	£000
CA 20X0	70,500
Less depreciation 20X1	(6,500)
	64,000
CA 20X1	73,000
Purchases	9,000

Test your understanding 5

Task 1

Eigg Ltd

Reconciliation of profit before tax to net cash from operating activities

	£000
Profit before tax	6,735
Adjustments for:	
Depreciation charges	4,458
Finance costs	105
Gain on disposal of property, plant and equipment	(448)
Dividends received	(120)
Operating cash flows before working capital changes	10,730
Increase in inventories (5,914 – 4,928)	(986)
Decrease in trade and other receivables (4,480 – 5,376)	896
Decrease in trade, and other payables (2,464 – 4,435)	(1,971)
Cash generated from operations	8,669
Tax paid	(887)
Interest paid	(105)
Net cash from operating activities	7,677

Task 2

Eigg Ltd
Statement of cash flows for the year ended 31 March 2008

	£000
Net cash from operating activities	7,677
Investing activities	
Proceeds on disposal of property plant and equipment (W1)	992
Purchases of property, plant and equipment (W2)	(11,552)
Dividends received	120
Net cash used in investing activities	(10,440)
Financing activities	
New bank loans raised	1,000
Proceeds of share issue	2,500
Dividends paid during year	(277)
Net cash from financing activities	3,223
Net increase in cash and cash equivalents	460
Cash and cash equivalents at beginning of year	(180)
Cash and cash equivalents at end of year	280

Workings

(W1) Proceeds of property, plant and equipment:

	£000
CA (878 – 334)	544
Add profit	448
	992

(W2) Purchase of property, plant and equipment:

	£000
PPE at start	21,340
Less depreciation	(4,458)
Less CA of assets sold	(544)
PPE at end	(27,890)
PPE additions (β)	(11,552)

Test your understanding 6

Task 1

Adlington Ltd
Reconciliation of profit before tax to net cash from operating activities

	£000
Profit before tax	6,230
Adjustments for:	
Depreciation charges	4,398
Finance costs	595
Gain on disposal of property, plant and equipment	(455)
Operating cash flows before working capital changes	10,768
Increase in inventories (6,552 – 4,914)	(1,638)
Decrease in trade and other receivables (4,550 – 4,641)	91
Decrease in trade and other payables (3,822 – 4,368)	(546)
Cash generated from operations	8,675
Tax paid	(658)
Interest paid	(595)
Net cash from operating activities	7,422

Task 2

Adlington Ltd
Statement of cash flow for the year ended 31 October 2009

	£000
Net cash from operating activities	7,422
Investing activities	
Proceeds on disposal of property plant and equipment (W1)	797
Purchases of property, plant and equipment (W2)	(14,483)
Net cash used in investing activities	(13,686)
Financing activities	
New bank loans raised	5,000
Proceeds of share issue	3,000
Net cash from financing activities	8,000
Net increase in cash and cash equivalents	1,736
Cash and cash equivalents at beginning of year	(1,286)
Cash and cash equivalents at end of year	450

Workings

(W1) Proceeds of property, plant and equipment:

	£000
CA (568 – 226)	342
Add profit	455
	797

(W2) Purchase of property, plant and equipment:

	£000
PPE at start	22,246
Less depreciation	(4,398)
Less carrying amount of sold assets	(342)
PPE at end	(31,989)
PPE additions	(14,483)

Consolidated accounts and the consolidated statement of financial position

15

Introduction

For this unit you may have to draft a consolidated statement of financial position using the financial statements of a parent and a subsidiary undertaking.

You also need to have an awareness of the legal factors and the IFRSs that affect the preparation of consolidated accounts, namely IFRS 3 *Business Combination* and IFRS 10 *Consolidated Financial Statements*. Note that accounting for joint ventures and investments in associates are not assessable.

ASSESSMENT CRITERIA

Explain the regulatory framework that underpins financial reporting (1.1)

Draft a consolidated statement of financial position for a parent company with one partly-owned subsidiary (4.2)

CONTENTS

1 Group accounts

1.1 Introduction

Until now, we have only dealt with the accounts of a single company. In this and the following chapter, we cover the major topic of group accounts.

In this chapter, we meet the basic principles of consolidation whilst preparing a consolidated statement of financial position. This will provide us with the foundation for studying the area in more detail in later chapters. In studying these chapters, you should always keep in mind these basic principles.

1.2 Groups

A group comprises a parent company and the undertakings (usually companies) under its control, which are called subsidiaries. The full legal definitions of a parent and subsidiaries are dealt with later and are not important at this stage.

For now, we shall assume that a parent has control of another company if it holds more than 50% of that company's ordinary shares.

1.3 Group accounts

In the UK, the Companies Act 2006 requires a parent company to produce group accounts which show a true and fair view of the whole group to the parent company's shareholders. The group accounts provide the parent's shareholders with information about the parent and the investments which it has made. Group accounts are intended for the parent's shareholders and are therefore prepared from the perspective of the parent company.

The parent's own individual statement of financial position shows the investment in the subsidiary, usually at cost, and its statement of profit or loss shows dividend income from the subsidiary in investment income. When the investing company has a controlling interest in another company, it is not sufficient merely to show the investment in this way as this does not reflect the substance of the relationship between a parent and its subsidiaries.

1.4 Control

As the parent has control, it can decide how a subsidiary's assets are used to generate income in the same way that it can decide how to manage its own resources. Hence, the Companies Act requires group accounts to be in the form of consolidated accounts, which combine the results and net assets of the group members into a single set of figures.

Group accounts comprise the following:

- a consolidated statement of financial position, which is presented in addition to the parent's own statement of financial position as an individual company
- a consolidated statement of profit or loss and other comprehensive income, which is usually presented instead of the parent's own individual statement, although the parent may choose to publish its own individual statement as well
- a consolidated statement of cash flow and statement of changes in equity (preparation of these for group accounts is beyond the scope of this unit)
- notes to the accounts, including accounting policies.

The requirement to produce group accounts is subject to exemptions, which are dealt with later.

1.5 Single entity concept

Group accounts consolidate the results and net assets of the individual group members to present the group to the parent's shareholders as a single economic entity.

This contrasts with the legal form that each company is a separate legal person. This is called the single entity concept and is an example of reflecting economic substance in financial statements rather than strict legal form.

Single entity concept

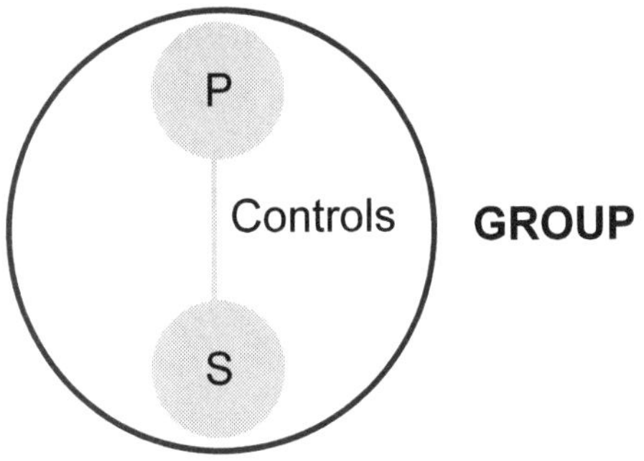

The group is viewed as a single entity.

2 IFRS 3 *Business Combinations*

2.1 Definition of a business combination

IFRS 3 says that a business combination as the bringing together of separate entities into one reporting entity. In most cases, when this occurs, one entity (the parent or acquirer) acquires control of the other entities (subsidiaries or acquirees).

There are different ways a business combination can be effected. In the examples we have seen so far, one company purchases the shares of another company. Other ways a business combination can occur include the purchase of the net assets of a business rather than the equity, or a reorganisation where a new company is created to control the newly acquired subsidiaries. However they are arranged, all business combinations are accounted for using the purchase method of accounting which we will see in the next two chapters.

3 IFRS 10 *Consolidated Financial Statements*

3.1 Definition of parent and subsidiary

A parent is an entity that controls another entity. A subsidiary is an entity that is controlled by another entity. An entity controls another if it has all of the following elements:

- power over the investee
- exposure, or rights, to variable returns from its involvement with the investee
- the ability to use its power over the investee to affect the amount of the investor's returns.

An undertaking is normally deemed to have power over an investee if it:

- holds a majority of voting rights
- controls the majority of voting rights through agreements with other investors.

3.2 Other points

IFRS 10 details the consolidation procedures that we have already seen in the previous chapters, such as the requirement to eliminate inter-company trading.

IFRS 10 says that **'a parent prepares consolidated financial statements using uniform accounting policies for like transactions and other events in similar circumstances.'** [IFRS 10, para 19].
All companies within the group need to follow the same policies otherwise the group accounts will be prepared with many differing policies which would not be useful to the users of those accounts.

4 The consolidation process

4.1 Introduction

A standard group accounting examination task will present you with the accounts of the parent company and the accounts of the subsidiary and will require you to prepare consolidated accounts.

The basic process is to add together the parent's and the subsidiary's accounts (e.g. revenues, expenses, assets and liabilities) on a line-by-line basis. However, there are a number of adjustments that need to be made, namely: goodwill; non-controlling interests; retained earnings; fair values; inter-group transactions and balances; and unrealised profit.

To tackle tasks of this kind we will use a formal pattern of workings required for the exam. These are detailed in the following pages.

4.2 The basic workings

We are going to use a formal pattern of basic workings to illustrate the approach to group questions and gradually build in complications.

The first step is to establish percentage ownership and control. The percentage ownership is calculated by dividing the number of shares owned by the parent in the subsidiary by the total number of shares the subsidiary has in issue and multiplying by 100. (**Note:** The number of shares is not shown on the statement of financial position. The SFP shows the nominal value of shares in issue).

Unless other information is provided it is assumed that a parent has control over another company if it owns more than 50% of the shares in issue. In these circumstances consolidated financial statements should be prepared.

Working 1: Goodwill

Goodwill is the difference between the price paid to acquire control of a subsidiary and the fair value of the net assets acquired. It represents the premium paid over and above the value of the assets in the business.

Goodwill	£
Consideration	X
Non-controlling interest (W1)	X
Net assets of subsidiary at acquisition date (W2)	(X)
Goodwill at acquisition	X
Impairment	(X)
Goodwill in SFP	X

Goodwill is capitalised on the consolidated statement of financial position. It is subject to an annual impairment review and this is adjusted in the working below as well as in W3.

Workings

1 NCI% × S's net assets at acquisition.

2 Subsidiary's (S's) share capital + S's retained earnings + S's other reserves + the difference between the fair value and the carrying amount of S's net assets at the acquisition date.

Note: Impairment may either be given as a percentage of goodwill at acquisition or in monetary terms.

Working 2: Non-controlling interests (NCI)

The non-controlling interest represents the shareholders that are not part of the group. For example, if the parent owns 80% of a subsidiary's shares the NCIs would own the remaining 20% of the shares.

The mechanics of a consolidation require that 100% of the subsidiary's revenues, expenses, assets and liabilities are added to the parent's in the consolidated statement of profit or loss and other comprehensive income and statement of financial position. This is performed regardless of the parent's % shareholding. If the parent owns less than 100% of the shares then an amount is calculated for both the SoCI and the SFP as attributable to the NCIs.

Non-controlling interest

Statement of financial position:

	£
Share capital attributable to NCI (W1)	X
Retained earnings attributable to NCI (W2)	X
Revaluation attributable to NCI (W3)	X
Total	X

Statement of profit or loss:

NCI% × subsidiary's profit after tax	X

Workings

1 NCI percentage ownership (NCI%) × subsidiary's (S's) share capital at the period-end.

2 NCI% × S's retained earnings at the period-end.

3 NCI% × S's other reserves (e.g. revaluation) at the period-end.

Working 3: Group retained earnings

In order to calculate group profits you cannot add together the retained earnings of the parent and the subsidiary because some of the retained earnings may have been earned before they were purchased by the parent company. The parent has no right to recognise profits earned before they controlled the subsidiary. You therefore need to work out the profit attributable to the parent after they gained control of the subsidiary.

Retained earnings	£
100% of the parent's retained earnings	X
Parent's share of the subsidiary's retained earnings (W1)	X
Impairment of goodwill (as per goodwill working)	(X)
Total	X

Workings

1 P% × (S's retained earnings at the period-end – S's retained earnings at the date of acquisition).

4.3 Buying shares in another company

When one company buys shares in another company the cash paid is recorded as an investment in the acquiring company's statement of financial position (Dr Investment Cr Cash). When the consolidated statement of financial position is prepared this investment is substituted by the net assets of the subsidiary, which are included in the consolidated statement of financial position on a line by line basis.

Example

Draft statements of financial position of Polar and Squirrel on 31 December.

	Polar Ltd	Squirrel Ltd
Assets	£000	£000
Property, plant and equipment	90	80
Investment in Squirrel at cost	110	
Current assets	50	30
Total assets	250	110
Equity		
Share capital	100	100
Retained earnings	120	–
	220	100
Current liabilities	30	10
	30	10
Total equity and liabilities	250	110

Polar Ltd has just bought 100% of the shares of Squirrel on the statement of financial position date.

Required:

Prepare a consolidated statement of financial position as at 31 December 20X1.

Solution

Step 1

- Set up a proforma for the answer, in this case the consolidated statement of financial position.
- Set up a separate proformas for the workings.
- Start with the workings then use these to construct the statement of financial position.

Step 2

Establish the percentage ownership and control. We are told that Polar owns 100% of Squirrel:

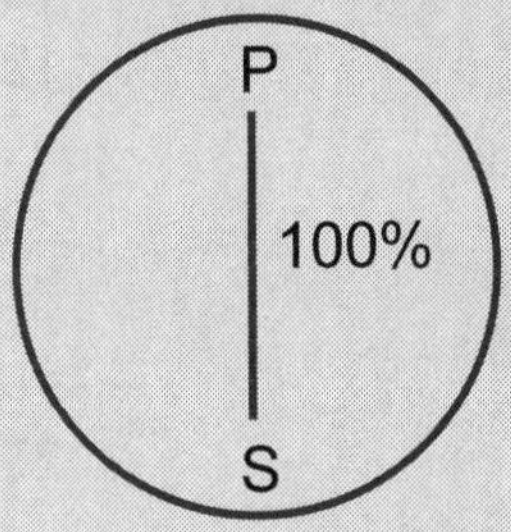

In the absence of any other information we can assume that P controls S by virtue of its 100% shareholding.

Step 3

Calculate goodwill.

Step 4

Calculate non-controlling interests.

As Polar owns 100% of the share capital of Squirrel there are **NO NCIs** to calculate in this question.

Step 5

Calculate group retained earnings.

As Polar owns 100% of Squirrel, there is no non-controlling interest. Squirrel has no retained earnings so there is no need for that working either.

Note:

- Do not include the investment in Squirrel in the consolidation.
- Do not consolidate the share capital of Squirrel.

Polar Group consolidated statement of financial position as at 31 December 20X1

	£000
Goodwill (W1)	10
Property, plant and equipment (90 + 80)	170
	180
Current assets (50 + 30)	80
Total assets	**260**
Equity	
Share capital (P only)	100
Retained earnings (W2)	120
	220
Current liabilities (30 + 10)	40
Total equity and liabilities	**260**

Workings

(W1) Goodwill

	£000
Purchase consideration	110
Non-controlling interest	
0% × 100	0
Net assets of Squirrel Ltd acquired	(100)
Goodwill	10

(W2) Retained earnings

	£000
100% Polar	120
Polar's share of Squirrel's retained earnings	0
Impairment of goodwill	0
	120

Note: Squirrel has no retained earnings to consolidate

Test your understanding 1

Puffin (I)

Draft statements of financial position of Puffin and Seagull on 31 December 20X1 are as follows:

	Puffin Ltd	**Seagull Ltd**
	£000	£000
Property, plant and equipment	146	35
Investment in Seagull at cost	90	
Current assets	24	15
Total assets	260	50
Equity		
Share capital	100	40
Retained earnings	130	–
	230	40
Current liabilities	30	10
Total equity and liabilities	260	50

Puffin Ltd has just bought 100% of the shares of Seagull on the statement of financial position date.

Required:

Prepare a consolidated statement of financial position as at 31 December 20X1.

5 Non-controlling interest

5.1 Control

We said earlier that we can 'control' a company without necessarily owning it 100%. In fact any holding of more than 50% of the equity shares is usually sufficient to give control. If we own more than 50%, but less than 100%, of the equity shares of another company we need an additional working: non-controlling interest. This calculation is necessary to reflect the third-party ownership in the net assets of the subsidiary. For the purpose of this assessment, non-controlling interest will always be valued at the subsidiary's proportionate share of net assets.

Example

Suppose that Polar's investment in Squirrel represents only 80% of Squirrel's equity, not 100%. All other details remain the same.

Required:

Prepare a consolidated statement of financial position as at 31 December 20X1.

Solution

We use exactly the same technique as before, following our standard pattern of workings.

Polar Group consolidated statement of financial position as at 31 December 20X1

	£000
ASSETS	
Non-current assets	
Goodwill (W1)	30
Property, plant and equipment (90 + 80)	170
	200
Current assets (50 + 30)	80
Total assets	280
EQUITY AND LIABILITIES	
Equity	
Share capital (100% P only)	100
Retained earnings (W3)	120
Non-controlling interest (W2)	20
Total equity	240
Current liabilities (30 + 10)	40
Total equity and liabilities	280

Note: Even though Polar only owns 80% of the share capital of Squirrel we still add together 100% of Polar's and 100% of Squirrel's revenues, expenses, assets and liabilities. This means there is a NCI% of 20% (100% – 80%).

Workings

(W1) Goodwill

	£000
Purchase consideration	110
Non-controlling interest at acquisition (20% × 100)	20
Net assets of Squirrel at acquisition	(100)
Goodwill	30

(W2) Non-controlling interests

	£000
Share capital attributable to NCI (20% × £100,000)	20
Retained earnings attributable to NCI	0
	20

(W3) Retained earnings

	£000
100% Polar	120
Polar's share of Squirrel's retained earnings	0
Impairment of goodwill	0
	120

Note: Squirrel has no retained earnings to consolidate.

Test your understanding 2

Puffin (II)

Using test your understanding 1, facts as before, but now assume that Puffin's investment in Seagull represents only a 90% interest.

Required:

Prepare a consolidated statement of financial position as at 31 December 20X1.

6 Accounting for reserves

6.1 Pre and post-acquisition reserves

The reserves which exist in a subsidiary company at the date when it is acquired are called its 'pre-acquisition' reserves. These are capitalised at the date of acquisition by including them in the goodwill calculation.

To see what this means, remember that we calculate the value of net assets acquired not by totalling the value of individual assets, but instead (as a short cut) by referring to the other side of the statement of financial position – equity.

Thus the value of net assets acquired is the value of share capital acquired plus the value of (pre-acquisition) profits acquired. By comparing this total with the amount of the purchase consideration we arrive at the value of goodwill.

In the previous examples the parent acquired its shares in the subsidiary on the reporting date. However in the case when the parent made the purchase some months or years prior to the reporting date, the subsidiary reserves must be split out into pre and post-acquisition.

The parent has influenced any change in reserves since the date of acquisition only.

Example

Draft statements of financial position of Piper and Swans on 31 December 20X1 are as follows.

	Piper Ltd	Swans Ltd
	£000	£000
ASSETS		
Property, plant and equipment	90	100
Investment in Swans at cost	110	
Current assets	50	30
Total assets	250	130

EQUITY AND LIABILITIES		
Equity		
Share capital	100	100
Retained earnings	120	20
	220	120
Current liabilities	30	10
Total equity and liabilities	250	130

Piper Ltd had bought 80% of the shares of Swans on 1 January 20X1 when the retained earnings of Swans were £15,000.

Required:

Prepare a consolidated statement of financial position as at 31 December 20X1.

Solution

We use our standard workings as before, but when we calculate net assets at the date of acquisition in W2 we include share capital and reserves at the date of acquisition.

If we follow our standard workings our answer will be as follows.

Piper Group consolidated statement of financial position as at 31 December 20X1

	£000
ASSETS	
Non-current assets	
Goodwill (W1)	18
Property, plant and equipment (90 + 100)	190
	208
Current assets (50 + 30)	80
Total assets	288

Equity	
£1 shares (100% P only)	100
Retained earnings (W3)	124
Equity attributable to holders of the parent	224
Non-controlling interest (W2)	24
Total equity	248
Current Liabilities (30 + 10)	40
Total equity and liabilities	288

Workings

(W1) Goodwill

	£000
Purchase consideration (price paid)	110
Non-controlling interest at acquisition (20% × 115)	23
Net assets of Swans Ltd at acquisition (100 + 15)	(115)
Goodwill	18

(W2) Non-controlling interests

Share capital attributable to NCIs (20% × £100,000)	20
Retained earnings attributable to NCIs (20% × £20,000)	4
	24

(W3) Group retained earnings

Profits earned by the subsidiary after the date of acquisition are called 'post-acquisition reserves'. At the date of acquisition Swans had retained earnings of £15,000. At the year-end they have retained earnings of £20,000. Therefore, Swans have earned £5,000 of profit post acquisition.

Piper includes their share of the post-acquisition profits in group retained earnings, as calculated below.

	£000
100% Piper's retained earnings	120
Piper's share of Swans' retained earnings (80% × £5,000)	4
	124

If the subsidiary had other reserves (e.g. a revaluation reserve or a general reserve) we would use the same basic calculation for each one separately.

Test your understanding 3

Pluto

Draft statements of financial position of Pluto and Snoopy on 31 December 20X8 are as follows.

	Pluto Ltd	**Snoopy Ltd**
	£000	£000
ASSETS		
Property, plant and equipment	120	150
Investment in Snoopy at cost	140	–
Current assets	40	50
Total assets	300	200
EQUITY AND LIABILITIES		
Equity		
Share capital	100	100
Retained earnings	160	70
Total equity	260	170
Current liabilities	40	30
Total equity and liabilities	300	200

Pluto purchased 75% of the shares of Snoopy on 1 January 20X7, when the retained earnings of Snoopy stood at £40,000.

Required:

Prepare a consolidated statement of financial position as at 31 December 20X8.

Test your understanding 4

Dublin

The following are the summarised statements of financial position of Dublin and Shannon at 31 December 20X9.

	Dublin Ltd	Shannon Ltd
	£	£
ASSETS		
Non-current assets		
Property, plant and equipment	100,000	60,000
Investments:		
24,000 shares in Shannon Ltd	50,000	
Current assets	215,000	50,000
Total assets	365,000	110,000
EQUITY AND LIABILITIES		
Equity		
Called up share capital (£1 ordinary)	190,000	40,000
Retained earnings	25,000	50,000
	215,000	90,000
Current liabilities	150,000	20,000
Total equity and liabilities	365,000	110,000

Dublin Ltd purchased 60% of its shares in Shannon Ltd on 1 January 20X9, when Shannon's retained earnings were £40,000.

Required:

Prepare the consolidated statement of financial position as at 31 December 20X9.

7 Fair values

7.1 Introduction

Goodwill is determined by comparing the value of the business as a whole with the aggregate of the fair values of its identifiable net assets. In our consolidation examples to date we have assumed that the fair value of the subsidiary's assets was equal to their carrying amounts. This approach is fine for assessment tasks where you are not given any information about the fair values.

If the fair value of the subsidiary's net assets, at the date of acquisition, is different from their carrying amount, the book amounts should be adjusted to fair value on consolidation. The fair value is value at which it could be sold for in an arm's length transaction.

Example

Hardy Ltd acquired 80% of the share capital of Woolf Ltd for £54,000 on 31 December 20X7. The draft statements of financial position of the two companies have been drawn up on that date.

	Hardy Ltd	**Woolf Ltd**
	£	£
ASSETS		
Non-current assets		
Property, plant and equipment	75,000	35,000
Investment in Woolf Ltd	54,000	
Current assets	35,000	39,500
Total assets	164,000	74,500
EQUITY AND LIABILITIES		
Equity		
Share capital – £1 ordinary shares	60,000	20,000
Retained earnings	62,000	38,500
	122,000	58,500
Current liabilities	42,000	16,000
Total equity and liabilities	164,000	74,500

You are given the following additional information:

The fair value of the property, plant and equipment of Woolf Ltd, on 31 December 20X7, was £42,500. This increase in value over the carrying amount of the assets can be attributed to freehold land.

Required:

Prepare the consolidated statement of financial position of Hardy Ltd as at 31 December 20X7.

Solution

Fair value adjustment

Looking at the property, plant and equipment of Woolf Ltd:

	£
Fair value at 31 December 20X7	42,500
Carrying amount at 31 December 20X7	35,000
Revaluation to fair value	7,500

On the face of the consolidated statement of financial position, property, plant and equipment will need to be increased by £7,500.

This extra £7,500 will also impact goodwill (W1) and non-controlling interest (W2).

Hardy Ltd: Consolidated statement of financial position at 31 December 20X7

	£
ASSETS	
Non-current assets	
Goodwill (W1)	1,200
Property, plant and equipment (75,000 + 35,000 + 7,500)	117,500
Current assets (35,000 + 39,500)	74,500
Total assets	193,200

EQUITY AND LIABILITIES	
Equity	
Share capital – £1 ordinary shares	60,000
Retained earnings (W3)	62,000
Equity attributable to equity holders of the parent	122,000
Non-controlling interests (W2)	13,200
Total equity	135,200
Current liabilities (42,000 + 16,000)	58,000
Total equity and liabilities	193,200

Workings

(W1) Goodwill

	£
Consideration	54,000
Non-controlling interest at acquisition (20% × 66,000)	13,200
Net assets of Woolf Ltd at acquisition (20,000 + 38,500 + 7,500)	(66,000)
	1,200

(W2) Non-controlling interests

	£
Share capital attributable to NCIs (20% × 20,000)	4,000
Retained earnings attributable to NCIs (20% × 38,500)	7,700
Revaluation adjustment (20% × 7,500)	1,500
	13,200

(W3) Retained earnings

	£
100% Hardy Ltd	62,000

(Note that there are no post-acquisition retained earnings for the subsidiary, since the consolidation is being performed immediately after acquisition.)

8 Intra-group balances

8.1 Introduction

Intra group balances must be eliminated in full, since the group as a single entity cannot owe balances to/from itself.

Intra-group balances may arise in the following situations:

- P and S trade with each other, resulting in current account balances i.e. receivables and payables
- Intra-group loans, resulting in a loan asset and loan liability.

If the current account balances between P and S agree, then these need to be eliminated. The entry for this is:

Dr Payables

Cr Receivables

Current account balances may disagree. This is most likely to be due to cash in transit or goods in transit.

8.2 Cash in transit

Cash has been sent by one group company, but has not yet been received and so is not recorded in the books of the other group company. The following adjustment will be required:

Cr Receivables
Dr Bank
Dr Payables

8.3 Goods in transit

Goods have been sent by one company, but have not yet been received and so are not recorded in the books of the other group company. The following adjustment will be required:

Dr Inventory
Cr Payables
Dr Payables
Cr Receivables

In effect, the cash and goods in transit, explained in sections 8.2 and 8.3, are treated as if they have been received by the recipient company to bring the intra-group balances to agreement.

Example

The following extracts are provided from the statements of financial position of P and S at the year-end:

	P Ltd	S Ltd
	£000	£000
Current assets		
Receivables	270	80
Cash	120	40
Current liabilities		
Payables	160	90

P's statement of financial position includes a receivable of £40,000 being due from S.

Shortly before the year-end, S sent a cheque for £4,000 to P, P did not receive this cheque until after the year-end.

Required:

Prepare extracts from the consolidated statement of financial position as at 31 December 20X1.

Solution

P Group extracts from consolidated statement of financial position as at 31 December 20X1

	£000
Current assets	
Receivables (270 + 80 – 40)	310
Cash (120 + 40 + 4)	164
Current liabilities	
Payables (160 + 90 – 36)	214

Start by adding across P and S's assets and liabilities for the consolidated statement of financial position.

For the cash in transit, neither entity is recording the cash so this needs to be amended i.e. add £4,000 to cash. Then eliminate the remaining intra group balances i.e. £40,000 from receivables and £36,000 from payables.

Cr Receivables	£40
Dr Bank	£ 4
Dr Payables	£36

9 Provisions for unrealised profits

9.1 Introduction

The parent and/or the subsidiary may sell goods to each other, resulting in a profit being recorded in the selling company's financial statements. If these goods are still held by the purchasing company at the year-end, the goods have not been sold outside the group. The profit is therefore unrealised from the group's perspective and should be removed.

The adjustment is also required to ensure that inventory is stated at the cost to the group.

Example

P sells goods to S for £400 at cost plus 25%. All goods remain in the inventory of S at the end of the year.

Mark up on cost

	%	£
Selling price	125	400
Cost of goods	100	320 (400 × 100/125)
Profit	25	80 (400 × 25/125)

Individual FS

P records profit	80
S records inventory	400

Group financial statements should show:

Profit	0
Inventory	320

Provision for unrealised profit adjustment

Dr	Group retained earnings	(W3)	80
Cr	Group inventory	(CSFP)	80

The group profit figure for the parent will be reduced as it is the parent that recorded the profit in this case.

Example

Sat Ltd acquired 100% of the share capital of Shindo Ltd when the balance on Shindo's retained earnings stood at £250,000.

The draft statements of financial position of the two companies have been drawn up as at 30 June 2009.

During the year, Sat Ltd sold goods to Shindo Ltd for £120,000 at a mark-up of 20%. Half of these goods still remain in inventory at the year end.

Required:

Prepare the consolidated statement of financial position of Sat Ltd as at 30 June 2009.

	£000	£000
ASSETS		
Non-current assets		
Property, plant and equipment	4,000	2,000
Investment in Shindo Ltd	3,400	
Current assets		
Inventory	500	100
Other current assets	100	300
Total assets	8,000	2,400
EQUITY		
Equity		
Share capital – £1 ordinary shares	6,000	1,500
Retained earnings	1,600	700
	7,600	2,200
Current liabilities	400	200
Total equity and liabilities	8,000	2,400

Solution

We will now prepare the consolidated statement of financial position.

Sat Ltd: Consolidated statement of financial position at 30 June 2009

	£000
ASSETS	
Non-current assets	
Goodwill (W1)	1,650
Property, plant and equipment (4,000 + 2,000)	6,000
Current assets	
Inventory (500 + 100 – 10)(W4)	590
Other current assets (100 + 300)	400
Total assets	8,640
EQUITY AND LIABILITIES	
Share capital – £1 ordinary shares	6,000
Retained earnings (W3)	2,040
	8,040
Current liabilities (400 + 200)	600
Total equity and liabilities	8,640

Consolidated workings (all in £000)

(W1) Goodwill

Consideration	3,400
Non-controlling interest at acquisition (0% × 1,750)	0
Net assets of Shindo Ltd at acquisition 1,500 + 250	(1,750)
	1,650

(W2) Non-controlling interests

There are no NCIs: Sat owns 100% of the shares of Shindo.

(W3) Retained earnings

Sat Ltd	1,600
PUP adjustment (W4)	(10)
Shindo Ltd (100% × (700 – 250) (post acquisition reserves)	450
	2,040

(W4) PUP

	£
Selling price	120
Cost of goods (120 × 100/120)	(100)
Profit on sale	20

Half of these goods were sold outside, therefore only half remain. We adjust the unrealised profit for the half of the goods remaining within the group. Therefore 10 will be adjusted in (W3) and against inventory.

10 Other considerations

10.1 Other reserves

In many cases there is only one reserve, retained earnings, in the subsidiary's statement of financial position. The pre-acquisition retained earnings are taken to the goodwill computation and the parent's share of the subsidiary's post acquisition retained earnings are included in the group retained earnings calculation.

A subsidiary may have other reserves in its statement of financial position, such as a revaluation reserve. On consolidation, we treat these in exactly the same way as retained earnings. Hence, the subsidiary's reserves at acquisition are taken to the goodwill computation and the parent's share of the subsidiary's post-acquisition reserves is added to the parent's own reserves.

However, it is important not to mix up the different categories of reserve. Therefore, if a subsidiary has a post-acquisition revaluation reserve, for example, the parent's share goes in the consolidated statement of financial position under 'revaluation reserve' not 'retained earnings'.

10.2 Accounting policies

All balances included in consolidated accounts should be based on the same accounting policies. If a subsidiary uses different accounting policies to prepare its own accounts from those adopted by the group as a whole (e.g. regarding development costs), the subsidiary's accounts should be adjusted prior to consolidation for consistency. We should make any necessary adjustment to the subsidiary's retained earnings in a working prior to calculating goodwill, non-controlling interests and group reserves.

Test your understanding 5

1 P Ltd acquires 90% of S Ltd for £100,000 on a date when S Ltd's net assets total £80,000. What is goodwill arising on consolidation?

2 P Ltd owns 80% of S Ltd. S Ltd's net assets total £100,000 on the statement of financial position date. What figure for non-controlling interests will appear in the consolidated statement of financial position?

3 What accounting treatment does IAS 36 require for purchased goodwill?

4 S Ltd has net assets of £60,000 at the date of acquisition. However the land of S Ltd has been revalued upwards by £30,000. This has not been included on S Ltd's statement of financial position. What is the fair value of S Ltd's net assets at the date of acquisition?

Test your understanding 6

The following are the statements of financial position of Dunsley Ltd and its subsidiary undertaking Ravenscar Ltd as at 31 December 20X1.

	Dunsley Ltd	Ravenscar Ltd
	£000	£000
ASSETS		
Non-current assets	5,210	1,250
Investment in Ravenscar Ltd	1,800	
	7,010	1,250
Current assets		
Inventories	1,520	610
Trade receivables	1,120	520
Cash	120	85
	2,760	1,215
Total assets	9,770	2,465
EQUITY AND LIABILITIES		
Equity		
Share capital	3,000	500
Share premium	1,000	100
Retained earnings	4,160	1,155
Total equity	8,160	1,755
Current liabilities	1,610	710
Total equity and liabilities	9,770	2,465

Additional information:

- The share capital of both companies consists of ordinary shares of £1 each.
- Dunsley Ltd acquired 60% of the shares in Ravenscar Ltd on 31 December 20X1.
- The fair value of the property, plant and equipment of Ravenscar Ltd at 31 December 20X1 was £1,750,000.

Task

Prepare a consolidated statement of financial position for Dunsley Ltd and its subsidiary undertaking as at 31 December 20X1.

Consolidated statement of financial position, Dunsley Ltd as at 31 December 20X1

	£000
ASSETS	
Non-current assets	
Property, plant and equipment	
Current assets	
Total assets	
EQUITY AND LIABILITIES	
Equity	
Total equity	
Current liabilities	
Total equity and liabilities	

Workings

(W1) Goodwill

	£000

(W2) Non-controlling interest

	£000

(W3) Retained earnings

	£000

Test your understanding 7

Shireoaks Ltd acquired a 60% holding in Harkhill Ltd on 1 January 20X1.

The statements of financial position as at 31 December 20X1 showed the following:

	Shireoaks Ltd	Harkhill Ltd
	£000	£000
ASSETS		
Non-current assets		
Property, plant and equipment	17,500	5,750
Investment in Harkhill	5,100	
Current assets	4,750	1,520
Total assets	27,350	7,270
EQUITY AND LIABILITIES		
Equity		
Share capital	8,000	1,000
Share premium	1,500	500
Retained earnings	11,500	3,830
Non-current liabilities		
Debentures	4,100	1,000
Current liabilities	2,250	940
Total equity and liabilities	27,350	7,270

Additional information:

- The share capital of both companies comprises ordinary shares of £1 each and there have been no changes during the year.
- Shireoaks Ltd acquired 60% of the shares in Harkhill Ltd.
- At 1 January 20X1 the balance of retained earnings of Harkhill Ltd was £3,000,000.
- The fair value of freehold land at Harkhill Ltd as at 1 January 20X1 was £3,500,000 as compared with a carrying amount of £3,100,000. This revaluation has not been reflected in the books.

Task

Prepare a consolidated statement of financial position as at 31 December 20X1.

Consolidated statement of financial position as at 31 December 20X1

	£000
ASSETS	
Non-current assets	
Property, plant and equipment	
Current assets	
	–––––
Total assets	
	–––––
EQUITY AND LIABILITIES	
Equity	
	–––––
	–––––
Non-current liabilities	
Current liabilities	
	–––––
Total equity and liabilities	
	–––––

Workings

(W1) Goodwill

	£000

(W2) Non-controlling interest

	£000

(W3) Retained earnings

	£000

Test your understanding 8

Data

The managing director of Tolsta Ltd has asked you to prepare the statement of financial position for the group.

Tolsta has one subsidiary undertaking, Balallan Ltd. The statements of financial position of the two companies as at 31 October 2008 are set out below.

Statement of financial positions as at 31 October 2008

	Tolsta Ltd	Balallan Ltd
	£000	£000
ASSETS		
Property, plant and equipment	47,875	31,913
Investment in Balallan Ltd	32,000	
	79,875	31,913
Current assets		
Inventories	25,954	4,555
Trade receivables	14,343	3,656
Cash	1,956	47
	42,253	8,258
Total assets	122,128	40,171
EQUITY AND LIABILITIES		
Equity		
Share capital	45,000	12,000
Share premium	12,000	6,000
Retained earnings	26,160	11,340
Total equity	83,160	29,340
Non-current liabilities		
Long term loans	20,000	7,000
Current liabilities		
Trade and other payables	14,454	3,685
Tax liabilities	4,514	146
Total equity and liabilities	122,128	40,171

Further information:

- The share capital of Balallan Ltd consists of ordinary shares of £1 each. Ownership of these shares carries voting rights in Balallan Ltd. There have been no changes to the balances of share capital and share premium during the year. No dividends were paid or proposed by Balallan Ltd during the year.
- Tolsta Ltd acquired 70% of the shares in Balallan Ltd on 1 November 2007.
- At 1 November 2007 the balance of retained earnings of Balallan Ltd was £9,750,000.
- The fair value of the non-current assets of Balallan Ltd at 1 November 2007 was £31,100,000. The carrying amount of the non-current assets at 1 November 2007 was £26,600,000.

  The revaluation has not been recorded in the books of Balallan Ltd (ignore any effect on the depreciation for the year).
- Included in trade and other receivables for Tolsta Ltd and in trade and other payables for Balallan Ltd is an inter-company transaction for £2,000,000 that took place in early October 2008.
- The directors of Tolsta Ltd have concluded that goodwill has been impaired by 20% during the year.

Task

Using the proforma which follows, draft a consolidated statement of financial position for Tolsta Ltd and its subsidiary undertaking as at 31 October 2008.

Proforma consolidated statement of financial position

	£000
ASSETS	
Non-current assets	
	______
	______
Current assets	
	______
	______
Total assets	______
EQUITY AND LIABILITIES	
Equity	
Non-controlling interest	______
Total equity	______
Non-current liabilities	
Current liabilities	
	______
Total equity and liabilities	______

Workings

(W1) Goodwill

	£000
Goodwill impairment 20%	
Goodwill on CSFP	

(W2) Non-controlling interest

	£000

(W3) Retained earnings

	£000

11 Summary

In this chapter, we have met main legal and professional requirements in respect of group accounts are set out in:

- IFRS 3 *Business Combinations*
- IFRS 10 *Consolidated Financial Statements*

We have also seen the basic principles of preparing a consolidated statement of financial position. Make sure that you understand the concept of the group as a single entity and the distinction between control and ownership.

To reflect the fact that the parent controls the subsidiary and its operating policies, all of the subsidiary's assets and liabilities are consolidated in to the group statement of financial position. Even if the parent only holds say 60% of the shares, this is enough to give it control and all of the assets and liabilities are consolidated.

To reflect the ownership of the subsidiary in the group statement of financial position, in the equity section of the statement of financial position the share capital and reserves are effectively split into reserves of the group and the non-controlling interest. The group can only take its share of the post-acquisition reserves, whilst the non-controlling interest shows its share of net assets. This reflects the fact that whilst the group controls all of the assets and liabilities it does not own them all.

This last point is summarised in the following proforma:

Consolidated statement of financial position

		£
Net assets		X
P + S (100%)		
CONTROL		X
OWNERSHIP:		
Equity:		
Share capital	(P only)	X
Reserves	(P + P% × S post-acq)	X
Owned by P's shareholders		X
Non-controlling interest		X
(NCI% × S's net assets consolidated)		
Total equity		X

Key

P = parent

S = subsidiary

P% = parent share of subsidiary

NCI% = Non-controlling interest share of subsidiary

If you remember the single entity concept and use the standard workings then exam tasks should be achievable.

Test your understanding answers

Test your understanding 1

Puffin (I)

Consolidated statement of financial position as at 31 December 20X1

	£000
ASSETS	
Non-current assets	
Goodwill (W1)	50
Property plant and equipment (146 + 35)	181
Current assets (24 + 15)	39
Total assets	270
EQUITY AND LIABILITIES	
Equity	
Share capital	100
Retained earnings	130
	230
Current liabilities (30 + 10)	40
Total equity and liabilities	270

Workings

(W1) Goodwill

	£000
Purchase consideration	90
Non-controlling interest at acquisition (0% × 40)	0
Net assets of Seagull Ltd at acquisition	(40)
Goodwill	50

Test your understanding 2

Puffin (II)

Consolidated statement of financial position as at 31 December 20X1

	£000
ASSETS	
Non-current assets	
Goodwill (W1)	54
Property plant and equipment (146 + 35)	181
Current assets (24 + 15)	39
Total assets	274
EQUITY AND LIABILITIES	
Equity	
Share capital	100
Retained earnings	130
Non-controlling interest (W2)	4
Total equity	234
Current liabilities (30 + 10)	40
Total equity and liabilities	274

Workings

(W1) Goodwill

	£000
Purchase consideration	90
Non-controlling interest at acquisition (10% × 40)	4
Net assets of Seagull Ltd at acquisition	(40)
Goodwill	54

(W2) Non-controlling interests

Share capital acquired (10% × £40,000)	4

Test your understanding 3

Pluto

Consolidated statement of financial position as at 31 December 20X8

	£000
ASSETS	
Non-current assets	
Goodwill (W1)	35
Property plant and equipment (120 + 150)	270
Current assets (40 + 50)	90
Total assets	395
EQUITY AND LIABILITIES	
Equity	
Share capital	100
Retained earnings (W3)	182.5
Equity attributable to equity holders of the parent	282.5
Non-controlling interest (W2)	42.5
Total equity	325
Current liabilities (40 + 30)	70
Total equity and liabilities	395

Workings

(W1) Goodwill

	£000
Purchase consideration	140
Non-controlling interest at acquisition (25% × 140)	35
Net assets of Snoopy Ltd at acquisition 100 + 40	(140)
Goodwill	35

(W2) Non-controlling interest

	£000
Share capital attributable to NCIs (25% × £100,000)	25
Retained earnings attributable to NCIs (25% × 70,000)	17.5
	42.5

(W3) Group retained earnings

	£000
100% Pluto Ltd	160
Pluto's share of Snoopy's retained earnings (75% × 30)	22.5
	182.5

Snoopy's retained earnings were £40,000 at acquisition and £70,000 at the year-end. Therefore post acquisition profits were £30,000.

Test your understanding 4

Dublin

Consolidated financial statement of financial position as at 31 December 20X9

	£
ASSETS	
Non-current assets	
Goodwill (W1)	2,000
Property, plant and equipment (100,000 + 60,000)	160,000
	162,000
Current assets (215,000 + 50,000)	265,000
Total assets	427,000
EQUITY AND LIABILITIES	
Equity	
Called up share capital	190,000
Retained earnings (W3)	31,000
Non-controlling interest (W2)	36,000
Total equity	257,000
Current liabilities (150,000 + 20,000)	170,000
Total equity and liabilities	427,000

Workings

(W1) Goodwill

	£
Purchase consideration	50,000
Non-controlling interest at acquisition (40% × 80,000)	32,000
Net assets of Shannon Ltd at acquisition 40,000 + 40,000	(80,000)
Goodwill	2,000

(W2) Non-controlling interest

	£
Share capital attributable (40% × 40,000)	16,000
Retained earnings attributable (40% × 50,000)	20,000
	36,000

(W3) Group reserves

	£
100% Dublin	25,000
Dublin's share of Shannon's retained earnings (60% × £10,000)	6,000
	31,000

Shannon's retained earnings at acquisition were £40,000 and at the year-end were £50,000. Therefore post acquisition profits were £10,000.

Test your understanding 5

1 Goodwill = £100,000 + (10% × £80,000) – £80,000 = £28,000.

2 Non-controlling interests = 20% × £100,000 = £20,000.

3 Purchased goodwill should be capitalised as a non-current asset and reviewed for impairment annually.

4 £90,000.

Test your understanding 6

Consolidated statement of financial position
Dunsley Ltd and its subsidiary undertaking, Ravenscar Ltd, as at 31 December 20X1

	£000
ASSETS	
Non-current assets	
Goodwill (W1)	447
Property, plant and equipment (5,210 + 1,750)	6,960
Current assets	
Inventories (1,520 + 610)	2,130
Trade receivables (1,120 + 520)	1,640
Cash and cash equivalents (120 + 85)	205
	3,975
Total assets	11,382
EQUITY AND LIABILITIES	
Equity	
Share capital	3,000
Share premium	1,000
Retained earnings (W3)	4,160
Non-controlling interest (W2)	902
Total equity	9,062
Current liabilities (1,610 + 710)	2,320
Total equity and liabilities	11,382

Workings

(W1) Goodwill

	£000
Consideration	1,800
Non-controlling interest at acquisition (40% × 2,255)	902
Net assets of Ravenscar Ltd at acquisition 500 + 100 + 1,155 + (1,750 – 1,250)	(2,255)
	447

(W2) Non-controlling interest

	£000
Share capital attributable to NCIs (40% × 600)	240
Retained earnings attributable to NCIs (40% × 1,155)	462
Fair value adjustment (40% × (1,750 – 1,250))	200
	902

(W3) Retained earnings

	£000
100% Dunsley Ltd	4,160
There are no post acquisition reserves of Ravenscar Ltd	0
	4,160

Test your understanding 7

Shireoaks Ltd and its subsidiary undertaking, Harkhill Ltd, as at 31 December 20X1

Consolidated statement of financial position as at 31 December 20X1

	£000
ASSETS	
Non-current assets	
Goodwill (W1)	2,160
Property, plant and equipment (17,500 + 5,750 + 400)	23,650
Current assets (4,750 + 1,520)	6,270
Total assets	32,080
EQUITY AND LIABILITIES	
Equity	
Share capital	8,000
Share premium	1,500
Retained earnings (W3)	11,998
Non-controlling interest (W2)	2,292
	23,790
Non-current liabilities	
Debentures (4,100 + 1,000)	5,100
Current liabilities (2,250 + 940)	3,190
Total equity and liabilities	32,080

Workings

(W1) Goodwill

	£000
Consideration	5,100
Non-controlling interest at acquisition (40% × 4,900)	1,960
Net assets of Harkhill Ltd at acquisition 1,000 + 500 + 3,000 + (3,500 – 3,100)	(4,900)
	2,160

(W2) Non-controlling interest

	£000
Share capital attributable to NCIs (40% × 1,500)	600
Retained earnings attributable to NCIs (40% × 3,830)	1,532
Fair value adjustment (40% × 400)	160
	2,292

(W3) Retained earnings

	£000
100% Shireoaks Ltd	11,500
60% Harkhill Ltd (3,830 – 3,000))	498
	11,998

Test your understanding 8

Tolsta Ltd
Consolidated statement of financial position as at 31 October 2008

	£000
ASSETS	
Non-current assets	
Goodwill (W1)	7,540
Property, plant and equipment (47,875 + 31,913 + 4,500)	84,288
Current assets	
Inventories (25,954 + 4,555)	30,509
Trade receivables (14,343 + 3,656 – 2,000)	15,999
Cash (1,956 + 47)	2,003
	48,511
Total assets	140,339
EQUITY AND LIABILITIES	
Equity	
Share capital	45,000
Share premium	12,000
Retained earnings (W3)	25,388
Non-controlling interest (W2)	10,152
Total equity	92,540
Non-current liabilities	
Long-term loan (20,000 + 7,000)	27,000
Current liabilities	
Trade and other payables (14,454 + 3,685 – 2,000)	16,139
Tax liabilities (4,514 + 146)	4,660
Total equity and liabilities	140,339

Workings

(W1) Goodwill

	£000
Consideration	32,000
Non-controlling interest at acquisition (30% × 32,250)	9,675
Net assets of Balallan Ltd at acquisition 12,000 + 6,000 + 9,750 + (31,100 – 26,600)	(32,250)
	9,425
Goodwill impairment 20%	(1,885)
Goodwill on CSFP	7,540

(W2) Non-controlling interest

	£000
Share capital and share premium attributable to NCIs 30% × (12,000 + 6,000)	5,400
Retained earnings attributable to NCIs (30% × 11,340)	3,402
Fair value adjustment (30% × 4,500)	1,350
	10,152

(W3) Retained earnings

	£000
100% Tolsta Ltd	26,160
70% Balallan Ltd (11,340 – 9,750)	1,113
Goodwill impairment	(1,885)
	25,388

Consolidated statement of profit or loss

16

Introduction

For this unit you may have to draft a consolidated statement of profit or loss from the financial statements of a parent and a subsidiary undertaking. In this chapter therefore we will build on the consolidation principles from the previous chapter and prepare a consolidated statement of profit or loss.

ASSESSMENT CRITERIA

Draft a consolidated statement of profit or loss for a parent company with one partly-owned subsidiary (4.1)

CONTENTS

1 Basic principles

1.1 Introduction

In this chapter, we switch our attention to the consolidated statement of profit or loss. This is prepared on the same basis as the consolidated statement of financial position and thus most of the key principles will already be familiar.

In particular, the single entity concept and the distinction between control and ownership are as important to the consolidated statement of profit or loss as they are to the consolidated statement of financial position.

The parent's own statement of profit or loss as an individual company will show dividend income from the subsidiary. The consolidated statement of profit or loss shows the incomes generated from the group's resources. Those resources are shown by the net assets in the consolidated statement of financial position.

1.2 Control and ownership

When we prepared the consolidated statement of financial position, we added together the net assets of the parent and subsidiary line by line to show the resources under the parent's control.

We apply exactly the same principle in preparing the consolidated statement of profit or loss by adding together the parent's and subsidiary's income and expenses line by line from revenue down to profit after tax. This will give us the profit after tax generated from the resources under the group's control.

In the consolidated statement of financial position, we showed the ownership of the group's net assets on the equity side, where we showed the non-controlling interests separately from the equity attributable to the parent's shareholders.

The parents and non-controlling interest's share of the profit after tax is shown in a note beneath the statement of profit or loss.

1.3 Intra-group items

We need to cancel out any intra-group trading i.e. sales from the parent to the subsidiary and vice versa and also intra group interest e.g. if the parent has made a loan to the subsidiary and is charging interest. If we are showing the results of the group as a single entity, then we cannot include transactions between the companies. If allowed, group companies might make sales between them in order to generate profit which would not give a true and fair view of the results. Therefore, we show the results of transactions which the group as a whole has made with third parties.

The journal to cancel out intra group trading is therefore:

Dr	Revenue	X	
Cr	Cost of sales		X

with the value of inter-company sales.

We shall now see in more detail how to prepare the consolidated statement of profit or loss.

1.4 Proforma consolidated statement of profit or loss

Work your way through the tutorial notes, which are referenced by letters in brackets in the pro forma that follows:

Tutorial notes:

(a) Intra-group sales must be eliminated from both the revenue of the selling company and the cost of sales of the buying company.

(b) Any intra-group interest must be eliminated from interest receivable and interest payable respectively (single entity concept).

(c) Similarly, dividends from subsidiaries must be eliminated since the profits of those subsidiaries are being consolidated and it would be double counting to include the dividends as well.

(d) Profit after taxation – Up to this point, 100% of all items for the parent company and all subsidiaries have been aggregated (subject to intra group adjustments). It is now necessary to compute the amount of the profit after taxation that is attributable to outside (non-controlling interests) shareholders.

(e) Non-controlling interest – This is calculated by taking the non-controlling interest's share of the subsidiary's profit after tax.

Consolidated statement of profit or loss for the year ended....

	£
Revenue (a)	X
Cost of sales (a)	(X)
Gross profit	X
Distribution costs	(X)
Administrative expenses	(X)
Other income(b)(c)	X
Profit from operations	X
Finance costs (b)	(X)
Profit before tax	X
Tax	(X)
Profit for the period (d)	X
Attributable to:	
Equity holders of the parent	X
Non-controlling interest (e)	X
	X

1.5 Key exam workings

(**Note:** The percentage of ownership will be given in the exam).

Workings

(W1) Revenue

	£000
P Ltd	X
S Ltd	X
Intercompany transaction	(X)
Total	X

(W2) Cost of sales

	£000
P Ltd	X
S Ltd	X
Intercompany transaction	(X)
Total	X

Example

Set out below are the draft statements of profit or loss of Smiths plc and its subsidiary company Flowers Ltd for the year ended 31 December 20X7.

On 31 December 20X5 Smiths plc purchased 75% of the ordinary shares and £10,000 10% debentures in Flowers Ltd. At that date the retained earnings of Flowers Ltd were £3,000.

The issued share capital of Flowers Ltd is 100,000 £1 ordinary shares, and it had £30,000 10% debentures outstanding on 31 December 20X7. Flowers Ltd pays its debenture interest on 31 December each year.

During the year Smiths plc sold goods to Flowers Ltd for £20,000, making a profit of £5,000. These goods were all sold by Flowers Ltd before the end of the year.

	Smiths plc	Flowers Ltd
	£	£
Revenue	600,000	300,000
Cost of sales	(427,000)	(232,000)
Gross profit	173,000	68,000
Distribution costs	(41,000)	(14,000)
Administrative expenses	(52,000)	(31,000)
Income from shares in subsidiary	7,500	–
Income from other non-current asset investments (dividends from UK quoted companies)	3,000	1,000
Other interest receivable – from group companies	1,000	–
Finance costs	–	(3,000)
Profit before tax	91,500	21,000
Tax	(38,500)	(8,000)
Profit for the period	53,000	13,000

Required:

Prepare the consolidated statement of profit or loss for Smiths plc and its subsidiary undertaking for the year ended 31 December 20X7.

Solution

Following through the pro forma, we will deal with the issues one at a time.

Where you are uncertain of the treatment, refer back to the earlier tutorial notes.

Steps 1 and 2

Revenue and cost of sales

The total revenue is £900,000 but the intra-group sale of £20,000 has been included as part of Smiths plc's revenue. It must be eliminated, leaving £880,000 (600,000 + 300,000 – 20,000).

Similarly, total cost of sales is £659,000 but the intra-group purchase of £20,000 has been included in cost of sales for Flowers Ltd. Eliminating it leaves £639,000 (427,000 + 232,000 – 20,000).

Step 3

Investment income and interest payable

- **Income from shares in group companies** of £7,500 represents the dividend receivable from the subsidiary (75% × £10,000). It must be excluded from the consolidated statement of profit or loss.
- **Interest receivable from group companies** of £1,000 is Smiths plc's share of the debenture interest paid by Flowers Ltd (10% × £10,000). It must be cancelled against the finance cost in Flowers Ltd's statement of profit or loss to leave the net finance cost to people outside the group of £2,000.

Step 4

Non-controlling interest

The non-controlling interest is 25% of Flowers Ltd's profit after tax figure (25% × £13,000 = £3,250).

Step 5

Prepare the consolidated statement of profit or loss.

Smiths plc

Consolidated statement of profit or loss for the year ended 31 December 20X7

	£
Revenue (600,000 + 300,000 – 20,000)	880,000
Cost of sales (427,000 + 232,000 – 20,000)	(639,000)
Gross profit	241,000
Distribution costs (41,000 + 14,000)	(55,000)
Administrative expenses (52,000 + 31,000)	(83,000)
Income from other NCA investments (3,000 + 1,000)	4,000
Finance costs (3,000 – 1,000)	(2,000)
Profit before taxation	105,000
Tax (38,500 + 8,000)	(46,500)
Profit for the period	58,500
Attributable to:	
Equity holders of the parent	55,250
Non-controlling interest (25% × 13,000)	3,250
	58,500

Key exam style workings are below:

(W1) Establish the group structure

The percentage of ownership will be given in the exam

Smiths plc

75%

Flowers Ltd

(W2) Revenue

	£000
Smiths plc	600,000
Flowers Ltd	300,000
Intercompany transaction	(20,000)
Total	880,000

(W3) Cost of sales

	£000
Smiths plc	427,000
Flowers Ltd	232,000
Intercompany transaction	(20,000)
Total	639,000

Test your understanding 1

Pulp plc

Given below are the draft statements of profit or loss of Pulp plc and Saxon Ltd for the year ending 31 March 20X2. Pulp plc purchased 60% of the share capital of Saxon Ltd on 1 April 20X0 at which date Saxon Ltd had a balance on its retained earnings of £20,000.

	Pulp plc	**Saxon Ltd**
	£000	£000
Revenue	650	380
Cost of sales	(320)	(180)
Gross profit	330	200
Distribution costs and administrative expenses	(190)	(90)
Dividend from Saxon Ltd	24	–
Profit before tax	164	110
Tax	(50)	(30)
Profit for the period	114	80

During the year Pulp plc sold goods costing £80,000 to Saxon Ltd and all of these had been sold outside the group by the end of the year.

You are required to prepare the consolidated statement of profit or loss for the Pulp plc group for the year ending 31 March 20X2.

Test your understanding 2

Aswall plc

Statements of profit or loss for the year ended 31 March 20X4

	Aswall plc	**Unsafey Ltd**
	£000	£000
Revenue	32,412	12,963
Cost of sales	(14,592)	(5,576)
Gross profit	17,820	7,387
Distribution costs	(5,449)	(1,307)
Administrative expenses	(3,167)	(841)
Dividends received from Unsafey Ltd	1,500	–
Profit from operations	10,704	5,239
Finance costs	(1,960)	(980)
Profit before taxation	8,744	4,259
Tax	(2,623)	(1,063)
Profit for the year	6,121	3,196

Further information:

- Aswall plc owns 75% of the ordinary share capital of Unsafey Ltd.
- During the year Unsafey Ltd sold goods which had cost £1,200,000 to Aswall plc for £1,860,000. All of these goods had been sold by Aswall plc by the end of the year.

Required:

Draft a consolidated statement of profit or loss for Aswall plc and its subsidiary undertaking for the year ended 31 March 20X4.

2 Inter-company trade and unrealised profits

2.1 Inter-company trade and unrealised profit

Earlier we cancelled out trade between group companies. The whole amount of the intercompany trade was deducted from both sales and purchases (cost of sales). An additional problem can arise if some of this inventory is unsold at the year end.

The provision for unrealised profit is calculated in the same way for both the statement of profit or loss and the statement of financial position.

The effect on the statement of profit or loss is that the reduction in the value of closing inventory will increase the cost of sales, and thereby reduce the group profits.

When the group reserves are calculated the reserves of the selling company will be reduced by the provision for unrealised profit.

If the subsidiary sold the goods then the non-controlling interest will also be reduced in respect of their share of the provision for unrealised profit.

This section will look at the impact this has on the statement of profit or loss.

Example

Sat plc acquired 90% of the issued share capital of Shindo Ltd on 1 January 20X7.

Set out below are the extracts from their statements of profit or loss for the year ended 31 December 20X7.

	Sat plc	**Shindo Ltd**
	£000	£000
Revenue (W1)	81,600	37,200
Cost of sales (W2)	(48,400)	(14,600)
Gross profit	33,200	22,600
Other income – dividend from Shindo Ltd	(3,600)	–
Distribution costs and administrative expenses	(5,000)	(3,200)
Profit before tax	24,600	19,400

The following additional information is relevant:

During the year Shindo Ltd sold goods which had cost £200,000 to Sat plc for £960,000.

Half of these goods still remain in inventory at the end of the year.

Required:

Prepare the consolidated statement of profit or loss for Sat plc and its subsidiary undertaking up to and including the profit before tax line for the year ended 31 December 20X7.

Solution

Following through the pro forma, we will take the issues one at a time. Where you are uncertain of the treatment, refer back to the earlier tutorial notes. All workings are in £000.

Step 1

Group structure

Sat plc

90%

Shindo Ltd

Step 2

Revenue, cost of sales and provision for unrealised profits (PUP)

The total revenue is £118,800 but the intra-group sale of £960 has been included as part of Shindo Ltd's revenue.

It must be eliminated, leaving £117,840 (81,600 + 37,200 – 960).

Similarly, total cost of sales is £63,000 but the intra-group purchase of £960 has been included in cost of sales for Sat plc.

Eliminating it leaves £62,040 (48,400 + 14,600 – 960).

The cost of sales needs to be adjusted for the unrealised profit. Shindo Ltd sold goods to Sat plc, so closing inventory will need to be adjusted by £380 because half of the goods have not been sold outside the group, the provision for unrealised profit is calculated below.

	£
Selling price (960/2)	480
Cost of goods (200/2)	100
Unrealised profit	380

Step 3

Investment income

Income from shares in group companies.

Dividends from Shindo Ltd of £3,600 must be excluded from the consolidated statement of profit or loss.

Step 4

Non-controlling interest

The non-controlling interest is 10% of Shindo Ltd's profit after tax figure, this does not need to be calculated in this question as the information for profit after tax is not been given.

Step 5

Prepare the extracts from the consolidated statement of profit or loss.

Sat plc

Consolidated statement of profit or loss for the year ended 31 December 20X7

	£
Revenue (W1)	117,840
Cost of sales (W2)	(62,420)
Gross profit	55,420
Other income – dividend from Shindo Ltd	–
Distribution costs and administrative expenses (5,000 + 3,200)	(8,200)
Profit before tax	47,220

Workings

(W1) Revenue

	£000
Sat Ltd	81,600
Shindo Ltd	37,200
Intercompany transaction	(960)
Total	117,840

(W2) Cost of sales

	£000
Sat Ltd	48,400
Shindo Ltd	14,600
Intercompany transaction	(960)
PUP adjustment (W3)	380
Total	62,420

(W3) PUP workings

	£000
Selling price	960
Cost of goods sold	(200)
Profit	760
Provision for unrealised profit (760 × ½)	380

Half the goods remain in inventory and therefore half the profit remains in the books. This unrealised profit needs to be eliminated.

Test your understanding 3

1 P Ltd owns 80% of S Ltd. During 20X4, P Ltd reported revenue of £100,000 while S Ltd reported revenue of £50,000. What revenue will be reported in the consolidated statement of profit or loss?

2 What is the journal entry for the consolidation adjustment to eliminate intra-group sales?

3 P Ltd owns 80% of S Ltd. S Ltd has profit after tax of £60,000. What is the non-controlling interest reported in the consolidated statement of profit or loss?

Test your understanding 4

You work as an accounting technician for Malton Ltd which has a single subsidiary, Whitby Ltd.

The statements of profit or loss for the two companies for the year ended 31 December 20X1 were:

	Malton Ltd	Whitby Ltd
	£000	£000
Revenue	14,100	5,100
Cost of sales	(7,150)	(2,750)
Gross profit	6,950	2,350
Distribution costs	(1,600)	(450)
Admin costs	(1,450)	(375)
Dividends received from Whitby Ltd	360	
Profit from operations	4,260	1,525
Finance costs	(760)	(125)
Profit before tax	3,500	1,400
Taxation	(1,200)	(400)
Profit for the year	2,300	1,000

Additional information:

- Malton Ltd acquired 80% of the ordinary share capital of Whitby Ltd on 1 January 20X1.
- During the year Whitby Ltd sold goods which had cost £500,000 to Malton Ltd for £800,000. All the goods had been sold outside the group by the end of the year.

Task

Draft a consolidated statement of profit or loss for Malton Ltd and its subsidiary for the year ended 31 December 20X1. Ignore goodwill.

Consolidated statement of profit or loss for the year ended 31 December 20X1

	£000
Revenue	
Cost of sales	
	______
Gross profit	
Distribution costs	
Admin costs	
	______
Profit from operations	
Finance costs	
	______
Profit before tax	
Tax	
	______
Profit for the year	
	______
Attributable to:	
Equity holders of the parent	
Non-controlling interest (W3)	
	______
	______

Workings

(W1) Revenue

	£000

(W2) Cost of sales

	£000

(W3) Non-controlling interest

	£000

Test your understanding 5

Data

The Managing Director of Wraymand plc has asked you to prepare the statement of profit or loss for the group. The company has one subsidiary undertaking, Blonk Ltd. The statements of profit or loss for the two companies prepared for the year ended 31 March 20X7 are set out below.

Statements of profit or loss for the year ended 31 March 20X7

	Wraymand plc	Blonk Ltd
	£000	£000
Revenue	38,462	12,544
Cost of sales	(22,693)	(5,268)
Gross profit	15,769	7,276
Other income – dividend from Blonk Ltd	580	–
Distribution costs	(6,403)	(2,851)
Administrative expenses	(3,987)	(2,466)
Profit from operations	5,959	1,959
Finance costs	(562)	(180)
Profit before taxation	5,397	1,779
Tax	(1,511)	(623)
Profit for the period	3,886	1,156

Additional information:

- Wraymand plc acquired 75% of the ordinary share capital of Blonk Ltd on 1 April 2006.
- During the year Blonk Ltd sold goods which had cost £1,100,000 to Wraymand plc for £1,600,000. Half of these goods remain in inventory at the end of the year.

Task

Using the proforma provided, draft a consolidated statement of profit or loss for Wraymand plc and its subsidiary undertaking for the year ended 31 March 20X7.

Wraymand plc
Consolidated statement of profit or loss for the year ended 31 March 20X7

	£000
Revenue	
Cost of sales	
	–––––
Gross profit	
Distribution costs	
Administrative expenses	
	–––––
Profit from operations	
Finance costs	
	–––––
Profit before taxation	
Tax	
	–––––
Profit for the period	
	–––––
Attributable to:	
Equity holders of the parent	
Non-controlling interest	
	–––––
	–––––

Workings

(W1) Revenue:

	£000

(W2) Cost of sales:

	£000

(W3) Non-controlling interest:

	£000

(W4) PUP adjustment:

	£000

3 Summary

The key thing to remember is that the consolidated statement of profit or loss gives the results of the group trading with third parties.

Therefore the following adjustments are necessary:

- Eliminate any intra-group sales from revenue and cost of sales.
- Exclude dividends and interest received from the subsidiary.
- Include non-controlling interest, being the non-controlling interest's share of the subsidiary company's profit after tax.
- Eliminate unrealised profit on inventory.

Test your understanding answers

Test your understanding 1

Pulp plc

Consolidated statement of profit or loss for the year ending 31 March 20X2

	£000
Revenue (650 + 380 – 80)	950
Cost of sales (320 + 180 – 80)	(420)
Gross profit	530
Expenses (190 + 90)	(280)
Profit before tax	250
Tax (50 + 30)	(80)
Profit for the period	170
Attributable to:	
Equity holders of the parent	138
Non-controlling interest (40% × 80)	32
	170

Test your understanding 2

Aswall plc

Consolidated statement of profit or loss for the year ended 31 March 20X4

	£000
Revenue (W1)	43,515
Cost of sales (W2)	(18,308)
Gross profit	25,207
Distribution costs (5,449 + 1,307)	(6,756)
Administrative expenses (3,167 + 841)	(4,008)
Profit from operations	14,443
Finance costs (1,960 + 980)	(2,940)
Profit before taxation	11,503
Tax (2,623 + 1,063)	(3,686)
Profit for the year	7,817
Attributable to:	
Equity holders of the parent	7,018
Non-controlling interest (W3)	799
	7,817

Workings

(W1) Revenue

	£000
Aswall plc sales	32,412
Unsafey Ltd sales	12,963
Less Inter-company sale	(1,860)
	43,515

(W2) Cost of sales:

	£000
Aswall plc cost of sales	14,592
Unsafey Ltd cost of sales	5,576
Less Inter-company purchase	(1,860)
	18,308

(W3) Non-controlling interest:

25% × 3,196 =	799

Test your understanding 3

1 £100,000 + £50,000 = £150,000.

2 Debit group turnover, Credit group cost of sales.

3 NCI = 20% × £60,000 = £12,000.

Test your understanding 4

Consolidated statement of profit or loss for the year ended 31 December 20X1

	£000
Revenue (W1)	18,400
Cost of sales (W2)	(9,100)
Gross profit	9,300
Distribution costs (1,600 + 450)	(2,050)
Admin costs (1,450 + 375)	(1,825)
Profit from operations	5,425
Finance costs (760 + 125)	(885)
Profit before tax	4,540
Tax (1,200 + 400)	(1,600)
Profit for the year	2,940
Attributable to:	
Equity holders of the parent	2,740
Non-controlling interest (W3)	200
	2,940

Workings

(W1) Revenue:

	£000
Malton Ltd	14,100
Whitby Ltd	5,100
Less inter-company sales	(800)
	18,400

(W2) Cost of sales:

	£000
Malton Ltd	7,150
Whitby Ltd	2,750
Less inter-company purchase	(800)
	9,100

(W3) Non-controlling interest:

20% of £1,000	200

Test your understanding 5

Consolidated statement of profit or loss for the year ended 31 March 20X7

	£000
Revenue (W1)	49,406
Cost of sales (W2)	(26,611)
Gross profit	22,795
Distribution costs	(9,254)
Admin costs	(6,453)
Profit from operations	7,088
Finance costs	(742)
Profit before tax	6,346
Tax	(2,134)
Profit for the year	4,212
Attributable to:	
Equity holders of the parent	3,985
Non-controlling interest (W3)	227
	4,212

Workings

(W1) Revenue:

	£000
Wraymand plc	38,462
Blonk Ltd	12,544
Less inter-company sales	(1,600)
	49,406

(W2) Cost of sales:

	£000
Wraymand plc	22,693
Blonk Ltd	5,268
Less inter-company purchase	(1,600)
Provision for unrealised profit adjustment	250
	26,611

(W3) Non-controlling interest:

25% of (£1,156 – 250)	227

(W4) PUP adjustment

Selling price	1,600
Cost of goods sold	(1,100)
Profit	500
Provision for unrealised profit (500 × ½)	250

MOCK ASSESSMENT

1 Mock Assessment Questions

TASK 1.1 (24 marks)

Ice is a limited liability company. An initial trial balance for the year ended 31 December 20X1 is presented below.

	Debit	Credit
	£	£
Revenue		600,000
Purchases	240,000	
Administrative expenses	185,000	
Distribution expenses	75,000	
Plant and machinery – cost	120,000	
Plant and machinery – accumulated depreciation at 1 January 20X1		15,000
Trade receivables	20,500	
Allowance for receivables – 1 January 20X1		2,000
Inventory – 1 January 20X1	24,000	
Share capital		10,000
Trade payables		29,000
Retained earnings – 1 January 20X1		43,500
6% Loan – repayable 31 December 20X4		100,000
Cash	130,000	
Dividends paid	5,000	
	799,500	799,500

The following notes are relevant to the preparation of the financial statements for the year ended 31 December 20X1:

- The current year tax bill has been estimated at £6,000.
- It has been determined that trade receivables of £1,000 are irrecoverable. No adjustment is required to the allowance for receivables.

- Depreciation on plant and machinery is charged at 20% per annum on a reducing balance basis. Depreciation is charged to cost of sales.
- The loan was taken out on 1 April 20X1. No interest has been accrued.
- Closing inventory has been correctly valued at £30,000.
- A customer bought a good on credit from Ice Ltd for £500 on 10 December 20X1. They returned this good on 30 December 20X1. No entries have been posted for this return.
- Ice Ltd is being sued by an ex-employee for unfair dismissal. Legal advisers think it is probable that Ice will lose the case and that they will have to pay damages of £50,000 in 20X2. Legal costs are charged to administrative expenses.

(a) Draft the statement of profit or loss for Ice Ltd for the year ended 31 December 20X1. **(16 marks)**

(b) Draft the statement of changes in equity for Ice Ltd for the year ended 31 December 20X1. **(8 marks)**

Note: Additional notes and disclosures are not required.

TASK 1.2 **(16 marks)**

This task is a continuation of task 1.1 and uses the same data.

Draft the statement of financial position for Ice Ltd as at 31 December 20X1.

Note: Additional notes and disclosures are not required.

TASK 1.3 **(10 marks)**

You are an AAT student working for Piecefold Accountants. You have been asked to prepare the financial statements of Tribold Ltd, a manufacturer of science equipment, for the year ended 31 December 20X3.

Write a response to both matters in the box provided below.

Matter 1

Tribold Ltd had inventories at 31 December 20X3 which had cost £228,000. During 20X3, a competitor company offered similar scientific equipment products for sale at very competitive prices, some of which were below Tribold Ltd's normal selling price.

Explain to the directors of Tribold Ltd why inventories should be recognised as an asset in the statement of financial position.

Explain how IAS 2 requires inventories to be measured in this situation.

Matter 2

One of the senior managers, Jason, at Tribold Ltd has asked you to apply for a job working in the accounts department within the firm.

Explain how the fundamental ethical principle of objectivity may be threatened in this situation, including the nature of the threat.

TASK 1.4 **(12 marks)**

The directors of Caroline plc are concerned about the performance of a machine. The machine has a carrying amount of £500,000. The directors believe that the machine has a fair value of £400,000 and a value-in-use of £420,000. If the machine was to be sold, Caroline plc would have to incur selling expenses of £2,000.

Prepare brief notes to the directors of Caroline plc that address the following:

1 According to IAS 36 *Impairments of Assets*, when are impairment reviews required?

2 Using the figures from above, illustrate how an impairment loss is calculated and recognised in the financial statements.

TASK 1.5 **(15 marks)**

SlowMo Ltd bought a new building on 1 January 20X1 for £300,000. It was decided to depreciate this over fifty years on a straight line basis.

On 31 December 20X8, the building is re-valued to £750,000.

(a) Per IAS 16 *Property, plant and equipment,* what is the revaluation gain that will be recorded in other comprehensive income? **(3 marks)**

A £450,000

B £456,000

C £498,000

D £492,000

At 31 December 20X1, Imp Ltd has an item of inventory which cost £100 to manufacture. Due to damage, the business will need to spend £50 to repair the item. Once repaired, the item could be sold for £120.

(b) Per IAS 2 *Inventories*, what should be the value of this item of inventory in the statement of financial position? **(3 marks)**

A £100

B £150

C £120

D £70

Murray Ltd has a year end of 31 December 20X1.

(c) According to IAS 10 *Events after the reporting period*, which of the following is not an adjusting event? **(3 marks)**

A A major credit customer goes bankrupt on 3 January 20X2

B Inventory which cost £3,000 to purchase was sold for £2,000 on 5 January 20X2

C A fire destroyed the company's warehouse on 6 January 20X2

D On 10 January 20X2, a regulator announces that the company must pay £10,000 in fines as a result of health and safety regulation breaches that occurred during the year ended 31 December 20X1

Bob's Bakery Ltd is taking legal action against one of its suppliers and is hoping to receive £1m in compensation. Legal advisors have advised that Bob's Bakery Ltd will probably win the case.

(d) Per IAS 37 *Provisions, contingent liabilities and contingent assets*, Bob's Bakery should recognise a £1 million asset in respect of the legal action.

Is this statement true or false? **(1 mark)**

A True

B False

(e) Which one of the following items is not part of the 'five step' approach for revenue recognition as outlined in IFRS 15? **(2 marks)**

A Allocate the total price between the separate performance obligations in the contract

B All contracts must be in writing

C Recognise revenue when a performance obligation is satisfied

D Identify the contract

(f) According to IFRS 16 *Leases*, which of the following is the correct calculation for the initial recognition of a right-of-use asset? **(3 marks)**

A The present value of lease payments not yet made + lease payments made at or before the commencement date – initial direct costs

B The present value of lease payments not yet made – lease payments made at or before the commencement date + initial direct costs – estimated costs of removing or dismantling the asset

C The present value of lease payments not yet made + lease payments made at or before the commencement date + initial direct costs + estimated costs of removing or dismantling the asset

D The present value of lease payments not yet made + lease payments made at or before the commencement date + initial direct costs – estimated costs of removing or dismantling the asset

TASK 1.6 (30 marks)

ABC plc acquired 75% of the ordinary shares of XYZ Ltd for £200,000. At the acquisition date, the retained earnings of XYZ were £100,000.

The statements of financial position for ABC and XYZ as at 31 December 20X1 are presented below.

	ABC plc	XYZ Ltd
	£	£
Assets		
Non-current assets		
Property, plant and equipment	240,000	297,000
Investments	200,000	–
Current assets		
Inventories	75,000	56,000
Trade and other receivables	120,000	94,000
Cash and cash equivalents	5,000	52,000
Total assets	640,000	499,000
Equity and liabilities		
Equity		
Share capital	100,000	50,000
Retained earnings	342,000	334,000
Non-current liabilities		
Loans	100,000	50,000
Current liabilities		
Trade and other payables	98,000	65,000
Total equity and liabilities	640,000	499,000

The following notes are relevant to the preparation of the consolidated financial statements:

- The carrying amount of the net assets of XYZ Ltd approximated their carrying amounts, with the exception of some land. This land held in the accounts of XYZ at its cost of £60,000 but was estimated to have a fair value of £100,000. This land is still held at 31 December 20X1.
- During the year, ABC sold goods on credit to XYZ for £20,000 making a profit on the sale of £6,000. All of these goods are still included in the inventories of XYZ and the invoice has not yet been settled.
- Goodwill has not been impaired.
- The non-controlling interest will be valued at their proportionate share of net assets.

Draft the consolidated statement of financial position for ABC plc and its subsidiary undertaking as at 31 December 20X1.

TASK 1.7 (20 marks)

You have been asked to calculate ratios for MP Ltd in respect of its financial statements for the year ending 31 March 20X1 to assist your manager in his analysis of the company.

MP Ltd's statement of comprehensive income and statement of financial position are set out below.

MP Ltd – Statement of profit or loss for the year ended 31 March 20X1

	20X1
	£000
Revenue	48,000
Cost of sales	(28,000)
Gross profit	20,000
Distribution costs	(8,200)
Administrative expenses	(5,400)
Profit from operations	6,400
Finance costs	(1,250)
Profit before tax	5,150
Tax	(1,545)
Profit for the period	3,605

MP Ltd – Statement of financial position as at 31 March 20X1

	£000
ASSETS	
Non-current assets	
Property, plant and equipment	310,500
Current assets	
Inventories	15,000
Trade receivables	8,500
Cash and cash equivalents	3,725
Total assets	337,725
Equity	
Share capital	150,000
Retained earnings	152,795
Total equity	302,795
Non-current liabilities	
Bank loans	15,000
	15,000
Current liabilities	
Trade payables	17,100
Tax liabilities	2,830
	19,930
Total liabilities	34,930
Total equity and liabilities	337,725

(a) State the formulas that are used to calculate each of the following ratios: **(10 marks)**

(i) Gross profit percentage

(ii) Operating profit percentage

(iii) Current ratio

(iv) Trade payables payment period

(v) Interest cover.

(b) Calculate the above ratios to ONE DECIMAL PLACE. **(10 marks)**

TASK 1.8 **(23 marks)**

You have been given the following information by the management of CAP Ltd, for the years ended 31 December 20X1 and 20X2.

	20X2	**20X1**
Gross profit	14.9%	11.4%
Inventory holding period	26 days	22 days
Receivables collection period	50 days	43 days
Payables payment period	28 days	30 days
Gearing	70%	52%

Prepare a report to the management that includes:

- Comments on whether CAP Ltd has performed better or worse in 20X2 in terms of the calculated ratios, giving possible reasons, as compared to the prior year.
- Suggestions on steps CAP Ltd can take to reduce its receivables collection period and any problems that these steps may cause.

2 Mock Assessment Answers

TASK 1.1 (24 marks)

(a) Statement of profit or loss for year ended 31 December 20X1
(16 marks)

	£
Revenue (W1)	599,500
Cost of sales (W2)	(255,000)
Gross profit	344,500
Administrative expenses (W3)	(236,000)
Distribution costs	(75,000)
Operating profit	33,500
Finance costs (£100,000 × 6% × 9/12)	(4,500)
Profit before tax	29,000
Income tax expense	(6,000)
Profit after taxation	23,000

Workings

(W1) Revenue

	£
Revenue	600,000
Sales return	(500)
	599,500

(W2) Cost of sales

	£
Opening inventory	24,000
Purchases	240,000
Depreciation	21,000
((£120,000 – £15,000) × 20%)	
Closing inventory	(30,000)
	255,000

(W3) Administrative expenses

	£
Per trial balance	185,000
Irrecoverable debt	1,000
Provision	50,000
	236,000

(b) Statement of changes in equity for year ended 31 December 20X1 **(8 marks)**

	Share capital (£)	Retained earnings (£)	Total equity (£)
Balance at 1 January 20X1	10,000	43,500	53,500
Total comprehensive income		23,000	23,000
Dividends		(5,000)	(5,000)
Balance at 31 December 20X1	10,000	61,500	71,500

TASK 1.2 **(16 marks)**

Statement of financial position as at 31 December 20X1

	£
Non-current assets	
Property, plant and equipment (W1)	84,000
Current assets	
Inventories	30,000
Receivables (W2)	17,000
Cash and cash equivalents	130,000
Total assets	261,000
Equity	
Ordinary share capital	10,000
Retained earnings	61,500
Non-current liabilities	
Loan	100,000
Current liabilities	
Trade and other payables (W3)	33,500
Tax payable	6,000
Provision	50,000
Total equity and liabilities	261,000

Workings

(W1) Property, plant and equipment

	£
Cost per TB	120,000
Acc' Dep'n per TB	(15,000)
Depreciation for year	(21,000)
	84,000

(W2) Receivables

	£
Per trial balance	20,500
Allowance per trial balance	(2,000)
Irrecoverable debt	(1,000)
Sales return	(500)
	17,000

(W3) Trade and other payables

	£
Per trial balance	29,000
Loan interest	4,500
	33,500

TASK 1.3

(10 marks)

Matter 1

Inventories are recognised as an asset in the statement of financial position because they meet the definition of an asset – they are a present economic resource controlled by the entity as a result of past events. An economic resource is a right that has the potential to produce economic benefit. The inventories are controlled by Tribold Ltd because they own them and they have the potential to produce economic benefit as they can be sold.

IAS 2 requires inventories to be measured at the lower of cost and net realisable value for each separate product or item. Cost may be based upon specific unit cost, or determined by use of an acceptable method, such as 'first-in, first-out' or weighted average cost basis. The selling prices of Tribold and the competitor are an indication of the net realisable value of each product. If this is less than cost for some products, Tribold will need to reduce the inventory valuation of those items to their net realisable value. If net realisable value of an item is higher than its cost, then (i.e. it would normally be sold at a profit), these it should be measured at cost.

Matter 2

You face a self-interest threat. You may become biased in favour of Tribold Ltd when preparing the accounts for the company. You may prioritise the completion of the accounts for Tribold Ltd over that of other clients.

TASK 1.4 **(12 marks)**

1 An impairment review should be performed annually for:

- intangible assets which have been attributed an indefinite useful economic life
- goodwill acquired in a business combination.

For other assets, an impairment review should be performed if there are indicators of impairment. This would include:

- decreases in the market value of an asset
- evidence of damage
- a reduction in the usage of an asset
- evidence that an asset has performed worse than expected.

2 An impairment has occurred if the carrying amount of an asset exceeds the recoverable amount.

The recoverable amount is the higher of:

- fair value less costs to sell
- value-in-use.

In this scenario, fair value less costs to sell are £398,000 (£400,000 – £2,000) and the value-in-use is £420,000. Therefore, the recoverable amount if £420,000.

The asset is therefore impaired and will need to be written down by £80,000 (£500,000 – £420,000).

The impairment loss will be charged to the statement of profit or loss.

TASK 1.5 **(15 marks)**

(a) **C**

Cost	300,000
Accumulated depreciation	(48,000)
(300,000/50) × 8 years	
Carrying amount at 31/12/X8	252,000

£750,000 – £252,000 = £498,000 **(3 marks)**

(b) **D**

Cost = £100

NRV = 120 – 50 = £70

Per IAS2, inventory is valued at the lower of cost and NRV **(3 marks)**

(c) **C**

As at the year-end, the inventory was in a saleable condition. Therefore, no adjustments are made. **(3 marks)**

(d) **B**

An asset would only be recognised from the legal action if it was virtually certain that the money will be received. **(1 mark)**

(e) **B**

Contracts do not need to be in writing, although many business entities may prefer to have written contracts so that there is certainty as to what has been agreed with customers. **(2 marks)**

(f) **C**

A right-of-use asset is initially recognised at cost.

The initial cost of the right-of-use asset comprises:

- The present value of lease payments not yet made
- Lease payments made at or before the commencement date
- Any initial direct costs
- The estimated costs of removing or dismantling the underlying asset as per the conditions of the lease.

(3 marks)

TASK 1.6 **(30 marks)**

Consolidated statement of financial position as at 31 December 20X1

	£
Assets	
Non-current assets	
Property, plant and equipment (£240,000 + £297,000 + £40,000 FV uplift)	577,000
Goodwill (W1)	57,500
Current assets	
Inventories (£75,000 + £56,000 – £6,000 PUP)	125,000
Trade and other receivables (£120,000 + £94,000 – £20,000)	194,000
Cash and cash equivalents (£5,000 + £52,000)	57,000
Total assets	1,010,500
Equity and liabilities	
Equity	
Share capital	100,000
Retained earnings (W3)	511,500
Non-controlling interest (W2)	106,000
Non-current liabilities	
Loans (£100,000 + £50,000)	150,000
Current liabilities	
Trade and other payables (£98,000 + £65,000 – £20,000)	143,000
Total equity and liabilities	1,010,500

Workings

(W1) Goodwill

	£
Consideration	200,000
Non-controlling interest (25% × £190,000)	47,500
Net assets of XYZ Ltd at acquisition date £50,000 + £100,000 + (£100,000 – £60,000)	(190,000)
	57,500

(W2) Non-controlling interest

	£
Share capital attributable to NCI (25% × £50,000)	12,500
Retained earnings attributable to NCI (25% × £334,000)	83,500
Revaluation attributable to NCI (25% × £40,000)	10,000
	106,000

(W3) Retained earnings

	£
Parent	342,000
Parent's share of XYZ post-aqn' (75% × (£334,000 – £100,000)	175,500
PUP	(6,000)
	511,500

TASK 1.7 **(20 marks)**

(a) **(10 marks)** (b) **(10 marks)**

(i) Gross profit percentage

$\frac{\text{Gross profit}}{\text{Revenue}} \times 100$ $\frac{20,000}{48,000} \times 100$ = 41.7%

(ii) Operating profit percentage

$\frac{\text{Profit from operations}}{\text{Revenue}} \times 100$ $\frac{6,400}{48,000} \times 100$ = 13.3%

(iii) Current ratio

$\frac{\text{Current assets}}{\text{Current liabilities}}$ $\frac{27,225}{19,930}$ = 1.4:1

(iv) Trade payables payment period

$\frac{\text{Trade payables}}{\text{Cost of sales}} \times 365$ $\frac{17,100}{28,000} \times 365$ = 223 days

(v) Interest cover

$\frac{\text{Profit from operations}}{\text{Finance costs}}$ $\frac{6,400}{1,250}$ = 5.1 times

TASK 1.8 **(23 marks)**

Report

To: Management of CAP Ltd

From: AAT student

Subject: Performance of CAP Ltd

Date: xxxxxxxxxx

As requested I have looked into the financial situation of CAP Ltd.

- (i) The **gross profit ratio** has improved, which is a positive sign as more gross profit is being generated by sales.

  This improvement may be due to an increase in selling price, a reduction in the cost of goods purchased, or perhaps a change in the product mix with higher margin products being sold in greater quantities.

  (ii) The **inventory holding period** ratio has worsened as it now takes 26 days on average to sell inventory, compared with just 22 days in the previous year.

  This could be due to poor inventory management or a large purchase before the year end, (e.g. a special build-up of inventories for a marketing campaign at the start of the next year).

  (iii) The **receivables collection period** has worsened as it now takes more time to collect in the cash due from credit customers. This could be due to deterioration in credit control and debt collection procedures.

  (iv) The **payables payment period ratio** has gone down since the company is taking fewer days credit from its credit suppliers. This could be due to taking up the discounts offered by the suppliers, buying more goods for cash or credit suppliers reducing their credit period.

  (v) The **gearing ratio** has worsened, indicating that a higher proportion of long-term finance of the enterprise is now provided by debt, and a smaller proportion is financed by equity.

  This movement could be due to CAP Ltd taking out new loans. Another explanation may be that the company has paid a dividend in excess of its annual profits.

- In order to reduce receivables collection period, CAP Ltd could consider the following steps:
  - (i) Investment in the credit control function, perhaps by hiring more staff. However, the expense of this may outweigh the benefits.
  - (ii) Reducing the credit period offered to customers. This may cause customers to change to a supplier which offers longer credit terms.
  - (iii) Offering greater prompt payment discounts. Again, the cost of this might be deemed to outweigh the benefits of improved cash flow.

REFERENCES

The Board (2019) Conceptual Framework for Financial Reporting. London: IFRS Foundation.

The Board (2019) IAS 1 Presentation of Financial Statements. London: IFRS Foundation.

The Board (2019) IAS 2 Inventories. London: IFRS Foundation.

The Board (2019) IAS 7 Statement of Cash Flows. London: IFRS Foundation.

The Board (2019) IAS 10 Events after the Reporting Period. London: IFRS Foundation.

The Board (2019) IAS 12 Income Taxes. London: IFRS Foundation.

The Board (2019) IAS 16 Property, Plant and Equipment. London: IFRS Foundation.

The Board (2019) IAS 36 Impairment of Assets. London: IFRS Foundation.

The Board (2019) IAS 37 Provisions, Contingent Liabilities and Contingent Assets. London: IFRS Foundation.

The Board (2019) IAS 38 Intangible Assets. London: IFRS Foundation.

The Board (2019) IFRS 3 Business Combinations. London: IFRS Foundation.

The Board (2019) IFRS 10 Consolidated Financial Statements. London: IFRS Foundation.

The Board (2019) IFRS 15 Revenue from Contracts with Customers. London: IFRS Foundation.

The Board (2019) IFRS 16 Leases. London: IFRS Foundation.

INDEX